Fresh From
the Bible for
201

FRESH from the WORD

the Bible for a change

Foreword by J.John

Edited by Nathan Eddy

IBRA
International Bible Reading Association

MONARCH
BOOKS
Oxford UK, and Grand Rapids, USA

Published by Monarch Books (an imprint of Lion Hudson plc)
Wilkinson House, Jordan Hill Road, Oxford OX2 8DR, England
Email: monarch@lionhudson.com www.lionhudson.com/monarch
and by the International Bible Reading Association
5–6 Imperial Court, 12 Sovereign Road, Birmingham, B30 3FH
Tel: 0121 458 3313; Fax: 0121 285 1816
www.ibraglobal.org
Charity number 1086990

ISBN 978 0 85721 783 7
e-ISBN 978 0 85721 784 4
ISSN 2050-6791

First edition 2016

A catalogue record for this book is available from the British Library

Printed and bound in the UK, July 2016, LH36

Fresh From the Word aims to build understanding and respect for different Christian perspectives through the provision of a range of biblical interpretations. Views expressed by contributors should not, therefore, be taken to reflect the views or policies of the Editor or the International Bible Reading Association.

The International Bible Reading Association's scheme of readings is listed monthly on the IBRA website at www.ibraglobal.org and the full scheme for 2017 may be downloaded in English, Spanish and French.

Contents

Foreword

The Bible: the bestselling book in the world, and an incredibly personal and intimate word and way of life. The Bible is a source of huge joy and power, but reading it takes effort and commitment. That's where *Fresh From the Word* comes in. Here you will find daily reflections from a variety of writers, fresh perspectives, moving prayers, and themes to make you think. I encourage you to make this book, with the Bible nearby, a part of your daily ritual. But it's not just about good habits. How can the Bible make a difference in our lives?

First, we need to let God's word *save* us. It's easy to think that the Bible simply gives moral guidance. But we need more than the gentle physiotherapy of morality and ethics; we need desperate heart surgery. It is in reading the Bible that we see our situation revealed; and at the same time it holds out God's love to us in Jesus Christ. If there is a devastating judgement here for us in the Bible there is also the most wonderful good news: God loves us and in Christ has forgiven us.

Second, we need to let God's word *steer* us. The desire to go along with everybody else is particularly strong today when most of us are constantly connected digitally to each other and to the global culture of emails, tweets and Facebook. If we pay attention to it, the Spirit of God in scripture will steer us on a safe course. Reading the Bible regularly, thoughtfully and prayerfully will guide us through life. It may not be a comfortable direction – going against the flow never is – but it will be the right one.

Finally, we need to let God's word *strengthen* us. The Bible comes to our aid providing constant encouragement and reminding us that God has given his Spirit to support his people in even the most difficult of circumstances.

God has spoken to us through scripture and our grateful response should be to listen: to read it daily and let it save, steer and strengthen us – every day!

J. John

Revd Canon J.John

How to use *Fresh From the Word*

How do you approach the idea of regular Bible reading? It may help to see daily Bible reading as spiritual exploration. Here is a suggestion of a pattern to follow that may help you develop the discipline but free up your mind and heart to respond.

- Before you read, take a few moments – the time it takes to say the Lord's Prayer – to imagine God looking at you with love. Feel yourself enfolded in that gaze. Come to scripture with your feet firmly planted.

- Read the passage slowly before you turn to the notes. Be curious. The Bible was written over a period of nearly 1000 years, over 2000 years ago. There is always something to learn. Read and reread.

- If you have access to a study Bible, pay attention to any echoes of the passage you are reading in other parts of the biblical book. A word might be used in different ways by different biblical authors. Where in the story of the book are you reading? What will happen next?

- 'Read' yourself as you read the story. Be attentive to your reactions – even trivial ones. What is drawing you into the story? What is repelling you? Observe yourself 'sidelong' as you read as if you were watching a wild animal in the forest; be still, observant and expectant.

- What in the scripture or in the notes is drawing you forward in hope? What is closing you down? Notice where the Spirit of Life is present, and where negative spirits are, too. Follow where life is leading. God always leads into life, even if the way feels risky.

- Lift up the world and aspects of your life to God. What would you like to share with God? What is God seeking to share with you?

- Thank God for being present and offer your energy in the day ahead, or in the day coming after a night's rest.

Introduction from the Editor

The dream and ideal of being at one with each other has always been at the heart of the International Bible Reading Association. Our founding vision in 1882 was not simply reading the Bible, but reading it together in small groups. We never printed books, only tweet-sized daily 'Hints' designed to encourage the small groups that gathered in homes, factories and workplaces, and churches. It was a revolutionary idea, reflecting the conviction that being 'at one' is both the fruit of Bible study and also the preparation for it. We knew then, as we know now, that we can only understand the full richness of scripture when we read it together; yet we also confess that the unity we seek is a gift of God through Jesus Christ.

So it is fitting that 'at-one-ment' is our Lenten theme this year: 'at-one-ment' captures something special about what we are at IBRA, and what all Christians hope for. For five weeks, we lift up this theme to catch the light in many ways: how can we be at one with each other, with the environment, with God, and with ourselves, in our world today? Clare Nonhebel in Dorset, UK, Terry Lester in Cape Town, Lynne Frith in Auckland and Jennifer Smith in London will lead us into these vital issues. In IBRA it's something we practise every day, wherever we live in the world; yet it is also our prayer and sustaining hope, never more so than in Lent.

We have a whole range of themes on offer this year. This year's themes include dreams, longing to belong, the creativity of the Trinity, politics of food, friendship in the digital age and a series to mark the 500th Martin Luther anniversary. Continuous books we read this year include Isaiah 1–39, 1 and 2 Timothy, Esther, Matthew and Exodus.

Our writers include an Anglican Benedictine in New Zealand, a Presbyterian and Anglicans in South Africa, pioneers and seekers in the UK who blur church boundaries, Pentecostals, Roman Catholics, Baptists and many more. New writers reflect our desire to represent the diverse face of the church: Richard Benda from Rwanda, Simei Monteiro from Brazil and Raj Patta from India are featured for the first time. Rabbi Alexandra Wright also writes for us, for the first time, on some difficult passages in Judges. What all these writers share is a commitment to reflect on the history, theology and message of the Bible, and on their own lives and the places they live.

Last year, we were able to grow our social media presence and use it to strengthen the bonds that make us one. May those bonds grow even more this year, both through our daily effort and through the grace of the One who makes us one.

Yours in Christ,

Nathan Eddy

Acknowledgements and abbreviations

Some writers use the abbreviations CE and BCE to indicate Common Era/before the Common Era according to modern convention. No disrespect is intended.

The use of the letters a or b in a text reference, such as Luke 9:37–43a, indicates that the day's text starts or finishes midway through a verse, usually at a break such as the end of a sentence. Not all Bible versions will indicate such divisions.

We are grateful to the copyright holders for permission to use scriptural quotations from the following Bible versions:

MSG   The Message. Copyright © 1993, 1994, 1995, 1996, 2000, 2001, 2002. Used by permission of NavPress Publishing Group.

NIV   THE HOLY BIBLE, NEW INTERNATIONAL VERSION® Anglicised, NIV® Copyright © 1979, 1984, 2011 by Biblica, Inc.® Used by permission. All rights reserved worldwide.

NKJV   New King James Version®. Copyright © 1982 by Thomas Nelson. Used by permission. All rights reserved.

NRSV   New Revised Standard Version Bible, copyright © 1989 the Division of Christian Education of the National Council of the Churches of Christ in the United States of America. Used by permission. All rights reserved.

RSV   Revised Standard Version of the Bible, copyright © 1946, 1952, and 1971 the Division of Christian Education of the National Council of the Churches of Christ in the United States of America. Used by permission. All rights reserved.

Hymn quotations from *Alleluia Aotearoa*, *Faith Forever Singing* and *Hope is Our Song* are used with the permission of the New Zealand Hymnbook Trust.

Reading the Bible

Notes based on the New Revised Standard Version by **Catrin Harland**

 Catrin Harland is the Methodist chaplain to the University of Sheffield, where she spends her time discussing life and faith with students and staff, usually over a coffee and a slice of cake. She is passionate about equipping young adults to live out their calling in the church and the world. She has a doctorate in New Testament studies, a passion for reading, walking and comedy (watching, rather than performing, much to the relief of all who know her), and three children who fill her time fairly effectively between them.

Sunday 1 January
All human life: singing with the God of poetry

Psalm 1:1–6

Happy are those who do not follow the advice of the wicked, or take the path that sinners tread, or sit in the seat of scoffers; but their delight is in the law of the LORD, and on his law they meditate day and night. (verses 1–2)

This week, we shall look at some of the types of writing in the Bible – the kinds of texts that we will encounter during the year. We'll find letters, stories, history, teaching, wisdom and prophecy. But we begin with a psalm, as the Psalms in many ways sum up all the rest.

The Bible is, in one sense, an account of human interaction with God – God at work through historical events, people learning about God through stories and teaching, God present in the believers' fellowship, divine inspiration in wise or prophetic speech. And the Psalms are a collection of poetic hymns which express human emotion and human relationship with God.

They reflect humanity at its most raw – people struggling to follow God, wrestling with a sense of betrayal, or desperately pleading for justification, revenge or forgiveness. They show people celebrating God's creative activity, rejoicing in God's love, singing in worship or (as here) declaring a commitment to follow God's law. They include expressions of wisdom, community, broken fellowship, hatred, love and anger. Like the prophets, they demand justice. And they rehearse the history of God's people.

In short, whether good or bad, in the Psalms all human life is found.

† God, give me honesty to shed my tears before you, courage to bring my questions to you, and commitment to sing my joy to you.

Monday 2 January
Older and wiser?
Celebrating the God of wisdom

Proverbs 8:22–31

When he marked out the foundations of the earth, then I was beside him, like a master worker; and I was daily his delight, rejoicing before him always, rejoicing in his inhabited world and delighting in the human race. (verses 29b–31)

Wisdom, we often hear, comes with age. I hope this is true – that one day, if I live long enough, I will become truly wise. But I'm not so sure. Experience and knowledge may come with age, but does wisdom not relate more to how this is applied? I have met some very wise young people (and a few foolish elders), who learn from their experience, understand the limits of their knowledge and are aware of the consequences of their actions.

The book of Proverbs is dedicated to the pursuit and celebration of wisdom. Much of it is a collection of insights – perhaps reflecting the collective applied experience of a community, written down for the benefit of future generations. It is the biblical equivalent of the culturally-shaped little sayings many of us remember hearing from our parents or grandparents.

But this part of the book is simply a celebration of the very nature of wisdom. It celebrates wisdom not only as a part of God's creation, but as the first work of creation. Before shaping the heavens and earth, God made wisdom. Wisdom is intimately bound up in the relationship between Creator and creation. It has been there from the very beginning of that relationship, rejoicing in it.

Perhaps wisdom is even more than understanding how to apply our experience to live better. Wisdom is a part of godliness. It comes from living in relationship with God. God's wisdom is deeper than ours can ever be, however long we live, and any of us, at any age, can know God and live wisely.

† God of wisdom, make us wise enough to seek your will, wise enough to choose your ways, wise enough to trust in you. Draw us deeper into you, until your wisdom lives in us.

For further thought
• Paul says, 'For the wisdom of this world is foolishness with God.' (1 Corinthians 3:19) What do you think he meant by this?

Tuesday 3 January
Does God care? Challenging the God of history

Ezra 1:1–11

In the first year of King Cyrus of Persia, in order that the word of the Lord by the mouth of Jeremiah might be accomplished, the Lord stirred up the spirit of King Cyrus of Persia so that he sent a herald throughout all his kingdom. (verse 1)

Open any newspaper and you might find yourself wondering where God is. Does God even care? It is a question which has troubled humans since we began to think about our relationship with the divine. Even in the Bible we find people and nations demanding an answer to it.

The history writers of the Bible, however, are clear that God can – and does – intervene in people's lives, acting through the good news and the bad, shaping history according to a divine plan. When things were not going well, when powerful nations conquered Israel and exiled her people, when the Temple was destroyed, these were presented as the consequences of human unfaithfulness and divine anger. And now that anger has subsided, God is using a foreign leader as an agent of grace.

This is not without its problems, of course. What are we to think when we see whole communities destroyed by natural disasters, or vulnerable children apparently abandoned to the mercy of the merciless? If this is God's doing, what does it say about God's compassion? If it is not, what does it say about God's power?

These are difficult questions, with no easy answers. Sometimes, like the Israelites in exile, all we can do is wrestle and cry out. But for Ezra, there was a message of hope. Through the generosity (or the careful political calculations) of Cyrus, ruler of the Persian Empire, Israel is restored to her homeland, Temple, worship and relationship with God. This is no accident, we are clearly told. This is the love of God.

† King of heaven, comfort those who feel themselves at the mercy of rulers or of the forces of nature. Give us courage to wrestle with difficult questions, and faith to see you at work.

For further thought
- Where does all this leave those who are not lucky enough to see an end to their suffering? Is God's grace selectively bestowed?

Wednesday 4 January
Weapons into beauty:
responding to the God of prophecy

Micah 4:1–7

For out of Zion shall go forth instruction, and the word of the Lord from Jerusalem. He shall judge between many peoples ... they shall beat their swords into ploughshares, and their spears into pruning hooks; nation shall not lift up sword against nation, neither shall they learn war any more. (verses 2b and 3b)

In the British Museum, in London, there is a remarkable set of sculptures. They include trees, animals and a royal throne. And all are made of guns – the instruments of death and war – turned into things of beauty and expressions of peace.

For Micah, as for many of the prophets, contemplation of the future of Jerusalem offers an all-embracing, peaceful vision. The prophets promise the Israelites that their spiritual home will become a focal point for all people, bringing peace and harmony between the nations. But this is not strictly a relationship of equals. Israel has a special place in this vision, instructing all the nations in the ways of the Lord.

This must have been a comforting message for an occupied and exiled people. It promises a future in which they will no longer be oppressed, but will have power. And significantly, they will not use that power to oppress others, but to invite others to share in the joy of knowing and worshipping God, in peace and harmony.

How sad, then, that although Jerusalem has indeed become a spiritual home for many people, in the process it has become one of the most fought-over cities in the world. Perhaps, once again, we need to hear that vision of hope from the prophets. A vision of hope, of peace, of nations learning war no more. A vision in which bridges are built on the ruins of tanks, and hands empty of guns are extended in love.

† God of Abraham, Isaac, Ishmael and Jacob, bring peace to Jerusalem, that holy city in a holy land. Bless all who work for peace there and elsewhere – give them courage, strength and hope.

For further thought

- Where in your own life, in your local community or globally do swords need to be beaten into ploughshares? What can you do to help?

Thursday 5 January
Love and best wishes: writing the God of community

Romans 16:1–16

Greet Asyncritus, Phlegon, Hermes, Patrobas, Hermas, and the brothers and sisters who are with them. Greet Philologus, Julia, Nereus and his sister, and Olympas, and all the saints who are with them. Greet one another with a holy kiss. All the churches of Christ greet you. (verses 14–16)

I am a terrible letter-writer. As a child, I could never keep up a pen-pal relationship and was relieved that my birthday's closeness to Christmas meant I could get away with one set of thank-you letters each year. Even now, I frequently forget to reply to emails and no doubt often cause offence as a result.

Not so for Paul, who appears to have been an enthusiastic letter-writer. His output includes the short note to Philemon and the lengthy theological treatise which is the Epistle to the Romans. But even in Romans – a text whose complex theology has engaged Christians over many hundreds of years – we find a personal touch. Most of the final chapter comprises a long list of greetings. We can almost see Paul wracking his brains to make sure he has left no one out.

This list of names, affectionately remembered, shows not Paul the great theologian, but Paul the valued member of the community of faith. He had probably never visited the Roman Church at this point, but he is known to them by reputation. And through the networks of Christians around the Roman Empire, he knows many of its members personally.

We are shaped in our discipleship to a large extent by our faith community – not merely by those we see on a day-to-day basis, but by the worldwide community of Christians, and by those who have gone before us and set us an example. Thanks be to God for the love and fellowship of others!

† Thank you, God, for the love, care and encouragement which has shaped me as a disciple. Thank you for those who have loved, challenged and corrected me. Give me the grace to support others too.

For further thought

• Who have you not written or spoken to recently? Is there someone who would benefit from your encouragement?

Friday 6 January
Finding wonder:
going deeper with the God of stories

Mark 4:26–34

With many such parables he spoke the word to them, as they were able to hear it; he did not speak to them except in parables, but he explained everything in private to his disciples. (verses 33–34)

I always enjoy reading stories with children. I love sharing picture books with toddlers, and discussing more complex stories with pre-teens. I enjoy young children's complete acceptance for a story. They do not need to know whether it really happened or is true to life – it's a story, to be enjoyed. They learn from it and grow through it, without even realising it.

But an older child might have questions. Why did this happen to that character? Will it happen to me? What does this mean? Does it point to something deeper? These questions lead into other thoughts, ideas and questions – for some of which, there are no simple answers.

So it is with Jesus and his followers. He offers stories. He points to ordinary things – the crops growing unseen in the soil, or the huge mustard trees which start so small. He fills people's minds with pictures. He doesn't need to explain them – the image is enough for now, and will gradually become more and more meaningful. As his hearers walk past the mustard tree each day, they will be reminded of his teaching; their understanding will deepen and questions will arise.

But with those who have been following for longer, who have learnt more, he shares a little more. He explains, asks questions, discusses and teaches.

Sometimes, I long for answers and explanations, and want to wrestle with the deeper meaning. But sometimes, it's enough just to know that the kingdom of God is like the things that grow, and I can look, enjoy and learn a little without even realising it.

† Christ, who took the children in your arms and blessed them, help us to become more childlike in our learning and our growing, that we too may enter the kingdom of heaven.

For further thought

- Where can you see pictures of the kingdom in the ordinary things you see around you? Can you use the everyday to illustrate the eternal?

Saturday 7 January
Following our Rabbi:
learning from the God of teaching

John 14:15–24

You will know that I am in my Father, and you in me, and I in you. They who have my commandments and keep them are those who love me; and those who love me will be loved by my Father, and I will love them and reveal myself to them. (verses 20–21)

Yesterday, we considered how, through stories, Jesus inspires people to discover the kingdom. And how, for those who are his closer followers, Jesus teaches, explains and elaborates.

Today, Jesus is drawing together much of that teaching for his very closest disciples, at the end of his earthly ministry. He promises to send the Holy Spirit; he teaches them how to live together in community; he describes his closeness to the Father; and in the very same breath and the same language, he describes the closeness of his followers to him. We are 'in Christ' and he is 'in us', just as he is 'in his Father'.

This is the closeness of a rabbi and disciple. Like the best teachers, Jesus has taught his disciples not just information or facts, but a whole way of being. He has taught them to love learning from him. He has taught them through his own life of self-giving service. He has taught them the meaning of the kingdom and shown them the very nature of the King. And now he is leaving them, supported by the Spirit, to continue his work and teach those who come after. He is leaving them with a reminder of their closeness to him – the disciples walking in the way of the Rabbi and showing others how to do likewise.

This is our calling – to walk in his way, to follow where he leads, to learn from his teaching, to show others the way of love, and to seek to grow daily more like him. The simplest and yet most challenging lesson of all – and one to be contemplated and practised year long.

† Heavenly teacher, give me the humility to learn, the love to put my learning into practice, and the grace to share what I have learnt with others. Make me a faithful disciple.

For further thought

• What lesson do you struggle to learn from Jesus the Rabbi? What is he trying to teach you? And what lessons have you learnt well?

Readings in Matthew (1)
Secrets of the kingdom

Notes based on the New International Version (UK) by **Jan Sutch Pickard**

Jan Sutch Pickard is a writer and storyteller living on the Isle of Mull, and a former Warden of the Abbey in Iona. In the last few years she has served twice with the Ecumenical Accompaniment Programme in Palestine and Israel, based in small West Bank villages but with a chance to spend time in Jerusalem and reflect on its divisions today. A Methodist Local Preacher, she leads worship for the Church of Scotland on Mull.

Sunday 8 January
A bright cloud

Matthew 17:1–13

A bright cloud covered them, and a voice from the cloud said, 'This is my Son, whom I love … Listen to him!' (verse 5)

This week's Gospel stories are about seeing – and not seeing; wonder – and fear; hearing – and questioning; beginning to understand what is beyond words. It is about the unbearable beauty of God's presence, the mystery of God at work in our lives: the 'secrets of the kingdom'.

First, the 'transfiguration': on the mountaintop his disciples looked at Jesus and saw him changed in ways they could not understand. Coming down from the mountain, later, he told them about his coming suffering and death – a message hard to hear. But then and there they were in the cloud, a 'bright cloud', and I'm trying to imagine what that was like.

A card came to me in the post as I was writing this: a piece of encaustic wax art, like a burst of light, like a swirling cloud. I find it beautiful, but hard to describe. Pat, the artist-friend who made it, is very creative, using paint and craft materials rather than words. She is also registered blind. Details of the world around are obscured, often baffling, sometimes threatening. But Pat knows the value of light. Light speaks to her of God's presence. Listening to it, she wants to share it.

† Mysterious God, from the bright cloud of your presence you speak to us, help us to hear and to share the light of your love.

Monday 9 January
Moving mountains

Matthew 17:14–27

Truly I tell you, if you have faith as small as a mustard seed, you can say to this mountain, 'Move from here to there,' and it will move. Nothing will be impossible for you. (verse 20)

On the mountaintop, three friends of Jesus had experiences beyond words. But on the way down, Jesus began talking to them about his death. Then at the foot of the mountain baffled disciples, who had watched Jesus healing a sick child, wondered why they could not do the same. He told them that they needed enough faith to move mountains. Impossible! And yet with God nothing is impossible.

In 2015 the Scottish celebrations of 70 years of Christian Aid focused on how many 'mountains' (for instance, of disease, debt, poverty) have been climbed and how many there are still to conquer. Staff members set themselves the challenge of climbing seventy 'Munros' – mountains of over 3000 feet (approximately 914 metres). On the island where I live, I saw supporters of the charity and local congregations joining them, raising money through sponsorship, but raising awareness too. People will have been challenged and changed by this experience. Mountains of not-caring have begun to move.

The Gospel account follows with another conversation: Jesus talking again about his death: '"The Son of Man is going to be delivered into the hands of men. They will kill him, and on the third day he will be raised to life." And the disciples were filled with grief.' Of course they were distressed to imagine his death. That third day, when the stone would be rolled away from the tomb, was still beyond their believing.

† Huge and hostile as mountains, problems can be overcome; small as a mustard seed, faith can make a difference – God, with you nothing is impossible. Thank you!

For further thought
• What good cause or charity do you support, and what are the mountains it needs to move?

Tuesday 10 January
These little ones

Matthew 18:1–14

Your Father in heaven is not willing that any of these little ones should perish. (verse 14)

Two scenes come alive in my mind. One, a few years ago, had only a few witnesses – a remote Palestinian village where life is hard, under pressure of poverty and politics, and the threat of violence. But this was a hopeful scene: a group of children had found a lamb in the fold with a broken leg, and brought it to one of the shepherds. He sat on the ground – they all did – and carefully felt and manipulated the leg, then sent one child running for salve, another for cloth to bandage it, another for a splint. They quietly watched and learned as he cared for this little life.

I was present there, watching and learning too.

I wasn't on a Turkish beach in 2015, when a boat carrying Syrian refugees (one of many) overturned. Some of the passengers made it to shore, others were drowned, including a three-year-old, Aylan Kurdi, with his mother and brother. Pictures of the child's body on the tide-line moved people all over the world. Would their pity make any difference to the huge tragedy of the Syrian people, or of desperate migrants from many other places, seeking a better life? Some relief agencies were doing what they could. But where was God in all this?

Surely God was grieving too: the God who weeps for a world broken and divided by human sinfulness; God, the good shepherd, who, with human help, can seek out and save the little and the lost.

† Loving God, you rejoice in children, grieve for those who are lost; may we share your hands-on caring, knowing that we too are your children.

For further thought

• When has a picture or story in the news moved you? What did you do? Is this another way of God speaking to us?

Wednesday 11 January
Face to face, heart to heart

Matthew 18:15–20

'Where two or three gather in my name, there am I with them.' *(verse 20)*

The words above can be used by members of very small congregations as consolation. But the meaning goes deeper. In small groups, people can give more support, listen more carefully and be more honest with each other. Christians meeting in small groups can help each other to grow spiritually. The disciples were a small group. Jesus invited them to imagine a situation that might arise.

The story goes like this: one of your group is doing wrong – others are well aware of that. One response would be silent disapproval. Another would be to talk about the person behind their back, in a judgemental way. Another would be to have a major confrontation, involving the whole community. What is the loving thing to do – and what will be most effective in changing bad behaviour?

Jesus encouraged his friends to see the value of speaking to someone, rather than about them. A face-to-face conversation is the best way to broach a difficult subject. In some situations, it may help to involve others as witnesses. Take every chance of dealing with the problem fairly, and treat each other with respect. Pray together, too.

The way that any group deals with conflict has bigger implications and impact, like a stone dropped into a pool, creating widening circles. But at the heart of the story that Jesus invites us to imagine here are two human beings face to face, glimpsing in each other the presence of God.

† God-with-us, help us to find ways of being more fully with each other: in honesty, in fairness, in love.

For further thought

• Think prayerfully about someone who has made you disappointed or angry. How can you raise the problem and solve it together?

Thursday 12 January
Heartfelt forgiveness

Matthew 18:21–35

Then Peter came to Jesus and asked, 'Lord, how many times shall I forgive my brother or sister who sins against me? Up to seven times?' Jesus answered, 'I tell you, not seven times, but seventy-seven times.' (verses 21–22)

Exaggeration adds zest to this conversation about another imaginary situation. Peter was thinking that forgiving seven times would show great forbearance. 'What?' we can imagine Jesus exclaiming, 'Just seven times, Peter? Seventy-seven times!'

Then Jesus told a parable – one that's a tall story. A man owed the king 10 000 bags of gold – an unimaginable sum of money. His merciful master cancelled the debt. But this man learned nothing from this experience and, finding a fellow servant who was in debt to him – owing a mere hundred silver coins – demanded it with menaces. Jesus will have told this story much better – with a twinkle in his eye, with the humour that can drive home a point. But suddenly it's not funny anymore: the unmerciful man in the story is punished.

What are we to make then of today's financiers and governments, whose policies have driven poor people and developing nations into debt – who demand repayment and impose heavy penalties? What are we to make of the powerful, who believe that they are entitled to expenses and bonuses which are paid with money taken unforgivingly from their fellow citizens? It is hard to see the funny side of such selfishness, such impunity.

Of course Jesus' parable isn't just about money. We (who are so aware of the way that others offend us) need to see ourselves as the servant who owed a great deal, whose huge debt was completely forgiven.

God forgives us over and over again. And we, with our brothers and sisters, need to do the same. Right, Peter?

† Forgiving God, Father of all, forgive us our debts, as we forgive those who are in our debt.

For further thought

• We all need forgiveness. What do you want to say 'sorry' for – to someone else? To God?

Friday 13 January
The kingdom of heaven

Matthew 19:1–15

Then people brought little children to Jesus for him to place his hands on them and pray for them. But the disciples rebuked them. Jesus said, 'Let the little children come to me, and do not hinder them, for the kingdom of heaven belongs to such as these.' (verses 13–14)

Erin, 3 years old, watched a rainbow forming, a curve of vivid colours: 'It's a rainbow – and it's come to stay!' The rainbow didn't last, but I hope her sense of wonder will. 'The kingdom of heaven belongs to such as these.'

What is the kingdom of heaven like? The Pharisees didn't think of asking that, having other things on their minds. They were trying to trap Jesus by asking what was lawful. Later his disciples tried to protect him by asking mothers to take their distracting children away.

But the kingdom of heaven has a way of breaking through, and widening all our horizons.

The Pharisees asked legalistic questions about divorce. In a society where women were often seen as the property of – and problems for – men, divorce seemed a solution. Jesus responded that men and women were both created by God; in marriage, when they have become one, human beings should honour that, not try to undo God's work. And what about those whose sexuality is different? If eunuchs, castrated or born that way, cannot reproduce, are they outside God's plan for humankind? Jesus reminded his hearers that some 'choose to live like eunuchs for the sake of the kingdom of heaven', which can include – and be honoured by – our differences.

Women and eunuchs were both outsiders. Children, also, in many cultures have been seen as second-class citizens, the property of adults, exploited, abused, often ignored. Jesus welcomed them with care, celebrating their innocence and joy. Children are very close to God. Their wonder holds the secrets of the kingdom.

† God whose love includes and transforms all, widen our horizons, teach us to respect those who are different, help us to rediscover a child's wonder.

For further thought
- Have you ever felt an outsider? Who are the outsiders in your community now? How can they be included?

Saturday 14 January
Treasure in heaven

Matthew 19:16–30

Jesus answered, '… Go, sell your possessions and give to the poor, and you will have treasure in heaven. Then come, follow me.' (verse 21)

When the young man heard this, he went away sad, because he had great wealth.

The picture of this rich young man going sadly away hangs heavy on my mind, as I hear Jesus say: 'It is easier for a camel to go through the eye of a needle than for someone who is rich to enter the kingdom of God.'

That proverb has a long history in Jewish midrash and wise sayings of different faiths. Featuring camel or elephant, it's absurd and impossible – except if God intervenes. Jesus may have known a gateway in the old city of Jerusalem, a narrow wicket gate through which a camel could only pass without its load. But no one is sure of that gate's location.

The significant thing, though, would be the load. That young man, like any rich person, had too much stuff, was weighed down with possessions. Jesus' instruction to sell his belongings, give away his money, was like unloading the camel. Then the next step might be possible. And then how light his steps would be …

I watch that young man walking away heavy-hearted: not a bad man, he knew and kept the commandments, wanted to live in God's way. He just had too much stuff. But what would have happened once he started to let go? Leaving behind homes, families, land, for 'eternal life' isn't easy. In the process, values are reversed, life is turned back to front and upside down. The first shall be last, and the last first … Could the rich young man, weighed down with possessions and ways of thinking that allowed little freedom of movement, have coped with such radical change?

† Pray for people living in poverty, and those who have more than they need; for those who yearn for change, and those who don't know how to begin; for a just sharing of the world's resources.

For further thought

• Could this be me? How can I change? How do I let go? And what for me would be 'treasure in heaven'?

Readings in Matthew (1)
From Galilee to Jerusalem

Notes based on the New International Version (UK) by **Mark Woods**

Mark Woods is a Baptist minister and journalist who has worked for *The Baptist Times* and the *Methodist Recorder*. He currently writes mainly for the online magazine *Christian Today* and is on the leadership team of his church in Cheltenham. Aside from reading everything he can lay his hands on, he enjoys walking, photographing birds and running, though more when it's over than when he's doing it. He is the author of *Salvation Songs: Seventy Great Hymns and their Stories*, published by Verité CM.

Sunday 15 January
God is more generous than we are

Matthew 20:1–16

I want to give the man who was hired last the same as I gave you. Don't I have the right to do what I want with my own money? Or are you envious because I am generous? So the last will be first, and the first will be last. (verses 15–16)

As this week's readings begin, Jesus is on his last journey to Jerusalem. On his way he encounters people whose stories give us deep spiritual insights, like the Pharisees and the rich young ruler in chapter 19. He also tells parables, including this story of the workers in the vineyard.

However, it hardly seems right. A denarius was a day's wage for a labourer, so it was fair enough for those who worked all day. But the owner seeks out unemployed workers and offers them the same pay even if they only worked a couple of hours. That wasn't just bad business, it seemed to go against natural justice.

However, the story is about God's generosity. God is just, but he gives without calculating. God reaches out to all, deserving it or not.

The background to the story is the troubled times in which Jesus lived, with much poverty and social disruption. The landowner is an image of God, but he also stands for a real landowner, who gives work to the poor at his own cost. In a time of austerity in which poor people are squeezed, this story also speaks of the responsibilities of the rich.

† God, help us not to be jealous of your generosity to others, but to rejoice in it; and teach us to be generous too.

Monday 16 January
The first shall be last

Matthew 20:17–34

Whoever wants to become great among you must be your servant, and whoever wants to be first must be your slave – just as the Son of Man did not come to be served, but to serve, and to give his life as a ransom for many. (verses 26–28)

This passage seems to have three sections: Jesus predicts his death, James and John ask to be seated in places of honour in his kingdom and two blind men are healed. In fact, it's a unity. Jesus is going to the cross. His followers win honour by taking up their cross and suffering with him, not by worldly success. James and John are blind to this until Jesus opens their eyes, a 'miracle' echoed and reinforced by the physical healing in verses 29–34.

The lure of success, of money and power, is very strong. Perhaps that's particularly true today, when we're surrounded by images of beautiful and wealthy people living lives that most of us could never aspire to. It can make us discontented and jealous.

But Jesus offers a different way of looking at the world altogether. He says that James and John will share his suffering or 'drink from my cup' – a reference to their martyrdom. Their privilege is to walk in his footsteps, wherever that leads them.

It isn't wrong to want to excel at our chosen career. Sometimes that will lead to success and recognition. But Jesus says these shouldn't be our reason for wanting to excel. Our motivation in this, as in everything, should be our discipleship.

This is particularly true for Christian leaders, whom Jesus has in mind in this teaching. Authority and leadership should always be exercised lovingly and humbly. The word 'minister' means 'servant' and even Jesus 'did not come to be served but to serve'.

† God, I pray that you will forgive me if I have wanted worldly success more than I should. Open my eyes to what is really important and help me to put following Jesus first.

For further thought
- Which of the world's values do I blindly take for granted instead of judging them by the standards of Jesus?

Tuesday 17 January
An odd sort of triumphal entry

Matthew 21:1–11

The crowds that went ahead of him and those that followed shouted: 'Hosanna to the Son of David!' 'Blessed is he who comes in the name of the Lord!' 'Hosanna in the highest!' When Jesus entered Jerusalem, the whole city was stirred and asked, 'Who is this?' (verses 9–10)

The entry of Jesus into Jerusalem on what we now call Palm Sunday is the beginning of the last act in the drama. It has all sorts of biblical and historical echoes. The crowd waved palms as they did when Jehu was made king in 2 Kings 9:13 and when Simon Maccabaeus entered Jerusalem after his victory (1 Maccabees 13:51). The crowd shouted 'Hosanna!', from Psalm 118:25, which means 'Save now!' For many, these words might have been just a cheer – Hooray! – but they carry a weight of meaning whether they knew it or not.

It was a very dangerous moment. Jerusalem was overflowing with Passover pilgrims (one estimate is around two and a half million). The feast was a focus of nationalistic feelings and the Romans would be very nervous. If Jesus were ever to start a popular rising against them, this would be the time.

However, he chose to enter the city not on a warhorse, but on a donkey – a rather absurd animal. The crowd still cheered him, but he made his point. His mission was much, much greater than the liberation of a small Middle Eastern province from its alien ruling powers.

The great tests of our faith come when everyone is telling us that the easy and obvious thing is also the right thing. Jesus could easily have avoided a terrible death by going along with the crowd. Instead of listening to them, he chose the hardest way because he knew that God had called him to it.

† God, when everything around me is pointing to the easy and popular way, help me to keep my mind focused on you. Help me do what's right, even when it's hard.

For further thought

• Conquerors come and go, and their names are barely remembered. Billions of people have heard of Jesus – because he rode a donkey, not a warhorse.

Wednesday 18 January
Jesus cleanses the Temple

Matthew 21:12–17

Jesus ... overturned the tables of the money-changers and the benches of those who were selling doves. 'It is written,' he said to them, "My house will be called a house of prayer," but you are making it a den of robbers.' (verses 12–13)

When Jesus went to the Temple and overturned the tables of the money-changers he was taking on the most entrenched interests of the city. Every Jew had to pay a Temple tax near the Passover time and it had to be in a certain currency. So if people had money in a different currency – if they'd come on pilgrimage from another country, for instance – it would have to be changed, at a ruinous rate of exchange. And doves were a common sacrifice, but they had to be certified acceptable. If you bought a dove outside the Temple you risked its rejection, but pre-certified doves cost a lot more.

It was a racket, and Jesus was outraged. His attack on the money-changers and rip-off traders was popular with the people, but it struck at the root of the power and wealth of the priestly class. This, more than anything, was what led them to call for his death.

Matthew tells us that Jesus drew attention to the children who were shouting his praise. For children, right and wrong are very clear. They haven't learned to compromise or to see things in shades of grey. Elsewhere in Matthew (13:34–30) Jesus tells the parable of the wheat and the tares as a way of encouraging people not to be too quick to judge. But sometimes we have to judge and we have to act, because a situation is intolerable. If it means annoying powerful people, so be it; God calls us to be faithful to him.

† God, help me to be brave enough to stand up for what's right when I see things that are wrong. Help me not to be daunted by powerful people, but to trust in you.

For further thought
• Have I become so used to wrong things that I no longer recognise them? Do I need to start seeing like a child again?

Thursday 19 January
Faith that moves mountains?

Matthew 21:18–27

Truly I tell you, if you have faith and do not doubt ... you can say to this mountain, 'Go, throw yourself into the sea,' and it will be done. If you believe, you will receive whatever you ask for in prayer. (verses 21–22)

The story of the cursing of the fig tree is a strange one. The point of it, however, is to illustrate the power of faith – or rather, the power of the one in whom we have faith.

Jesus' words about being able to command a mountain to cast itself into the sea are hyperbole, not intended to be taken literally. This should caution us against taking verse 21, in which he promises that 'If you believe, you will receive whatever you ask for in prayer' literally either. Much spiritual harm has resulted because this verse is misunderstood. Prayer and faith do nothing by themselves; God chooses to do what God does. It's not as if faith can be measured by weight. In Mark 9:24 the father of a demonised boy says, 'I do believe; help me overcome my unbelief!' There's not much faith there, but Jesus heals the lad.

Nevertheless, Jesus is calling us to trust in God completely, for whatever we need. No matter how hard something seems, he will bring us through it. There's a sharp contrast here with the attitude of the chief priests and the elders who try to catch him out by asking him by what authority he taught. His question in reply throws them into confusion. They try to avoid incriminating themselves and have to reply with a feeble, 'We don't know.'

These priests and elders have no real faith at all. They are just playing games. The faith Jesus has in mind moves mountains.

† God, help me to believe that you will answer my prayers. Give me the faith to believe you can move mountains, and walk round them with me when you choose not to.

For further thought

• What are the 'mountains' – the obstacles, threats or challenges – we're facing in our lives now? Do we believe that God can deal with them?

Friday 20 January
Better late than never

Matthew 21:28–32

Jesus said to them, 'Truly I tell you, the tax collectors and the prostitutes are entering the kingdom of heaven ahead of you. For John came to show you the way of righteousness, and you did not believe him, but the tax collectors and prostitutes did'. (verses 31b–32)

Jesus was indifferent to money, power and respectability. For him, in those class-ridden times, everyone was equal before God. We see this in the parable of the two sons: one was told to go and work in the vineyard, refused and then went; the other said he'd go, and didn't. The one who initially refused stood for the 'sinners' – the tax collectors, prostitutes and similar low-lives. The one who said he'd go but stayed comfortably at home stood for the 'righteous', or self-righteous, who thought themselves far superior to those who were so morally compromised.

The point, though, is that they were both called to go and 'work in the vineyard'. Jesus relates this to the message of John the Baptist, who called people to repent of their sins and turn to God.

There are sins which are plain to everyone. We are all quick to condemn people who lie or cheat, or who are violent or greedy. But Jesus is speaking to the same chief priests and elders who have just tried to catch him out to get him into trouble. They are respectable citizens and Jesus is saying that tax collectors and prostitutes are better than they are, because they repented and believed.

What are the easy, comfortable sins of respectable people? Perhaps pride, or spiritual laziness or a condemning spirit. We may not be guilty of gross immorality (though we may) but we are all vulnerable to these other temptations. We are no better than anyone else, Jesus says; what matters is obedience.

† God, I'm sorry if I have looked down on people and thought that I'm better than they are because my sins are different. Help me to see myself as you see me.

For further thought

- What counts as 'working in the vineyard' for us today? How does God want us to serve him in our daily lives?

Saturday 21 January
The stone the builders rejected

Matthew 21:33–46

Therefore I tell you that the kingdom of God will be taken away from you and given to a people who will produce its fruit. Anyone who falls on this stone will be broken to pieces, anyone on whom it falls will be crushed.
(verses 43–44)

The parable of the tenants has a sort of stern sadness about it. It is aimed at the chief priests and the Pharisees – the experts in religious law and custom, who believed that their knowledge and status gave them authority over lesser mortals. Jesus is placing them firmly in the line of unfaithful Israel, who again and again had failed to respond to the prophets God sent them. And in the end, they would reject him too.

But the wonderful thing about the parable is how wrong they were. Jesus asks what the owner of the vineyard will do to the murderers. They say that he will 'bring those wretches to a wretched end' and rent the vineyard to someone else.

In fact, after the death of Jesus there is no judgement, just a call to repentance. Peter explains what has happened and the people, cut to the heart, say: 'Brothers, what shall we do?' Nobody dies; everyone is welcome to repent and be part of God's new community.

We should be careful how we read this story. It is not that God takes away the 'vineyard' from the Jews and gives it to (mainly Gentile) Christians. The contrast is between those who do what God says – keeping the spirit of the law rather than the letter, loving their neighbours as themselves and loving God with all their heart – and those who don't.

Jesus teaches here that God wants people who will bear fruit. There is no future in selfishness or pride.

† God, thank you for your mercy to me and to all the world. Thank you that nothing can separate us from your love and that no sin is beyond forgiveness.

For further thought
• Read some of the stories of Jesus and see how he treated people, and ask God to show you how you can be like him.

Dreams
Any dream will do?

Notes based on the New Revised Standard Version by **Paul Nicholson SJ**

Paul Nicholson is a Roman Catholic priest, a member of the Society of Jesus, also known as the Jesuits. Since ordination in 1988 he has worked in community development, as a spiritual director and retreat guide, and in the training of ordinands. He is currently assistant to the Jesuit Provincial in Britain. He is editor of *The Way*, a journal of Christian spirituality, and author of *Growing Into Silence* (2011) and *An Advent Pilgrimage* (2013). He lives at the UK Jesuit headquarters in central London.

Sunday 22 January
Tested by dreams

Deuteronomy 13:1–5

If prophets or those who divine by dreams appear among you and promise you omens or portents, and the omens or the portents declared by them take place, and they say, 'Let us follow other gods' (whom you have not known) 'and let us serve them', you must not heed the words. (verses 1–3)

How does God communicate with you? You can probably think of different ways. You might first look to the words of scripture – you wouldn't read these notes unless you believed that God has a message to be found in the Bible. Then, maybe, you expect to hear God's word through your church leaders, or to discover God's will in the events of your everyday life. But there is another way that God speaks to people, and that's the way that we'll be looking at during the next two weeks. That way is through dreams.

This week we will look at six dreams recorded in the book of Genesis, asking what God is saying in each of them and what that might in turn say to us today. But we start with a warning. Dreams cannot be accepted uncritically. They need to be tested, to see whether they can be trusted as a guide for action. Indeed, in this passage from the book of Deuteronomy, the author suggests that God is testing the people through the dreams they are presented with. Where do your own dreams lead you? To a closer following of God, or in some other direction?

† O God, whose dreaming brought the world and all it contains into being, shape my dreams so they lead me to follow you more faithfully.

Monday 23 January
When the pieces fall into place

Genesis 20:1–7

Then God said to him in the dream, 'Yes, I know that you did this in the integrity of your heart; furthermore it was I who kept you from sinning against me.' (verse 6)

In 1865 the German chemist August Kekulé was working out the structure of various chemical compounds. He knew the elements of one such compound, benzene, but he couldn't see how they fitted together. Then one night he had a dream, of a snake circling round to bite its own tail. On waking, he realised that he had his solution. The atoms in benzene were arranged in a ring, a structure that explained well the observed properties of the compound.

Sometimes dreams can bring together different aspects of a situation or problem, to resolve it in a way that the waking mind has not been able to. This is one way of thinking about Abimelech's dream here. He has offered hospitality to two strangers, Abraham and Sarah, seemingly brother and sister. Finding himself attracted to the woman, he takes her for his own. Perhaps, even then, he sensed there was something not quite right here, that all was not exactly as it seemed. In his dream, the pieces fall into place. Despite what he has been told, this woman is not the sister of the traveller he has made welcome, but his wife. With the clarity that the dream gives him, Abimelech sees what he must do. In the morning, he returns Sarah to Abraham and sends them on their way, laden with gifts.

Can you recall a time when, in dreaming, your own vision has clarified, so that on waking you know what you must do or where you must go? Can you recognise God speaking to you through your own dreams of this kind?

† 'Muddy water, left still, grows clear.' Lord, help me see clearly when the situation is unclear, the outlook misty and the way ahead obscure.

For further thought

• For the next few days, keep a notepad by your bed, and quickly note down when you wake any dreams you can then recall.

Tuesday 24 January
Surely the Lord is in this place

Genesis 28:10–22

Jacob left Beer-sheba and went toward Haran … He dreamed that there was a ladder set up on the earth, the top of it reaching to heaven; and the angels of God were ascending and descending on it. (verses 10 and 12)

In Jacob's dream, the ladder with angels is simply a prelude to a great promise that God makes: that he and his descendants will be given the land on which he lies, as far as the eye can see, and that everyone on earth will be blessed in Jacob's offspring. Yet the ladder is not incidental. It shows that from now on heaven and earth are not separate realms, going their own ways. Rather, they are intimately connected, with messages and messengers passing freely from one to the other.

In the Gospels, the Son of God, travelling from heaven to earth in the incarnation, is named Emmanuel; 'God-with-us'. Centuries before, Jacob senses this truth in his dream. On waking he sees God has been here with him, unrecognised, and prays that this presence of God will continue to go with him. The blessing Jacob's descendants will bring to all peoples will consist precisely in this, that they will demonstrate to everyone the presence of God in their midst. Sometimes that will be a glorious presence, as when the prophet Isaiah pictures people from all over the world flocking to the Temple in Jerusalem. At other times, it will be a silent, suffering presence, exemplified by the persecution of the Jews in the Holocaust of the Second World War. Either way, God will be there.

The invitation of this dream is to join with Jacob's response, wherever you find yourself and in whatever situation you face. Can you exclaim with him today: 'Surely the Lord is in this place – and I did not know it!'

† Lord, my head knows that you are present in all times and all places; open the eyes of my heart to see your presence, to feel that you are truly Emmanuel.

For further thought

• If you can, search out Francis Thompson's poem 'In no strange land', a meditation on Jacob's dream brought into our own time.

Wednesday 25 January
All that you need, and more

Genesis 31:1–16

The angel of God said to me in the dream, 'Jacob,' and I said, 'Here I am!'
And he said, '... I have seen all that Laban is doing to you ... Now leave
this land at once and return to the land of your birth.' (verses 11–13)

The dream in this passage is a strange one, of striped, speckled
and mottled goats. Its effect is to remind Jacob of the way in
which God has helped him prosper, despite the years he has spent
serving his cheating uncle, Laban. Now, God tells him, his time of
servitude is over, and he can return to his homeland with his wives
and children.

Once again a dream acts to underline the reality of a situation that
might be lost sight of in the course of everyday, more conscious
living. It reminds Jacob of what he already knows to be true in his
heart of hearts, and suggests to him a course of action he should
take as a result. It might well seem safer to stay with Laban, to
remain with the familiar pattern of living, despite its discomforts.
But God promises that if he makes a break with all this, he can
count on God taking care of him, as God has in the past.

Every now and then it can be good to review our lives, to notice
where, perhaps, we have become stuck in a rut, and consider
whether God is calling us out into something new. It may well
seem scary even to become aware of such a call, let alone to follow
where it leads. Where might you find the strength you need for
this? Perhaps, like Jacob, you are invited to recall how God has
already given you all that you need, and more. With that assurance,
it becomes easier to contemplate a move into pastures new.

† O God, giver of all good gifts, open my eyes to recognise more clearly all the ways
in which you uphold and provide for me; let me be grateful for your loving care.

For further thought

• Count your blessings! List ways God has taken care of you
recently, gifts he has given you and people he has sent to help
you.

Thursday 26 January
A time to speak, a time to be silent

Genesis 37:5–11

Joseph had another dream, and told it to his brothers, saying, 'Look, I have had another dream: the sun, the moon, and eleven stars were bowing down to me.' But when he told it to his father and to his brothers, his father rebuked him. (verses 9 and 10)

Some of the stories that we are considering describe perplexing dreams. No one has any difficulty in interpreting Joseph's dreams here. Their meaning is perfectly plain. Joseph, youngest of twelve brothers, is destined to outshine the other members of his family, to the extent that they will have no option but to bow down before him. Unsurprisingly, his brothers aren't delighted to hear this. Indeed, it only increases the dislike they already feel for their spoilt brat of a brother.

It will be many years before these dreams are realised, years in which Joseph will have suffered greatly. But during this time he will have learnt from his suffering, so that when he is finally united with his brothers he is no longer the swaggering figure of his youth. By then he will indeed be a great man, second only to Pharaoh in Egypt. Yet he will then treat his impoverished family with great tenderness and compassion.

It can be easy, in pursuit of your own dream, to ride roughshod over others, failing to take their feelings into account. The more clearly you see how things should be, the more tempting it is to push your own ideas through. The ideas may indeed be good; the dream may well be a true one. But maybe Joseph's sufferings would have been less acute if he had been able to learn a little tact and subtlety earlier in his career?

† Lord, as I follow the dreams that you plant within me, help me to be sensitive to the feelings of others.

For further thought

• What are the dreams that you're currently following in your own life? What effect does this have on those nearest to you?

Friday 27 January
The imagery of dreams

Genesis 40:5–19
*One night they both dreamed – the cupbearer and the baker of the king
of Egypt, who were confined in the prison – each his own dream, and
each dream with its own meaning. When Joseph came to them in the
morning, he saw that they were troubled. (verses 5 and 6)*

In *The Interpretation of Dreams,* Sigmund Freud considered at
length the symbolic meaning of dream images. As we see in today's
passage, this work is part of a long tradition. Joseph is presented
by his two fellow prisoners with stories rich in imagery. In one he
sees a path to life, and in the other to death. Yet, as he insists, 'Do
not interpretations belong to God?'

I worked for some years as a full-time retreat director. As well as
describing their prayer, some retreatants would want to talk about
their dreams. Indeed, the two were often closely related. In sleep,
the mind could throw up images that would cast light upon the
prayer of the preceding day. And what was experienced in prayer
could continue to unfold and be explored as the retreatant slept.

There was not, nor can there be, I believe, any easy one-to-one
correlation between a dream image and a meaning. A cup or a bird
will have different meanings for different people at different times.
Yet God can use these images to get a message through to me,
just as the images in the parables of Jesus are used. As I stay with
them, and ponder them prayerfully, I might come to an insight or
realisation that God has wanted me to grasp.

What is needed here is time – time to be still, to reflect. Such time is
in short supply for many today. But without it, I risk missing a word
or a gift that God may be anxious to give me.

† O Lord, to whom no language is foreign and no tongue unknown, help me to
understand you as you speak to me through the images of my dreams.

For further thought
• Is there an image from a recent dream staying with you at
  present? Or one that captures something of your own dreams
  for the future?

Saturday 28 January
How you gonna have a dream come true?

Genesis 41:15–36

I saw in my dream seven ears of grain, full and good, growing on one stalk, and seven ears, withered, thin, and blighted by the east wind, sprouting after them; and the thin ears swallowed up the seven good ears. (verses 22–24)

In the musical *Joseph and his Amazing Technicolor Dreamcoat*, Pharaoh, bearing a startling resemblance to Elvis Presley, tells a bemused Joseph two dreams. But Joseph is not bemused for long. Soon he is commandeering Egypt's wealth to lay up supplies for the years of famine the dreams forecast. So successful is he that the peoples of the Middle East, including his estranged brothers, flock to Egypt for relief supplies.

The musical highlights well, if playfully, the contrast between the magnificence of Pharaoh and the insignificance of the imprisoned Joseph. But here lies the paradox at the heart of this story. Pharaoh has no reason to trust Joseph. As far as he knows, the man is no more than an ungrateful adulterer, deserving of punishment. Yet unless he trusts him here, Egypt will share in the coming famine and destruction. Nor is he being invited to trust, initially, in a carefully considered, costed scheme, but rather in an idea based on an interpretation of a pair of strange dreams.

It's easy to dismiss dreams, contrasting the dreamer with the practical man or woman of action. Dreams are viewed as idle, fanciful, as fleeting and unreal. Yet, as a song in another musical *South Pacific* insists, you have got to have a dream to experience a dream coming true.

Followers of Christ are called to be dreamers, sharing the dream that Jesus called the kingdom of God. Only by trusting that dream in even the darkest of times can we commit ourselves to working alongside God to bring it into being.

† Lord Jesus, you inspired your followers with your dream of the kingdom of God. Help us to share that dream, and to work for its fulfilment.

For further thought

• How would you describe the dream of the kingdom of God to someone who knew nothing of it?

History of IBRA and the International Fund

The International Bible Reading Association (IBRA) was founded by the Sunday School Union (SSU) committee under Charles Waters in 1882. At the time Waters was the manager of a bank in King's Cross. As a devout young man and Sunday school teacher, Waters had arrived in London in 1859 to further his career and had encountered the brilliant and inspirational teaching of Charles Spurgeon. He threw himself heart and soul into working with Spurgeon and the Sunday School Union. In 1882, the SSU wrote to all members in Britain and overseas inviting them to join the newly formed International Bible Reading Association, circulating lists of daily Bible readings, supported by brief commentary notes.

The response was amazing. Readers appreciated that each day they were provided with a portion of scripture that was thoughtfully brief, selected with the utmost care to link to the week's topic. There was a living personal touch which was seemingly the secret of its success.

Charles Waters at his desk

By 1910 the readership had exceeded a million people and was touching the lives of soldiers fighting wars, sailors on long voyages to Australia, colliers in the coal mines of Wales, schools in Canada, Jamaica and Belfast, prisoners in Chicago – people all over the world, alone or in groups, felt comforted and encouraged by the idea of joining other Christians throughout the world in reading the same Bible passages. And they still do!

Today, over 130 years later, this rich history lives on, touching the lives of hundreds of thousands of people across the world. IBRA is now part of the Birmingham-based charity Christian Education and is working to continue the legacy, providing support to our global community of IBRA readers. Our aim is still to enable Christians from different parts of the world to grow in knowledge and appreciation of each other's experience of God through our international contributors and writers.

The original mission continues today and will do into the future!

Dreams
Dreams and dreamers

Notes based on the New Revised Standard Version by **Erice Fairbrother**

Erice Fairbrother (Associate of the Holy Cross) is a Benedictine solitary in Napier, New Zealand where she is director of the Order of the Holy Cross NZ Spirituality Centre. She teaches Benedictine formation and supports those in ministry through holy companioning, pastoral supervision and the leading of retreats. She is an editor, writer of theology (preferring to use the genre of poetry) and liturgy, and a poet. Her work has been published internationally, and she is currently the Poet at Napier Creative Arts Centre.

Sunday 29 January
Dreaming with God

1 Kings 3:5–15

The Lord appeared to Solomon in a dream by night, and God said, 'Ask what I should give you.' (verse 5)

Follow your dreams! Whether beginning life's journey, or older and reshaping futures, such calls to create our own dreams are everywhere. Where dreams were once thought to belong to the world of art and poetry, now everyone is encouraged to dream; to dream for whatever we desire or want.

Our scriptures this week challenge such thinking.

Today we meet Solomon as he dreams, but it's a dream that begins with God, where Solomon finds his own hopes in the desires God has for him. When the dream is over, he recognises it as a call from God on his life and begins to follow it. How well he ends up following is in the story that unfolds beyond this reading, but we leave him beginning to live into the reality of the dream he has dreamed with God.

In the week ahead we will encounter dreams and dreamers whose lives are developed when they, too, dream with God, finding dreams are not confined to poets and artists, or even belong to the dreamer. Dreaming with God is to be open and vulnerable with God, with the stuff of our own lives, for the work of establishing God's world on earth.

† God who dreamed with the prophets, open my inner ears and eyes to see and hear your presence in my dreams so that I may live for you more faithfully.

Monday 30 January
More than fantasy

Daniel 2:31–49

The great God has informed the king what shall be hereafter. The dream is certain and its interpretation trustworthy. (verse 45b)

Special effects movies pale beside this dream! Here is a statue of gigantic proportions that causes cataclysmic happenings for the whole kingdom! I wonder if you, like me, are thinking this one is more the stuff of nightmares than dreams.

Yet this is a dream that tells us some important things about God and what happens when we are open to God being part of our lives. While the dream provides images and metaphors pointing to the future of Nebuchadnezzar's kingdom, it also reveals the authority and power of God in the world. It is something the king recognises, and as a result he honours the dreamer Daniel then responds to God who is the 'certain' author of the dream. It tells us that when dreams are more than fantasy they reveal God; they reveal the reality of our relationship with God. It tells us God is intimately connected with life.

Sometimes as we follow our dreams, hard things, challenging things can assail us and it is tempting to think we've made the wrong decisions or haven't listened well. Perhaps it is then we reassess our original dream. Did we see where God was in it, or was our dream about self-fulfilment, rather than the fulfilment of living as people of the kingdom of God? Are the dreams we are following building a world of peace and justice, a place that is good, not only for ourselves, but for all we share it with?

† God of all, fill me with the trust that will keep me faithful to the dream of your realm being established on earth.

For further thought

• Take time to recall when something about God has been revealed to you in a dream.

Tuesday 31 January
Peace – Live the dream!

Daniel 4:10–18

I continued looking … and there was a holy watcher, coming down from heaven. This is the dream that I saw. … and now you Belteshazzar [Daniel] declare the interpretation. (verses 13 and 18)

The dream we encounter today reminds us that God dreams with leaders and others we least expect; in today's instance, with a foreign, non-believer in his own dream, on his own terms. His response indicates he recognised something more than a human dream had come to him. Eager to seek out the truth he discerns it carries, he turns to Daniel, in whom over time he's come to trust, instead of consulting his own spiritual advisers.

We have watched and experienced in recent times, persecution of the Christian church, and attempts to erase it from places and history. This dream challenges us in these times, not to lose sight of the truth that Christ came to save the whole world, not just some of us! As we read this story of the dream we meet two people who are very differently positioned in relation to God, and yet between whom there is a developing trust. It is a trust that has come out of a commitment to seek and consult with one another truthfully over time.

We might not understand how God is dreaming with others for the sake of his realm being established on earth. To whom God speaks is God's prerogative, not ours. I wonder who we identify with in this story. Are we, like Daniel, able to recognise where God might be dreaming into the hearts of the least likely (perhaps whom we least like) and see God at work? Perhaps Daniel is one of those whom Jesus recognised as peacemaker and called blessed.

† God of all peoples, strengthen my trust that you have the whole world in your hands, and deepen my love for all people everywhere.

For further thought

• Look for opportunities to be part of interfaith meetings and live out the holy dream of peace on earth.

Wednesday 1 February
Dreams that reveal, challenge and heal

Daniel 4:19–27

May my counsel be acceptable to you: atone for your sins with righteousness and your iniquities with mercy to the oppressed, so that your prosperity may be prolonged. (verse 27)

Sometimes dreams do not appear to promise all will be well. Following these ones leads us into places and situations that are hard, challenging and test the very heart of us. Yet it is in the outworking of these dreams that we find the true value of friendship, of other companions on the way of Christ. These are times when honest scrutiny can lead to new growth.

The king in this story opens his dream up for scrutiny with a trusted companion. The revelations are not positive and we can only imagine what would have gone through his mind as he began to understand the cost of living this dream. Perhaps the fact that he could get on with his life nonetheless was because he knew he was not alone. That there were things he could do – and it seems Daniel gave good counsel – to atone for what he had done and act mercifully going into the future.

Perhaps you have set out with high hopes on a path you have chosen. On the way however things have not gone well; the dream, the hopes seem dashed, and nothing seems to make sense anymore. These are times when we tend to turn again to God, to seek the wise advice of another. It is not that we necessarily made terrible choices, or got God wrong. As we live these dreams, the things that can't be carried forward arise and must be dealt with. Dealing with them cannot be avoided and may take time, but in the end, we find ourselves healed and restored.

† God of my past, my present and my future, give me grace to offer companionship and care to others with whom I share this journey of life in you.

For further thought

• Recall others who have given you wise counsel and through whom you have found your way back to spiritual wellness and wholeness. Give thanks for them.

Thursday 2 February
Living the just dream

Daniel 7:1–18

But the holy ones of the Most High shall receive the kingdom and possess the kingdom forever – forever and ever. (verse 18)

Those who suffer from violence, war, abuse and oppression live through terrible trauma and long after are left with many impacting effects. Flashbacks, just one such form of trauma's ongoing presence, come without conscious recall, interrupt thoughts and terrorise memory, threatening hope and destroying dreams.

Perhaps that is part of what Daniel is experiencing in this dream of death and violence. Like many in our own time, Daniel was living under traumatic national persecution, in a situation where his life was determined by the will of others. To deny freedom of innocent people, to cause nations to live under a rule of fear is a modern anathema that Daniel would have recognised.

Victims of domestic violence know the long-term impact of trauma. It is sign of grace and of hope that many men and women in our own societies are seeking to overcome violence by working for justice and peace in homes and communities. To act justly is a life priority that God requires of us. Jesus modelled it; our dream for world peace rests on it. Like Daniel we can look at all that surrounds us in the world and 'be troubled' and 'terrified' by what we see. Or we can choose to grasp the promise of the one who said 'Peace, my peace I leave with you'!

Daniel is not left comfortless, and neither are we. The resurrection proclaims that those who cause suffering will not have the last word, and that those who have known suffering will be comforted. In Christ we will be overcomers. Through Christ, justice will prevail.

† Pray with the words popularly attributed to St Francis, 'Make me an instrument of your peace'.

For further thought

• How can I support those who work to stop violence in my own community? How can I show the peace of Christ through my own life?

Friday 3 February
Not just any dream will do

Jeremiah 23:23–32

Let the prophet who has a dream tell the dream, but let the one who has my word speak my word faithfully. (verse 28)

I have a dream! When Martin Luther King began his speech to the crowd who had marched on Washington, he was describing something more than his own imagining. His was a dream that was instantly recognised. It didn't need any discussion, except on how it might be fulfilled. The dream had integrity because it brought together the authentic shared hopes of a people longing for peace and justice. It was as if he was drawing on the dream that was already among them, a dream that they were somehow collectively dreaming together.

The prophet Jeremiah warns that not all dreams are so collectively shared. Not all dreams lead to God's will being done in our own lives and on earth. But how do we discern the difference? How do we know which dreams and visions are enabling of others in our church and society?

God makes it clear that his dreams are trustworthy because they benefit all (verse 32b). They are dreams that are recognisable as connecting with the hopes of the community. God's dreams resonate with us because they are founded in the reality of our lives – they aren't 'reckless'. Dreams grounded in God lead us more deeply into faithfulness and service. God's dreams keep us close to God; they don't take us to places where we might forget what God has done for us in the past. The words at communion 'do this to remember me' are a good guide. Will this dream help me remember Christ's call on my life? Will that dream bring life to others?

† May I never forget what God has done in my life, and may that be the source of my future directions on my journey of faith and service.

For further thought

• Recall dreams that have had positive impact on your life. Take a moment to identify where the voice of God was present in them.

Saturday 4 February
The reality test – following!

Ecclesiastes 5:1–7

With many dreams come vanities and a multitude of words; but fear God. (verse 7)

Dreams are part of life. They can bring awareness of needs to address. They can challenge, disconcert or inspire. They open us up to change and their outworking in the life of faith communities are marked by acts of peace and mercy, of justice and compassion. Where they lead us to weave the threads of community hopes, our faith develops a confidence which draws others to us and to God.

Dreaming with and in God is both empowering and inspirational. However, at this point Ecclesiastes addresses his community with a warning. It is not the dream that is important, but the one from whom the dream comes. It is not what we say about our dreams but how others see the way we live the dream. It is not the insight (prophecy) of the dream we are to pay attention to, but what it tells us about God.

Dreams, like miracles, like Jesus himself, lead us to God; show us more about our relationship with the divine. They cause us to 'fear' God. That is, to grow in ever deepening awareness of the holy, awareness that never fails to awaken us to the reality of our humanity and need of God's love.

As with all things, dreams will fade. Amazing moments of insight and understanding that come from so many sources in our faith need to be integrated into our lives. In the end it is not about the dream or the dreamer – for such is the beginning of vanity. It is always about the one who gave it. And always about how we follow.

† Pray for courage to follow the dreams for God's life in the world, out into your community and relationships.

For further thought

• Use the next dream you experience as the 'text' for your time of meditation.

1 and 2 Timothy
Dear Timothy

Notes based on the New Revised Standard Version by **Michael Jagessar**

 Michael Jagessar is a minister of the United Reformed Church. He is currently responsible for Global and Intercultural Ministry. More on Michael's biography and writings can be found at www.caribleaper.co.uk.

Sunday 5 February
Love from a pure heart

1 Timothy 1:1–11

Grace, mercy, and peace from God the Father and Christ Jesus our Lord. (verse 1)

These pastoral letters can make for challenging reading. There is much here that some may find uncomfortable and controversial. But the letters were intended to offer guidance for leadership of an early Christian community, and one can also sense both practice and vision of what an ideal Christian congregation and leadership should be like.

Attending and participating in the 2015 Parliament of the World's Religions, I was struck by the genuine commitment of people of various faith traditions and the wide-ranging ways they demonstrated the connection between belief and behaviour or teaching and practice. This is clearly on the mind of the writer of this pastoral letter, urging Timothy (and us) to invest in embodying and living out 'genuine love' free of self-interest. And, for the writer and his audience, this meant divesting themselves from idle and smooth talk, unhelpful conversations, and putting off arrogant attitude to matters of faith. All such habits just misrepresent the grace and generosity embodied and witnessed in the story of Jesus. 'Grace', amazing and abundant, sums up the way of God in Christ, and is the central message of this letter. The outworking of grace, manifested in genuine love, remains a challenge for all of us!

† God-who-loves-abundantly, may our living-out of your way in Christ always reflect your grace and generosity!

Monday 6 February
All because of Jesus

1 Timothy 1:12–20

The saying is sure and worthy of full acceptance, that Christ Jesus came into the world to save sinners – of whom I am the foremost. (verse 15)

Writing in the first century of the Christian Era about grace and God's saving work through Christ was no theory for Paul, who brilliantly evokes how the transforming power of grace works in the life of a person. If God can forgive, embrace and welcome such as him, imagine what God can do for any of us! So this personal encounter and transformation leads to thankfulness. As the writer puts it, 'the grace of our Lord overflowed for me with the faith and love that are in Christ Jesus'. It is all because of Jesus! Indeed, the re-centring continues as the passage keeps us centred on God the 'immortal, invisible, only wise' one, as we would sing today! To understand the depths of mercy and grace, it would be helpful if we can reflect on and recognise on our capacity to harm each other. There are those who intentionally plan to hurt and kill others; equally we who find such acts of terror despicable allow reason and love to disappear as we respond with our military might. We are all in need here. And, if we are unable to see our own need, can we ever be able to recognise and show appreciation for this amazing grace that embraces us? However fancy our God-talk may have evolved to be over the years, our calling is to bear witness to God's extravagant and overflowing love given for the whole of creation! The illogic of God's economy in Christ is that when we have encountered such reckless grace and love our instinctive response can only be to give praise and thanks. This is subversion at work!

† God-of-overflowing-grace-and-love, may our lives reflect the fullness of your grace and love. We pray in the name of abundant love, Jesus.

For further thought

• Give thought to ways we may continue to witness to the simple, dangerous and transforming fact of a God who loves and saves!

Tuesday 7 February
Pray for everyone

1 Timothy 2:1–15

I urge that supplications, prayers, intercessions, and thanksgivings be made for everyone. (verse 1)

Keep 'grace' as the orienting principle as you read and reflect on these verses. Praying for everyone is easier said than done: especially those we tend to disagree with or who may not be part of our 'immediate world'. The good intentions are there. It is in the practice that we miss out. In these verses the Christian community is invited to 'step out' beyond its own group and comfort zone to the 'cultures' beyond. Let me draw again from my experience of a full week at the Parliament of the World's Religions. In such an intense world of diverse faith-belonging and encounters, one was able to see oneself and the gospel of abundant grace differently through the living and interacting in this transient lived-space. While committed to the way of Jesus and the priorities of the 'good news', abundant grace means that we must pray for all and invest in learning about that which we consider alien and unfamiliar. Such is part of our witness to God's vision of a diverse world that God love intensely – a world of grace without bounds; peace without oppression, abundance without exploitation. What I learnt from religious neighbours during that week is what I know as fundamental to the way of Jesus. It is an invitation to be witnesses of God's generosity which releases us to be open, embracing and passing on what we have freely received. So remember well: there is one God who loves every single person. And pray always – for everyone. And lest we forget: 'prayer does not change God, but it changes the one who prays' (Kierkegaard).

† So, let us pray without ceasing for everyone, doing so with gratitude, for this is delightful in the sight of God who saves – who desires everyone to be saved and to share in full and abundant life …

For further thought

• During this week, consider what it means to pray for everyone in your context: how easy or challenging do you find such an invitation?

Wednesday 8 February
On leading and serving

1 Timothy 3:1–16

... I am writing these instructions to you so that, if I am delayed, you may know how one ought to behave in the household of God ... (verses 14–15)

I have found leading and serving in ministry humbling, daunting and challenging. Across the diverse geographical, varied and cultural contexts in which I have lived, this is what I can affirm. I have lost count of the many times I have failed to live out the demands of these verses on leading and serving. The words may have been meant as both encouragement and a reminder of what we are about, because the discomfort the text may cause us locates the costly nature of leadership in ministry. Given that most of the qualities required here suggest an inversion of the 'logic' of our prevailing cultures of leading and serving, I wonder who among us can assume any moral high-ground about our leading. If not for grace, what would become our leading and serving? Leading and serving demands of us integrity, living by example, generosity of spirit, gentleness, commitment and moderation. At the same time there is the need for toughness and resilience. Power and wealth-seeking, manipulation and personal gains are non-starters in the household of God. How can we re-learn what it means to be servants of the mystery of our faith, so that in our life together we can demonstrate life-affirming qualities of leading and serving? The world is waiting for something different!

† Loving God, may our exercise of the gifts we have received be a faithful reflection of your presence at work in our lives and deepen our desire to imitate the example of your child, Jesus, in whose name we pray.

For further thought

• Reflect on the calling to lead and serve (in and beyond church)? How does our leading and serving map on to the ideal of this pastoral letter? What do I need to do differently?

Thursday 9 February
By example

1 Timothy 4:1–12
Put these things into practice, devote yourself to them, so that all may see your progress. (verse 15)

I recall my ordination in July 1980 in a small village in Guyana – especially the speeches from family, friends and ordinary punters in the pews. I remember their words as these happened in the context of a prior oral examination on my knowledge of Luther and some of the teachings of the Lutheran Church in Guyana. Forget my knowledge of the Bible, I was largely thought of by my church as a dodgy Lutheran who knew little of Luther's writings. Their underlying message from their simple and to the point speeches were: live, preach and teach with your life. I have since discovered how difficult it is live, teach and preach with my life. I can think, reflect, speak and write the theology: that part is easy for me. The living-out calls for discipline in one's spiritual life, focus and courage to throw oneself at the mercy of grace! In retrospect, I can see the connection especially on the moments when I have been drawn into risky, uncomfortable, adventurous and grace-filled spaces. Whether I have followed sound teaching is another matter. Eugene Peterson puts it brilliantly in *The Message*: 'And that special gift of ministry you were given when the leaders of the church laid hands on you and prayed, keep that dusted off and in use.' I am still trying to do that as grace continues to sustain me in my failings!

† Lover-of-just-and-compassionate-acts, in Christ and through the encouragement of the Spirit re-shape us into living instruments of love, justice and peace.

For further thought
• During this week give thanks for a person whose example has influenced you. Consider ways in which you are and can be a better example – a witness to the Jesus way.

Friday 10 February
Family habits

1 Timothy 5:1–16

… whoever does not provide for relatives, and especially for family members, has denied the faith and is worse than an unbeliever. (verse 8)

I can picture my family of multiple religious heritages hearing these words and shaking their heads in assent. This is what they would consider a practical and common-sense outworking of their faith, which they tried to live out to the best of their abilities. Religious practices, rites and rituals were important to them. But they knew that all the chanting, regular prayers and rituals gain are empty if they were unable to demonstrate care and compassion starting with those closest to them. Religion and faith practice must begin at home. Neglect to care for family members – including the extended family – is a denial of faith. This was not premised on a neatly worked-out theological motivation: it just made sense! The prophets expressed this in their unique ways, while Jesus extended the family to include more than 'blood' relations. And as one of the pastoral letters reminds us: what sort of witness is that which talks of the 'love of God' that is not lived out relationally with sisters, brothers, friends or total strangers? And the practice of these habits are rightly linked to faith and faithfulness.

† God-who-delights-in-our-lived-out-faith, continue to deepen in us habits of care, love and compassion towards the most vulnerable in and around our communities.

For further thought

• Reflect on your family relationships: what is good and strong? What needs attention and intentional work? Make a commitment to act on one.

Saturday 11 February
Minding our leaders

1 Timothy 5:17–25

In the presence of God and of Christ Jesus and of the elect angels, I warn you to keep these instructions without prejudice, doing nothing on the basis of partiality. (verse 21)

Leading is never easy. Leading in the context of a community walking the Jesus way, with a different set of operating principles, is even more challenging. These verses capture some of contributing factors to stress, anxiety, quarrels and conflicts in our ecclesial communities: money, unsubstantiated charges, bullying, favouritism, process in electing leaders and injustices. We are also offered a whole raft of helpful guidelines. Order and proper functioning of early Christian communities and contemporary ones (like ours) is critical to our life together. We know how easy it is to fall into a routine of unhelpful habits and ways of operating. Some of these practices may be helpful, while others can chain us to ways that reflect a lack of grace and generosity. The high level of stress in ministry and among the leadership in churches suggests that we would do well to constantly reorient ourselves on the vocation of the ministry we are called to, including our collective responsibilities towards accountability to and with each other. What is God saying to us today?

† God-who-washes-feet-and-dries-up-tears, help us to discern the ways you seek to minister through our lives. Through your spirit give us courage to stand firm to what is faithful to your way and to lead with grace and compassion.

For further thought

• Consider our treatment of leaders in our churches: what are our expectations? Are they realistic and grounded on grace and generosity? In what ways will I show appreciation this week?

1 and 2 Timothy
Guard the treasure

Notes based on the New Revised Standard Version by **Michael Jagessar**

See Michael's biography on p. 37.

Sunday 12 February
The allure of wealth

1 Timothy 6:1–10

For the love of money is a root of all kinds of evil, and in their eagerness to be rich some have wandered away from the faith and pierced themselves with many pains. (verse 10)

Who does not love money? Money might be 'funny' to the rich, but most poor people cannot see the funny side. Money, wealth and riches have an interesting relationship with the Christian faith. At least since Moses smashed the golden calf, the borderland between the realms of faith and money has not been an altogether comfortable place to live: Mammon still competes with God for the loyalty of even the most devout. The message from churches that the 'love of money' distracts the faithful from what is most important, while the churches themselves administer millions of pounds, sounds somewhat hypocritical! Most of us will concede that our society is heavily materialistic, that we value products more than people and that greed is still a distortion of the way of God. Yet, only a few of us seem able to decide when enough is enough. Walking the way of abundant life brings wealth of a qualitatively different nature. If abundance is perceived primarily in terms of what can be counted, then it would only be a matter of time before the community self-destructs. Signs of this are all around us!

† God-who-loves-abundantly, heighten our awareness, deepen our understanding and broaden our horizons that we may discover your way of abundant life deep within us.

For further thought

• Reflect on the connection between the love of money and consumerist habits as enslavement. Is the writer too harsh here, given our complex relationship with money? If you are able, share your financial testimony with your community.

Monday 13 February
The race of abundant life

1 Timothy 6:11–21

Fight the good fight of the faith; take hold of the eternal life, to which you were called and for which you made the good confession in the presence of many witnesses. (verse 12)

Wealth can get in the way of putting one's trust in God. It can be a hindrance to walking the Jesus way. Yet the church's work depends on money, especially from those willing to share it. Hence the view that those blessed abundantly are 'to be rich in good works, generous, and ready to share'. This is equated as living 'life that really is life'. For us today, this may take the form of a call against a dominant trend which places the well-being of 'me' or self-interest above all else. Full life in Christ rests in connectedness: with God, with others and with our world. Our attention has to move beyond our needs to those of others. Around us the effects of a world groaning under the weight of self-interest and instant gratification is evident. The words of today's texts serve both as an encouragement and a call us to re-centre. This means placing our trust in God and being generous and ready to be rich in helping others. The good race of the faith means no slacking up, running the race of abundant life, and always mindful of the allure and distraction of material things. As Eugene Peterson writes in *The Message*: May 'overwhelming grace keep you!'

† Pour out in us, gracious God, the spirit of your love and then pour us out into the world, that we may know the true meaning of life in love for you and in service to others.

For further thought
• During this week, find one place/moment/person where you can demonstrate 'being generous and rich' in helping.

45

Tuesday 14 February
Remembering and bearing tradition

2 Timothy 1:1–18

I am reminded of your sincere faith, a faith that lived first in your grandmother Lois and your mother Eunice and now, I am sure, lives in you. (verse 5)

The pastoral letter is intended as an encouragement to 'keep the faith' in the midst of competing voices and other challenges Timothy and others were faced with. What an apt way to do so by drawing on the family heritage! This sort of encouragement both locates Timothy's identity and his responsibility to 'preserve' the faith. So he is reminded of the faith and faithfulness of his grandmother and his mother. Wherever the faith has spread one would find a connection with names. At another level the encouragement underscores that there is no need to reinvent the wheel: we have the teachings and examples of those who have gone before. In humility we need to imitate their example. Their faith and perseverance in faithfulness can help overcome the struggles of the day. Faith, gifted to us by God in Christ, is not a solo matter: we need each other in the community of faith. As inheritors and bearers of this story we would do well to remember our heritage while living out the good news, never losing sight of our calling. We have been loaned a story to share and the cloud of witnesses are cheering us on!

| Spirit of God, enlighten our hearts to the reality of your divine presence in our midst. Equip us with courage to faithfully bear and witness to the faith you have gifted us through saints past and present. In the name of one whose story we embody and live out.

For further thought

- During this week, reflect on these words: 'For God did not give us a spirit of cowardice, but rather a spirit of power and of love and of self-discipline' (verse 7). How do these words encourage you?

Wednesday 15 February
Our best for God

2 Timothy 2:1–19

Do your best to present yourself to God as one approved by him, a worker who has no need to be ashamed, rightly explaining the word of truth.
(verse 15)

How are Christians able to face situations of conflict and change while carrying convictions from the faith they have received? How have they managed to do so carrying the good news of Jesus Christ into new, uncertain and sometimes unsettling settings? Perhaps the answers offered here may not be what we may wish to hear. They include: remain steadfast to established conventions, preserve received tradition, hold it in trust for future believers, and avoid practices and ideas that may offend cultural conventions, especially about what counts as respectable behaviour. And if these are not enough, how about: deploying words carefully, avoiding wrangling and speaking 'the word of truth' (verse 15). How timely for us today, in the midst of our own word-wrangling over hot issues and as we keep striving to get the words just right, God accompanies us, claiming us and loving us even when words may fail us. In the meantime, our vocation is clearly put: focus on doing and offering our very best for God, mindful of pious talk that lacks the walk.

† Pray with thankful hearts for all that God has given you, remembering that your wealth lies in what you can give away. Pray that God's Spirit will lead you to give openly and generously of what is your very best.

For further thought

• What do these verses tell us of our faith and faithfulness (how we live out that faith)?

Thursday 16 February
A kind of container

2 Timothy 2:20 – 3:9

And the Lord's servant must not be quarrelsome but kindly to everyone, an apt teacher, patient, correcting opponents with gentleness. (verses 24–25)

I have lost count of how often I have failed to live up to the instructions in these verses. How about you? Though I have grown more helpful and affirming habits over the years, I still struggle with being patient. I am better at listening intently to views of those around me that I may not agree with. However, 'gentleness' in conversations on topics for which I hold strong views is hard work! I can surely testify to this costly and demanding nature of the vocation of attempting to walk the Jesus way. Being a 'kind of container God can use to present any and every kind of gift to his guest for their blessing' (as *The Message* puts it in verse 21) is demanding work. In our current situation of hate, fear, suspicion, aggression, impulsive reacting and lack of compassion, this is a necessary and timely calling. In such times, the need to invest and yearn after mature righteousness – especially in our nurturing habits of generosity and grace – is always greater than ever. And while the Jesus way of full life for all is demanding, the good news is that we are not left on our own. God accompanies us!

† God-always-present, you who give us strength in our weakness, peace and gentleness in times of anxiety, and words and boldness to proclaim more of you and of us, less, take hold of our lives and fill us with goodness to become your containers of love. In the name of love incarnate.

For further thought

• In what practical ways in church and beyond can we practise kindness, live out patience and embody gentle thoughts and kinds words with those who hold different views from us?

Friday 17 February
Sticking to the message

2 Timothy 3:10 – 4:8

But as for you, continue in what you have learned and firmly believed, knowing from whom you learned it. (verse 14)

While it is important to have many views and different voices in our life together, it is also crucially important to discern the 'voices' one can trust as 'truth'. This means that what we have learnt, hold strong convictions on, and our sources/nurturers are all crucially important – especially in complex and messy lives in churches. At the same time as we struggle to minister, persevere and strive to remain faithful to the way of God in Christ, these verses from 2 Timothy will also demand that what we have received as part of the inherited tradition must be questioned. In my current church family, I despair at the heavy administrative workload, numerous meetings and other sorts of perhaps legitimate matters that 'suck' ministers/church leaders dry, at the expense of 'stealing' time and thought given to worship, study and prayers. How then are we able to respond to or engage with the 'itching ears' syndrome of the punters in the pews, what they read, who are their reference points, what they are hauling from the online religious superstores and the new values they are embracing – all in the name of Christ? I agree with the writer: in spite of the complexities and messiness, we must faithfully keep the message simple – affirming, challenging, urging.

† Pray, giving thanks to God for the gifts of the Bible, scriptures and faithful servants of the Jesus way who have shaped and contributed to your spiritual and faith development. Pray, asking for humility and wisdom to continue to share what you have received in ways that are faithful, full of integrity and overflowing with generosity.

For further thought

• Reflect on the people who have 'lived the faith into us' whether we were aware of it at the time or not. Consider how such recalling may continue to inspire you.

1 and 2 Timothy – Michael Jagessar

Saturday 18 February
Yours in Christ

2 Timothy 4:9–22

The Lord be with your spirit. Grace be with you. (verse 22)

Timothy is urged to avoid shallow conceptions of heaven and oppressing others in order to get there. Yes, God is saving us now for heaven; none of us can say who belongs in heaven; never give up; see it through; finish the race. Lest we become distracted by unnecessary wrangling over who is in and who is out, how about examining our own commitment? For the only way to fight the good fight, keep the faith and finish the race, is through unflinching commitment. The concern here is not about 'winning': that would be a terrible misconception. The thrust here is about endurance and resilience. So how are you running or walking? Where is your source of encouragement? What about your ministry of encouraging? Given all the ambiguities that we embody, what can we do with the means we are blessed with to run or walk fully towards abundant life for all?

† Grace-giver-who-loves-extravagantly, in the midst of the rough and tumble of life and our own shortcomings, help us to not give up, to not tire out and to not give in. We pray in the name of the One who lifts tired arms and carries spent bodies.

For further thought
• During this week, consider three people you wish to encourage: write what you would like to say to them to encourage them in their Christian life.

Esther
The rise of Esther and Mordecai

Notes based on the New Revised Standard Version by **Noel Irwin**

Noel Irwin is a Belfast boy and a Methodist minister. In 2000 he moved to Sheffield: first working for the Church of England as a community outreach worker, then as superintendent of the Methodist Mission in the centre of the city. He and his family now live in Manchester. At present he divides his time as director of the Urban Theology Unit in Sheffield and as tutor in public theology at Northern College Manchester. In his spare time, he runs and coaches young runners – including his two children, who are much more talented than he ever was!

Sunday 19 February
Queen Vashti deposed

Esther 1:1–20

But Queen Vashti refused to come at the king's command conveyed by the eunuchs. At this the king was enraged, and his anger burned within him.
(verse 12)

When people say the Bible is irrelevant to their lives, they need to read the book of Esther: ethnic/religious cleansing, power politics, incredible wealth and greed, empires, dodgy characters, trouble in male/female relationships (indeed problems in all social relations) all appear – all with God nowhere in sight (secularism!).

Here we are drawn into the world of the story, the setting and some of the characters. The first person we meet is Xerxes (in some translations Ahasuerus). He is mentioned 190 times while, famously, God is not mentioned in the book – though for John Wesley the 'finger of God' does direct events. Despite the demonstration of Xerxes' majesty (verse 4) in the banquet, he is shown to have feet of clay (Daniel 2). Queen Vashti gets punished by having to do what she wanted to do in the first place (verses 10–20). This does not demonstrate authority but weakness! Then having the worst spin doctor ever, Memucan, the king's dirty linen is washed in public (verse 17), while the fragility of the power of the king is reflected in the fragile rule of all men over women (verse 18).

† Loving God, help us to discern your finger somehow directing things among the great ones of the world.

Monday 20 February
Esther is made queen

Esther 2:1–17

The king loved Esther more than all the other women … so that he set the royal crown on her head and made her queen instead of Vashti. (part of verse 17)

In the Soviet era under Stalin, it was common that if you fell out of favour you would be airbrushed out of official photographs. This is what happens to Queen Vashti as Esther makes her appearance in the story. When we look at this chapter we tend to focus on Esther being an orphan and then becoming queen. We perhaps see it as another version of Cinderella. Yet while we may sanitise the story, the Bible certainly does not airbrush the unpalatable and difficult parts of the narrative away.

In verse 4 it is clear that, for the king, women were simply another of the objects he possessed. Indeed, every year many boys were castrated to serve as eunuchs in the Persian court. Underneath our story lie assault, abuse and rape. Our news today speaks of powerful men (treated like gods?), who got away with things for many years as they abused vulnerable boys and girls; this should reinforce our horror at the institutional abuse that lies behind this chapter!

What do we make of Esther? Many feminists contrast her unfavourably with Vashti who is seen as a strong, independent woman, while Esther is both passive and submissive. So often we go to the Bible in order to find characters whose example we should follow. What I like about the book of Esther is that the folk in the story are not held up for us as paradigms of virtue. Rather there is a sense that God is working through dubious characters in order to bring about God's purposes.

† May we never see or use others as disposable commodities. Give us a sense that all are made in your image and likeness, O Lord.

For further thought

• www.antislavery.org/english/campaigns/ provides resources to campaign against the use of people as disposable commodities.

Tuesday 21 February
Mordecai uncovers a conspiracy

Esther 2:19–23

But the matter came to the knowledge of Mordecai, and he told it to Queen Esther, and Esther told the king in the name of Mordecai. (verse 22)

Funnily enough, later in life, poor old Xerxes ends up being 'done to death' by his own servants, despite this particular plot being foiled by Mordecai and Esther. One of the ways I relax is by reading murder mysteries. My pet hate in them is when there are far too many coincidences to be believable. Now in Esther there are loads of coincidences – in fact, it has been called a book of coincidences – you need to decide whether there are too many coincidences here for the plot to be credible. The theological question that comes to us is, 'What is the connection between coincidence and providence?' We know God is not mentioned in the book, but can we find God here not in the headlines of the book but almost hidden between the lines … in the coincidences of the text?

I had two friends who had very different conversion experiences. One was 'lights, camera, action', with God speaking very openly and dramatically to him at a certain moment in his life. For the other it was an ongoing process that took years with God being revealed through small things and speaking with a still, small voice. He gathered together his fragmentary contacts with God which only with hindsight formed a larger, clearer picture. At times in the Bible God appears sometimes in the foreground (Exodus) and other times in the background (the Joseph stories and Esther). The book of Esther should inspire us to listen between the lines, but never rule out miraculous Exodus liberation or an amazing road to Damascus experience.

† God of coincidences, with all the people I meet today, help me be an instrument of your hidden providence.

For further thought

• William Temple said that, when he prayed, coincidences happened. Let us look for coincidences after a time of prayer today.

Wednesday 22 February
Haman's plot

Esther 3:1–15

Letters were sent by couriers to all the king's provinces, giving orders to destroy, to kill, and to annihilate all Jews, young and old, women and children, in one day, the thirteenth day of the twelfth month, which is the month of Adar, and to plunder their goods. (verse 13)

The pantomime villain Haman arrives on the scene to catcalls and boos from the audience, which at least is what happens in the Jewish festival of Purim (see 9:24–32). Even in verse 1 he is identified as an enemy of the Jews because he is an Agagite. A Jewish audience immediately would identify him with King Agag of the Amalekites, who were ancient enemies of Israel. While there is no explanation as to why Mordecai refuses to bow to Haman (verse 2), there is a sense in the text that Mordecai immediately recognised Haman as an implacable enemy of Israel.

Haman discovers that Mordecai is a Jew (verse 4) and he makes the connection many of us have made throughout history; a personal problem with someone means there is an issue with everyone who shares that person's religion or race. So this book, which does not mention God or the law, becomes the most Jewish of books as one cannot help but think of the Shoah of the Jewish people under Hitler and the Nazis. The pogrom was due to take place the day before the Passover where Jews were delivered from the Egyptians. God had rescued the Jews in a particular way. Will they be saved again? Someone needs to stand up for their people and do what is right, no matter what the consequences. Mordecai and Esther will step up to the mark.

† Give me the courage, Lord, to stand up for those who are persecuted because of race or religion.

For further thought

• Research anti-Semitism and Islamophobia and reflect on how Christians have been like Haman.

Thursday 23 February
Esther decides to help

Esther 4:1–17

Mordecai then went away and did everything as Esther had ordered him.
(verse 17)

There are a lot of feasts in the book of Esther. The Gentiles feast and now the Jews fast as they face genocide. While questions of 'Where is God in the most painful moments of human life?' are not explicit, certain religious responses to pain and suffering do bubble up in the text. It is interesting that in the Greek version of the book prayers from Esther and Mordecai are added to 'enhance' the religious nature of the text. In verse 16 we have the efficacy of fasting with the implication of prayer here, because in Judaism those two things were so intricately connected. Verse 14 brings out the concept of providence; as 'another quarter' or 'another place' is used in Jewish writings to refer to God. Reflecting on that phrase, John Wesley has written that we must not let slip any opportunity of serving God in our generation.

Esther has two names (2:7), lives in two worlds, but makes a decision to identify with the people of God rather than the court of the Empire. This chapter is the turning point of the book, where Esther takes centre stage from Mordecai, in terms of the unfavourable comparison with Vashti, in verses 15–17 we have a role reversal where she commands Mordecai.

† God, let not any opportunity slip from me in which I might be part of your dream.

For further thought

• Do you think Esther represents coincidences, God's hidden action or both? Is it strange to have a book in the Bible that does not mention God? Find us on Facebook and share your thoughts today (www.facebook.com/freshfromtheword).

Friday 24 February
The plot thickens

Esther 5:1–14

The king said to her, 'What is it, Queen Esther? What is your request? It shall be given you, even to the half of my kingdom.' (verse 3)

If you remember the beginning of our story: Vashti risks her life by refusing to appear before the king. Here Esther (for the first time 'Queen Esther') risks her life by appearing before the king to put into action her plan to rescue her people. Xerxes is on the booze again (verse 6) and dangerous (1:10–11). To all intents and purposes he is the one in control, with all the power. But we will see in a story which likes to play around with appearance and reality that actually 'Queen' Esther has the more powerful weapons of wisdom and patience.

We all know the saying 'pride comes before a fall'. Never has that been so true than in this chapter. We should not forget the aura of racial hatred and menace here: 'that Jew' (verse 13). Esther is in a very deadly game, playing on the ego of powerful men. You cannot see how either Xerxes or Haman are fit to rule at all because it is all about them. Esther is the only one in the court who has a sense of obligation to others, as opposed to the gratification of selfish desires.

Appearing in the account for the first time is Zeresh, the wife of Haman (verse 14), who suggests, with her husband's mates, that he needs to build a gallows for Mordecai to put Haman in a better mood after once again Mordecai has not paid him enough respect. It seems Haman's idea of a good day is a banquet and a hanging! We shall see how his 'perfect' day turns out.

† Save us from pride, keep us humble, give us wisdom and patience, O God!

For further thought

• Where can you exercise Esther's wisdom and patience in your life?

Saturday 25 February
Mordecai honoured

Esther 6:1–14

So Haman came in, and the king said to him, 'What shall be done for the man whom the king wishes to honour?' Haman said to himself, 'Whom would the king wish to honour more than me?' (verse 6)

Esther steps away from the action in this chapter. Instead, we begin with one powerful man, Xerxes, trying to find a good book at bedtime, and finish with another powerful man in an even worse condition, Haman. Haman's wife Zeresh cheers him up (verse 13) by predicting his downfall and the vindication of Mordecai, which must have been an incredibly brave thing to do in the light of Haman's ego and arrogance … or is it a case of rats leaving a sinking ship?! In the middle of the chapter (verse 6) we have the only place in Esther where we get insight into someone's inner thought processes, as a way of showing how great pride can lead to an even greater fall.

The chapter also starts with coincidence and finishes with a banquet. Coincidences and banquets: themes in the book of Esther! Overall we have the story of the beginnings of a great reversal where Mordecai and his people triumph over their enemies. I particularly like the way Mordecai is not bothered by all the pomp and ceremony bestowed on him. He just goes back after his little tour and sits at the king's gate (verse 12), seemingly unaffected by it all. Two of the men in this chapter have everything, wealth and power, but cannot actually do anything to control events, while Mordecai 'the Jew' is under the threat of death and is not fussed about the trappings of wealth and power, but is about to be given the power and authority which the others desperately crave.

† When life is difficult and confusing may we walk in God's way and trust in his purposes.

For further thought

• What does the book of Esther have to say about religious toleration in your society today?

Esther
The triumph of the Jews

Notes based on the New Revised Standard Version by **Noel Irwin**

See Noel's biography on p. 51.

Sunday 26 February
Haman hanged

Esther 7:1–10
For we have been sold, I and my people, to be destroyed, to be killed, and to be annihilated. (part of verse 4)

The next reversal in the book is that the gallows made for Mordecai is used on Haman! We see again the deeply ironic nature of the book of Esther with Haman falling foul of the one sin that he does not seem to have been responsible for; a sexual sin, or a perceived sexual sin. This is a beautifully written account: in verse 8 there is a really nice play on the verb 'to fall' when Haman 'falls' onto Queen Esther, in 6:13 Zeresh warned him he has begun 'to fall' before Mordecai.

Esther is clever, in this chapter she becomes the saviour of her people. Only in verse 3 does she reveal her Jewishness and thus the fact she is under a death sentence from the decree of the king – though in 6:10 the king seems to have forgotten that he has condemned all the Jews to death. I love the development of the character of Esther. She was blindly obedient to Mordecai; she continues to be silent about her Jewishness; she then takes command of things herself. By leaving the comfort zone she is in, she becomes a great blessing to many other people.

† Lord you bless us to be a blessing to others. May we leave our comfort zones and come and follow you.

Monday 27 February
The king's edict

Esther 8:1–17

By these letters the king allowed the Jews who were in every city to assemble and defend their lives, to destroy, to kill, and to annihilate any armed force of any people or province that might attack them, with their children and women, and to plunder their goods. (verse 11)

Here we have the last reversal in the book, when the edict intended to bring about the destruction of the Jews is superseded by an edict which facilitates the slaughter of the enemies of the Jews. Both moral and translation issues are intertwined in the interpretation of verse 11. Haman's decree in 3:13 allowed the killing of all Jews, including women and children. The decree of Mordecai seems simply to parallel that and sanction the murder of women and children among the Jews' enemies. A minority of translations, and commentators, see the 'women and children' as being Jewish, so those who attack Jewish women and children are to be killed. For me, with so much of Esther being about reversals and parallels, the decree of Mordecai does allow the slaughter of women and children.

For many Christians and Jews this violence and destruction of innocent people will be deeply troubling. While for those who search the scriptures of religions to confirm their view that religion is all about murder and hate, these chapters in Esther will be manna from heaven. How can we respond? First, Esther and Mordecai have not been held up as saints for us to model our lives on. Second, you could argue that verse 11 is about defensive violence. But you still have the issue of non-combatants. Finally, as Christians and followers of Jesus, we are under a new covenant which places love and forgiveness at the heart of how God deals with humanity and thus as the way we should deal with one another – even with those we may see as enemies.

† Lord, help us to take your word to us in scripture seriously. May we struggle with heart and mind to understand what you are saying to us today through it.

For further thought

• 'Blessed are the peacemakers, for they will be called children of God' (Matthew 5:9). How can you live as a peacemaking child of God this coming week?

Tuesday 28 February
Triumph at last

Esther 9:1–17

When the king's command and edict were about to be executed, on the very day when the enemies of the Jews hoped to gain power over them … the Jews gathered in their cities throughout all the provinces … (part of verses 1–2)

From the beginning of this chapter to the end of the book the institution of the feast of Purim is explained to us. Whether it is the violence of our reading today, or the sexual exploitation of chapters 1 and 2, there is much to make us uneasy. Only so many of the difficulties in the book of Esther can be explained away. I have learnt in writing these notes that I need to engage with the Bible we have and not the one I wished we had.

So much in the book, with its setting in the imperial court of Persia, is incredibly alien to our situations and sensibilities today. One of the things that does shine out is in relation to the issue and exercise of power, whether that power is political, in the context of a country or an empire, or personal in a workplace or family. We see throughout this book how difficult it is for human beings to use power in a way that is fair, just and consistent. For answers to how to use power differently we need to go beyond the book of Esther. I want to turn to Jesus and see how God exercises power through weakness on the cross. I also think of another young Jewish woman, perhaps a similar age to Esther, who proclaimed even greater reversals in her Magnificat than those in the book of Esther – and in her weakness and powerlessness facilitated the salvation of the whole world by bringing the Saviour to birth.

† Wherever we find ourselves in our lives may we be faithful to you, O God.

For further thought
• Read the words of the Magnificat (Luke 1:46–55). What other texts from the Bible come to mind in relation to Esther? Share one on our Facebook group.

At-one-ment
The human dilemma

Notes based on the New International Version (UK) by **Clare Nonhebel**

 Clare Nonhebel is a novelist and writer on non-fiction topics including healing, homelessness and doubt. She is the co-author with a death row prisoner of his story: *Survivor on Death Row*. She writes to and visits death row inmates and has been involved in UK prison ministry, healing, discipleship and groups for adult survivors of childhood abuse.

Wednesday 1 March (Ash Wednesday)
My ways are not your ways

Isaiah 55:6–13

As the heavens are higher than the earth, so are my ways higher than your ways and my thoughts than your thoughts. (verse 9)

I once met a man who claimed he didn't need God because 'I've never really done anything wrong in my life.' After congratulating him on being the first perfect person I had ever met, we had a discussion about God's view of right and wrong.

The closer we get to God, the more we become aware that God's standards of goodness are rather higher than ours. Jesus says that evil takes place in the heart: contempt for a fellow human being is just as much murder as any outward sign of crime.

Comments on the Internet about death penalty prisoners often brand them as 'monsters' and call for vicious methods of ending their lives. The writers are unaware of their own violence or that they themselves have a murderous mindset.

It's clear, when someone commits a horrible crime, that something has gone seriously wrong with their humanity. If society then treats them inhumanely, we all become less humane and farther away from God.

Jesus says, 'Be perfect as your heavenly Father is perfect.' Our mindset, attitudes and judgements are so far from God's. Can human beings be perfect? The readings in the days to come will shed more light.

† Lord, I'm so far from perfect. Help!

Thursday 2 March
The tower of Babel

Genesis 11:1–9
Come, let us build ourselves a city ... so that we may make a name for ourselves; otherwise we will be scattered over the whole earth. (verse 4)

It's great to watch videos of 'flash mobs'.

A group of singers quietly mingles with the crowd in a busy city centre or shopping mall. One starts singing and heads begin to turn, wondering what's going on.

Then another member, some distance away, joins in – then more and more people, singing in unison. The astonished crowd can find it very moving. Everyone becomes drawn into the harmony.

But what happens when unity doesn't lead to harmony – when a football crowd turns from cheering its team to beating up the opposition? When a close-knit family bands together to terrorise neighbours?

The people on the Babel city-building project had no problem in communicating or co-operating; they were all on the same wavelength and spoke the same language. But their unity wasn't healthy.

As individuals and as a group, they lacked integrity – they were inwardly scattered, fragmented, in pieces. Rebellion against God causes a gang mentality, not real unity. It's a shaky foundation for any project, however community-minded it may appear.

God exposed the Babel discussions as meaningless nonsense and separated the planners before they could do real harm.

When communities, governments, businesses or even churches get together to plan great projects, everyone needs to take responsibility for asking the right questions, checking the foundations and the motives before giving their support. If it isn't God's plan, if it's founded on pride and self-interest. It may look and sound impressive, but it won't be in anyone's interest, ultimately.

† Lord, it's great to be part of a happy group or successful project. But don't let that sense of belonging draw me into anything that's not your plan.

For further thought
• Are there times when my 'yes' to God should involve saying 'no' to the group I'm in?

Friday 3 March
Cursed is the ground

Genesis 3:14–24

Man has now become like one of us, knowing good and evil. He must not be allowed to reach out his hand and take also from the tree of life and eat, and live for ever. (verse 22)

A common criticism of the church is that it is controlling – limiting people's freedom to experience life. Some religions or religious alternatives embrace everything in the universe, making no distinction between good and evil, believing this leads to natural freedom and balance.

The earliest experiment by man and woman reaching for all-embracing knowledge led, unexpectedly, to finding their options limited. Instead of experiencing life as God's gift, they found they had chosen to do it the hard way: the world became a painful place to bring children into and survival became heavy labour. Nothing came easily or naturally. Life could no longer last forever: no human being could cope if it did.

A friend of mine had motor neurone disease. Things he used to do without a second thought – scratching an itch, pulling up his socks – began to involve immense effort. Finally, he couldn't move, swallow or speak. If someone had promised him unending life, as he was experiencing it, it wouldn't be welcome.

Another friend, bringing up children in a violent neighbourhood, denied them the freedom of walking home alone after dark or playing outside when gangs of older boys were around.

Life without limits, in reality, doesn't bring freedom or the fullness of life promised by Jesus, but unwanted consequences. In a world that has chosen to break free from God these can be harsh, and harshest of all for the vulnerable.

† Father God, when your commands seem to limit my freedom, help me to trust that your way sets me free.

For further thought

• Do any of my choices 'curse the ground' for other people, making their lives more difficult?

Saturday 4 March
The warring self

Romans 7:14–25

I have the desire to do what is good but I cannot carry it out … Who will rescue me? (verses 18b and 24b)

Some years ago I prayed for a man struggling to overcome a sex addiction. Temptations tormented him until, hoping for some respite, he gave in. But the temptations returned, sooner and worse every time. He found himself, as Paul describes, doing the very things he most did not want to do. He reached the point of considering suicide, unable to live with the person he had become.

One day he had a phone call from someone whose business was to cater for such temptations, in a city considered one of the sex capitals of the world, inviting him to come over. He knew he should refuse. But he booked his flight for the next morning.

That night he cried out to God for help. He had tried willpower, fasting and a punishing schedule of exhausting physical exercise. Nothing had worked. He was about to sink deeper into his hated lifestyle.

Next morning, he turned on the early TV news and saw a huge fall of snow had blanketed the area around the airport and blocked all the roads round his house. All flights were cancelled. He fell on his knees and wept and thanked God.

Jesus promises to save us, and that means saving us from our darker self – the default mode we slide back into when discouraged, whether a major addiction or petty complaining, jealousy or gossip.

Who can rescue us from being drawn back into our default mode? Only a stronger attraction – the love of Jesus Christ for us.

† Jesus, you know me at my worst. And you know my desire for goodness. I trust you, when temptation exerts its power, to be a stronger power and rescue me.

For further thought

- God listens to our deepest desire. Is my deepest desire for good?

At-one-ment
At one with God

Notes based on the New International Version (UK) by **Clare Nonhebel**

See Clare's biography on p. 61.

Sunday 5 March
The disappointment of God

Genesis 6:5–8

The Lord said, 'I will wipe from the face of the earth the human race, whom I have created – and with them the animals, the birds and the creatures that move along the ground – for I regret that I have made them.' (verse 7)

Flying into Orlando airport, Florida, passengers had to walk past sniffer dogs. I thought they were checking for drugs, but it was for fruit! Even a speck of disease on an apple or orange could lead to the wipe-out of a whole crop and many farmers' livelihoods.

In this reading, spiritual disease had taken over God's people. They had brought such pollution to their souls and the whole world that there seemed to be nothing wholesome left to save. But in the very last line of this reading, a ray of light appears: one person still prepared to listen to God – Noah.

Sometimes it doesn't seem worth trying to lead a good life. What can one person do, in the face of the atrocities we see in our world? But God, although full of grief at the state of his people, thinks differently. Time and again, he demonstrates that even one soul willing to listen to him can overcome a whole tide of evil. Families who forgive the murderer of the child they loved so much, or people who risk their lives in peaceful campaigns against violence, are a small voice speaking against the clamour of evil. But God hears.

† Father God, even if no one seems to be listening, let our lives speak up for your goodness.

Monday 6 March
God's covenant with the earth

Genesis 9:8–17

I establish my covenant with you: never again will all life be destroyed by the waters of a flood; never again will there be a flood to destroy the earth. (verse 11)

Time and again, human beings have experienced a flood of evil that threatens to engulf every living soul. World wars, oppressive regimes, genocide, terrorism, environmental pollution and claims to supremacy by nations, races or religions have caused people to fear for their lives and for our planet's survival.

At times it seems impossible to halt the violent tide. But goodness has somehow never quite been extinguished. One person lies down in front of a tank. A writer speaks out. A group of students stages a protest. A small community sues a multinational company. A whistle-blower reveals corruption in a police force or government. A few people support them, though many more stay silent.

In an English seaside town, a cliff suddenly collapsed with no warning. Investigation revealed a network of tiny underground streams. Over time, the trickle of water had undermined the apparently solid rock until it gave way.

Even when trouble seems global and insurmountable, God promises that eternal life will prevail 'even though the earth may shake and mountains fall into the sea'. His justice will come 'like a mighty flood' to sweep away the more visible flood of evil. It is working away like underground streams in those insignificant people who stand against the tide.

We are not hopeless idealists clutching at straws. In believing that good will prevail over evil we rely on something unshakeable: God's covenant, made with every single person with a heart for God.

† Father God, you told human beings not to feed on knowledge of good and evil. When evil demands attention, keep my attention on you.

For further thought

• In conversation, do I focus more on the world's disasters or on hope in God's promise?

Tuesday 7 March
Atonement under the law

Leviticus 16:1–10, 29–34

On this day atonement will be made for you, to cleanse you. Then, before the Lord, you will be clean from all your sins. (verse 30)

In chapter 10 we read that two of Aaron's sons imitated their father's offering of fire at God's tabernacle, with no authority from God. Their arrogance resulted in Aaron's loss of freedom to come and go in God's presence, and the whole community's need to make changes in the way they approached him.

They could no longer take God for granted. Recognition of sin, repentance, sacrifice, washing, fasting and abstaining from normal activities were to be the preparation for meeting with God from now on.

It's easy, when Christian life is established, to become a bit casual about it. We can pray on autopilot or cut prayer time short, make excuses for lapses of patience or get too busy to put God first. Even major ministries fail because leaders keep repeating a formula that worked well yesterday or for the past 10 years, without consulting God about what he wants to do now.

How did Aaron feel, banned from the sanctuary he had been ordained to enter, unless he made all these elaborate preparations? We can only imagine. Humiliated? Or relieved that God would put the whole nation firmly in its place when his own sons took the law into their own hands?

Sometimes, when reverence and awe grow weak, law helps us get back on a firm footing with God. Tried-and-tested devotions, set times put aside for prayer and acts of kindness can remind us that God is God and our lives are his gift.

† Abba Father, you are also Sovereign Lord and Ruler of all. Keep reminding us that we owe our lives to you.

For further thought

• Do I presume, as a chosen friend of God, that God will be fine with whatever I do?

Wednesday 8 March
At one through Christ

Philippians 2:1–11

At the name of Jesus every knee should bow, in heaven and on earth and under the earth, and every tongue acknowledge that Jesus Christ is Lord, to the glory of God the Father. (verses 10–11)

Being punished for somebody else's crime is terrible. Many people have been executed under the death penalty before they were found to be innocent, or even in spite of evidence of innocence.

In accepting an agonising and shameful death with all its torture, abuse and public ridicule, Jesus not only submitted to the Father, who is just, and to human beings, who can be merciless, but reversed the human tendency to prefer to let others suffer rather than take their sufferings on.

True submission to God involves heart and soul, bodies and even, as in this reading, knees and tongues.

Once as a small child I was shut in a room till I finished my dinner, as a punishment for refusing food. After an hour or so my grandfather called round to visit and asked where I was. He came in, under strict instructions to 'make her do as she's told' and found me crying. The rice pudding was solid, congealed and disgusting. He encouraged me to imagine delicious strawberries and fed me a spoonful. I tried, but sobbed, 'It doesn't taste anything like them!'

So he picked up the spoon and ate the whole horrible mess himself, gagging slightly, then hugged me and sent me outdoors to play.

I've read many explanations of Jesus' atonement for our sins, all deeply theological. But – it may sound flippant – the image that still speaks most clearly to me today is somehow that rice pudding.

† Jesus, I can't comprehend the scale of your sacrifice for me and for the whole of humanity. Thank you.

For further thought

• If I had to atone for every offensive thought, impulse, action or attitude of my own – how long would my lifetime have to be?

Thursday 9 March
Reconciling work

At-one-ment – Clare Nonhebel

Ephesians 2:13–22
He himself is our peace, who has made the two one and has destroyed the barrier, the dividing wall of hostility. (verse 14)

There are sometimes good reasons for divisions between people. Jesus himself says he didn't commit to bring superficial peace even to families but to invite every person to stand alone before God. Children abused at home may need to make a complete break from family in order to heal. Warring factions of any kind may need to put distance between them before they can consider mediation.

But when division becomes a way of life, it can go on dividing into smaller and smaller units. My family is both English and Belgian. The English ones consider the Belgians foreigners. But other Belgians sometimes won't speak to my family because they are French-speaking, not Flemish-speaking Belgian.

Sometimes the strongest hostilities are between people who have the most in common. A friend lived in a small rural community in which people from one end of the village wouldn't pass the time of day with people from 'the wrong end' in which she lived!

In Jesus' day, Jews were set apart not only from Samaritans, Romans and Greeks but also among themselves: Pharisees, Sadducees and followers of different rabbis. Today some Christians still range themselves in theological groups and avoid or argue with each other.

Jesus' message is radical: there are no outsiders. God's kingdom is for everyone. He died for sinners. As soon as we claim that title, we're in.

† Jesus, admitting I'm wrong or that others can be different but still accepted by you is not easy – but you chose the hard way so we could enjoy real unity. Help me to choose that way, too.

For further thought
• Is there in my life at the moment any false union I should refuse? Or any division I need to work towards healing?

Friday 10 March
When God is absent

Psalm 22:1–11

Do not be far from me, for trouble is near and there is no one to help.
(verse 11)

This psalm supplied Jesus with words to pray when he was beyond words on the cross: 'My God, my God, why have you forsaken me?'

There are times for everyone when the Father seems to be an absent parent.

Psychologists say that our view of God reflects our view of our human father. As a child I used to think God had put us on the planet and left us to get on with life. It was years before I realised that this did not reflect God but the human father who abandoned the family.

People who turn against God or the fallible church have often been hurt by humans who could or should have helped them in their time of need but failed to, or made things worse. If God has invited but not forced those other people to offer assistance when it was needed, the sufferers can feel abandoned by God as well as by brothers and sisters.

But God cannot leave us. God is always near, even when we feel far removed from his sphere of influence. Like Jesus calling out, 'My God!' to the Father who seemed to have forsaken him, we can be sure he is there even when he doesn't seem near. When we can't hear him, he can still hear.

We are free to ignore the cry of our starving or suffering fellow human beings. We are free to ignore God if we prefer. But God is here.

† My God, when there is no one to help, come near. And when I ignore someone's cry for help, turn the volume up until I hear.

For further thought

• When someone feels forsaken by God, is there anything I can do to make him seem nearer?

Saturday 11 March
The new life in God

John 15:1–11

He cuts off every branch in me that bears no fruit, while every branch that does bear fruit he prunes so that it will be even more fruitful. (verse 2)

Pruning a fruitful branch doesn't feel like a good thing to do.

The plum tree in our garden looked flourishing until my husband noticed the leaves curling up and the fruit growing distorted. We resorted to ruthless pruning till most of the branches lay on the ground, some bearing fruit that looked promising. The remaining tree was skinny and forlorn.

Now it's still thin on branches but is heavily laden with beautiful juicy plums. And the new leaves are sparse but freshly green and healthy.

When God gets out the pruning shears, he may remove opportunities and cut down cherished projects. It's really hard to believe he knows best at those times. When we're asking for good things and all we see is dead ends, there's no way that the suffering feels like a route to a fuller life.

It's easier to see fruit in other people's lives: when someone has 'been through the mill' they may emerge as a gentler person, more understanding and less demanding.

Jesus invites, 'Remain in me and I will remain in you.' Stay with him and stick with his project, when your best dreams end up in a heap on the ground.

When the fruit of the Spirit comes – love, joy, peace, patience, kindness, goodness, faithfulness, gentleness and self-control – it will bring a new lease of life, worth the waiting and well worth living.

† Father, out of the least promising circumstances you can bring life that will last way beyond our lifetime. Keep us rooted in you and living a fruitful life.

For further thought
• What will 'remaining in Christ' involve today?

At-one-ment
At one with others

Notes based on the New Revised Standard Version by **Terry Lester**

Terry Lester has been a priest in the Diocese of Cape Town for over 30 years and has been serving in the Parish of Christ Church, Constantia, for five. He sees involvement in and commitment to community issues as the way faith communities can contribute to building the diverse Rainbow Nation. He believes that through engaged and vibrant communities of faith, reconciliation – a faith imperative – can become a living, everyday reality in a fractured society. He is married to Colleen and they have three adult children.

Sunday 12 March
All one in Christ Jesus

Galatians 3:23–29

There is no longer Jew or Greek, there is no longer slave or free, there is no longer male or female; for all of you are one in Christ Jesus. (verse 28)

Archbishop Desmond Tutu borrowed the term 'Rainbow Nation' to describe the new reality South Africans had arrived at with the dawn of a democratic order. The past was marked by the separate labels with its emphasis on racial and ethnic differences which separated each group from the other. But a new reality had dawned and it bathed and bound people of this new nation in the 'new colours' of the glorious rainbow.

Likewise, St Paul in Galatians is describing a new refracted reality from which a new nation had emerged; they are those who have come 'through Christ' in baptism and now live 'in Christ' where ethnicity, social standing or gender can destroy the new reality. Before encountering Christ, each group at Galatia had its own unique features, strengths and shortcomings – whether Jew or Greek or from slave or slave-owner class. Through Christ they are now bound together in a shared and common experience.

This week we explore what that rainbow nation looked like in Galatia – and could look like wherever we live.

† Lord God, in Christ you created a new order among us. Move us, too, through this same power that the world may move to embrace all others as you embrace humanity.

Monday 13 March
Being countercultural

Luke 6:27–36

Do to others as you would have them do to you. (verse 31)

It is said that in generations that experience trauma, cells in the body build up a memory of it and pass it on to their children. This memory of trauma resurfaces in illnesses like high blood pressure, anxiety and diabetes – proportionally higher than among those whose forebears were not subjected to such trauma. Slavery is an example used. What is done to others is therefore also visited upon their children and their children's children. Like ripples on a pond, the effects of an action continue long after. The gospel of Jesus Christ suggests that when love and goodness have their way, instead, the result is the spread of healing and wholeness.

It is said that Rabbi Hillel, in response to a question about the purpose and extent of the law, said that it is possible to stand on one leg and recite the entire law! When his incredulous enquirers asked how this could be, he said: 'What is hateful to you, do not do to your neighbour. That is the whole Torah. The rest is commentary. Go and learn.'

Just as each rabbi shaped and moulded his disciples through question and answer, forming them in the words and spirit of the Torah, so too does Jesus shape his newly called disciples (Luke uses 'apostles'). But Jesus is not just building on an established tradition; he is initiating his disciples into a new law – the law of love. Under this law there are no limits set.

† Lord Jesus, help me not to count the cost to myself but rather to anticipate the effect of my actions on unborn generations.

For further thought

• Find out something about your own ancestry and your family story.

Tuesday 14 March
Challenging hypocrisy

Luke 6:37–45

A good measure, pressed down, shaken together, running over, will be put into your lap; for the measure you give will be the measure you get back. (verse 38)

The image is of merchants weighing grain in the marketplace – but often they do not press it down and top it up and rarely does it overflow! But rather, with sleight of hand or other distractions, the grain is whipped off the scale and into your bag and an extended hand is ready to receive payment. Often these very people diligently observe all the religious feasts and occupy the best seats and are harsh in their judgement of those who don't.

The measure God uses for all is the one Jesus describes here. Just when you think it is enough, then it is well and truly pressed down and to the brim; but even that is not enough. It is then poured out so that it runs over. The measure is not to match money to quantity of product in comparable like measure but rather to set a new standard for generous action, an action initiated by God.

Countries that have inherited a legacy of injustice and violence have put processes in place which try to help victims to tell their story. It is a model which has worked in many contexts – South Africa, Rwanda, Peru – and is being tried in places like Sri Lanka. Jesus proposes a model of generous pouring out with nothing to match or counter in return. In the contexts mentioned it is like forgiving and forgetting; truth-telling without holding anything back and giving all without being enticed with a reward. Radical generosity is a precursor to experiencing radical grace.

† Spirit of the living God, rid me of all that I hold in for fear and empty me of all that I protect. Then fill me with your life-giving Spirit; shake me down till you overflow from and through me.

For further thought
• Is there a relationship which has become stuck by stinginess and may be unlocked through generous forgiving action?

Wednesday 15 March
Celebrating diversity

Romans 12:1–13

… so we, who are many, are one body in Christ, and individually we are members one of another. (verse 5)

These words from St Paul's letter to the church at Rome are repeated at each celebration of the Lord's Supper – when the bread is broken and the wine poured out. In the liturgy used by Anglicans, the presider states: 'The bread which we break, is it not a sharing of the body of Christ?' To which the people respond: 'We who are many are one body, for we all partake of the one bread.' This style of stating something and having it echo back is a method employed in learning. When we were growing up, our teachers used rote methods to drum things into us not only with questions and answers but also to a beat in a singalong way. Things were not only committed to memory but to the body as you swayed and tapped the knowledge into you. To this day we remember things because they were 'drummed into us' till we didn't even have to think about it; it became instinctive.

The first Christians were a diverse group. Each was shaped by that which was drummed into them from earliest days. St Paul is not suggesting a drumming out of the past and a drumming in of the new; that word 'individually' holds to the uniqueness of each but introduces another beat and rhythm: 'one body'. We have a practice in our liturgy where the bread and wine are held aloft and the minister says: 'Behold who we are'! To which the response is: 'May we become what we receive'.

† Lord, disturb my comfort with divisions in your body the church, and comfort us when we experience opposition as we seek to draw near to others.

For further thought

• Are you involved in ecumenical action and meeting others who worship differently to you? How do you speak of them so that unity of the body is enhanced?

Thursday 16 March
Healing the wounds of history

John 4:7–9, 19–26

But the hour is coming, and is now here, when the true worshippers will worship the Father in spirit and truth, the Father seeks such as these to worship him. (verse 23)

The coming of the light into the world brings judgement but also freedom from a dark past. Light and truth form the two-sided key which unlocks the chains which bind. Not everyone will rush towards the light for fear that what is hidden by darkness will be exposed. But it will bring relief and 'lightness' to those who embrace the chance to be freed from the burdens of darkness. For as St John issues a chilling warning that people prefer darkness, he introduces us to those who see it as an opportunity for relief. The Samaritan woman is burdened by a past which is both inherited and self-made. Her complicated domestic arrangements together with the intricacies of relations with the Jews leave her exhausted from hiding in the darkness of the mess it has all become. Her encounter with the 'prophet' begins a journey to wholeness and healing which had seemed out of reach for so long. Even though she had every reason to tread cautiously and with circumspection, she does not run and hide as she edges closer and closer to the light and to her own emancipation.

Each year on the anniversary of Nelson Mandela's death a national debate is ignited on what exactly his legacy is. Did he sell out on the pain of Black South Africans by signing up for nation-building and reconciliation, or did he ensure a better future for them? It is a debate which is far from over. What is clear, though, is that this man chose to step out of the darkness of resentment and hatred and to tread a different path. Those who hail him as the father of a new nation have found it far, far more difficult to walk that path!

† Lord Jesus, light of the world, quiet my fears and still my anxiety at being exposed by your light.

For further thought

• Imagine what comes to light when you shine a strong light into a dark corner. Now do it!

Friday 17 March
Celebrating women

Mark 14:3–9

She has done what she could, she has anointed my body beforehand for its burial. (verse 8)

Even in a liberated South Africa, women have found it harder to step out. Given the mix of cultural diversity and the place assigned to women, stepping out from the often menial roles of those deemed 'less than' takes courage. Too often women have been at the receiving end of this not only in patriarchal societies but also in Western democracies. It is almost excusable in the former, as one could argue that they 'know no better'. When found in modern societies that 'should know better', it is often a result of conditioning and culture.

But it takes more than simply courage to change the way things are. It also takes self-belief that a different order is possible, and one person can actually risk ridicule and shame to achieve it. To be culpable in condoning such actions or through our silence keeping systems in place which trap people in powerlessness – whether consciously or unconsciously, actively or passively – is a challenge we all face. In this story Jesus refuses the pull, even with eyes fixed on him, to be party to the demeaning of another. In this case, a woman. Instead he sees it as an act of love and compassion as a paying forward for what he too is about to do for all, including those very people who are insisting that he sends her away.

† Lord Jesus, grant me the courage and grace to step out and not use any excuse for being harsh to another person, no matter what the cost.

For further thought

• Light a candle for the many nameless women who have stood bravely through history for what they believe in.

Saturday 18 March
Paradox: Christ brings division

Luke 12:49–53

Do you think that I have come to bring peace on the earth? No, I tell you, but rather division! (verse 51)

In this statement, Jesus is setting the proverbial 'cat among the pigeons'. The traditions which have built up around Jesus seem to have avoided this image of him causing division and conflict and have preferred the one which presents him as 'gentle Jesus meek and mild' even when scriptural tradition does not shy away from him as controversial. Is it that we prefer a domesticated version of Jesus which is a soothing presence rather than one which challenges us to our core? It certainly suits those who see religion as an opiate with Jesus as the 'fix' keeping a nation docile and compliant.

In the 1980s religious leaders in South Africa produced the Kairos Document, which challenged this image and emphasised a Jesus who raged at injustice and at those who exploited God's children. The government acted swiftly in its clampdown on those responsible for the document, viewing it as a direct threat to their rule.

† Lord, it is possible to feel so right about something yet also be so wrong at the same time. Correct me where it is needed and necessary and help me move from rightness to righteousness.

For further thought

• What views which you held dearly have you been able to change your thinking about? Celebrate God's grace to you in bringing about change in your thinking.

At-one-ment
At one with creation

Notes based on the New Revised Standard Version by **Lynne Frith**

Lynne Frith loves playing with words – whether writing poems or prayers, playing scrabble, messaging friends – and has a secret longing to write on walls with a spray can. The rest of the time she is a Methodist presbyter in Auckland, Aotearoa, where she is privileged to serve with an inclusive, welcoming congregation.

Sunday 19 March
Sing green!

Genesis 2:4b–17

The Lord God took the man and put him in the Garden of Eden to till it and keep it. (verse 15)

This week we reflect on the relationship between humans and all creation, in particular the responsibility given to humankind. Some of the texts resonate with beauty, while others have some harsh undertones. All of them invite us to participate in the continuing work of creation.

We begin our reflections with a creation story. How different this is from the story in Genesis 1, in which humankind is given dominion over all living things. The creation account in Genesis 2 describes a different relationship, focused on care of the earth. The (male) human is formed 'from the dust of the ground', because there was no one to till the ground. Then a garden was planted. This suggests to me a relationship of connectedness, service and intimacy.

In the documentary *Gardening with Soul*, Sister Loyola, of the Sisters of Compassion in Wellington, exemplifies this close and caring relationship with the earth, and likens caring for a garden to the care and nurture of young children.

† Shirley Erena Murray invites us to 'Sing green for the good sweet earth, For creation's birth, for sky and sea, Sing green for the shining air, for the Maker's care, For the life in you and me' (in *Alleluia Aotearoa*, New Zealand Hymnbook Trust). Give thanks today and every day for those who care for the earth.

Monday 20 March
A mixed blessing

Genesis 9:1–7

The fear and dread of you shall rest on every animal of the earth … every moving thing that lives shall be food for you … I give you everything. (verses 2–3)

This text, in which the blessing conferred upon Noah and his sons with the injunction to 'be fruitful and multiply' is followed by the suggestion that all creation has been handed over for the benefit of Noah and his descendants, can be troublesome for twenty-first century readers. This uneasy relationship predicates the covenant that God will make. It potentially sets up an unequal situation that could be used to justify and excuse the exploitation of creatures for human gain.

At the same time, the climate of fear is intensified with the threat that for both humans and animals, the cost of consuming flesh containing blood is that life will be taken by their own kind – a reckoning required by God.

It challenges the notion of interdependence that threads through yesterday's reading. We might ask ourselves whether both the command to be fruitful and multiply and the attitude that all creatures exist for the benefit of humankind are relevant or appropriate, in an age in which the world population is burgeoning and the numbers of species nearing extinction is on the increase. In this small country alone there are several thousand endangered species.

† The hymn 'God of the Galaxies' by Shirley Erena Murray (in *Alleluia Aotearoa*, New Zealand Hymnbook Trust) draws attention to the way in which humankind has misused the gifts of creation, and concludes with a reminder: 'Life is a holy thing, life is a whole, Linking each creature and blessing us all, Making connections of body and soul.' Pray for those who misuse the gifts of creation.

For further thought

- Find out something about the endangered species in your area, and how you might contribute to their preservation.

Tuesday 21 March
Abundance beyond measure – for whose benefit?

Genesis 41:46–49, 53–57

The seven years of plenty that prevailed in the land of Egypt came to an end … there was famine in every country. (verse 53 and part of verse 54)

Prudent steward? Canny investor? Entrepreneur? Profiteer?

Any of these could describe Joseph's actions. He did well out of the disaster of famine. His prudent storage of grain in the years of abundance gave him a useful political tool in relation to both Pharaoh and to his family of origin. It is within Joseph's power to determine whether the people of Egypt, and of the world beyond, die of starvation. Survival requires resourcefulness.

People who live and work close to the land know that there will be good years and bad. Farmers know to be prepared for lean years – drought, harsh winters – and to maximise productivity in the years of abundance. Survival in difficult seasons is not only about soil and crops and livestock, but also about emotional and spiritual resilience.

Today's reading reminds us of the importance, whether we live in city or country, of using the years of plenty to build resilience and develop our resources so that we are better prepared for years of struggle and scarcity. It also says something about the politics of abundance and scarcity, and who benefits most from the stockpiling of resources.

† 'We are the voices for the earth, We who will care enough to cry, Cherish her beauty, clear her breath, live that our planet may not die' (Shirley Erena Murray in *Faith Forever Singing*, New Zealand Hymnbook Trust). Pray for those who are struggling to survive in times of natural disaster – drought, famine, flood, earthquake, bushfire, tsunami.

For further thought

• What have you 'stockpiled' that could be shared with a wider community?

At-one-ment – Lynne Frith

Wednesday 22 March
Restoring the land

Leviticus 25:23–24

Throughout the land that you hold, you shall provide for the redemption of the land. (verse 24)

Many indigenous peoples, including Maori in Aotearoa New Zealand, have understandings of land as being held in trust rather than owned. The land is a *taonga* or treasure for every generation, not the possession of any one individual. This is in contrast to the values of some other peoples in which land ownership is individualised and confers social status and power.

One of the hot political issues in my country is to do with foreign purchase and ownership of land, particularly large tracts of land, and the coastal margins. There is growing concern among the general population that in such an environment where the acquisition of land is a hallmark of individual success and wealth, the land itself, which is the source of all life, ceases to be a *taonga* and becomes a commodity.

We are reminded today of our responsibility to care for the land, whether it is the garden in our backyard, a smallholding, a large farm or the land that is our home, in such a way that it is nourished, cherished and renewed. We are also reminded of the temporary nature of human existence, and that the land is not ours to own.

† 'Touch the earth lightly, use the earth gently, nourish the life of the world in our care. Gift of great wonder, ours to surrender, trust for the children tomorrow will bear' (Shirley Erena Murray in *Alleluia Aotearoa*, New Zealand Hymnbook Trust). Pray for those whose traditional lands have been consumed by the demands of the wealthy one-third world.

For further thought
• What can you do to show that you cherish the land?

Thursday 23 March
Trees of life

> **Deuteronomy 20:19–20**
>
> *Although you may take food from them [the trees] you must not cut them down. (verse 19)*

These verses occur at the end of a chapter setting out the rules of conduct for warfare.

There is recognition of the devastation that war brings to the land. Perhaps the writer of this text also knew a thing or two about the vital role played by trees in ecological systems and climate control.

The trees that provide food must be protected, in order to continue their fruitfulness. Only the trees that do not bear food may be cut down for the purposes of war. In his book *The Covenanted Self*, Walter Brueggemann suggests that this text refers back to the creation narrative in Genesis 1 (p. 104). There is a reminder of the command for fruitfulness and abundance.

Even in times of war there is a duty to care for the earth and to ensure the continuation of all life.

In New Zealand there are laws that restrict both the logging of indigenous trees and the export of their timber. Trees are understood to be a precious part of our heritage, as well as an essential participant in the fragile ecology of these islands.

However, local authorities govern bylaws for the protection of trees in urban areas. In the city where I live, while protected or heritage trees may not be cut down without special consent, bylaws to prevent the indiscriminate cutting down of trees have recently been relaxed. Subsequently, one of my neighbours, who had a stand of mature trees on his property, had them all felled, with the result that the bird numbers have greatly reduced.

† Pray, with Shirley Erena Murray: 'God unnerve us, God, forgive us: how we plunder, waste and war! Give new meaning to earth's greening, that the beauty thrives once more' (from 'Look in Wonder', in *Hope is our Song*, New Zealand Hymnbook Trust).

For further thought

• What needs to happen in your community to sustain the ecological interdependence of all living things?

Friday 24 March
Gifts freely given

1 Chronicles 29:6–19

For we are aliens and transients before you, as were all our ancestors; our days on the earth are like a shadow. (verse 15)

There is a consistent theme throughout the First Testament in which the Israelites are exhorted to remember that they too have been strangers and aliens in a foreign land, whether through settling in Canaan, or being enslaved in Egypt. They are to remember what it was to be a foreigner and transient, in order to know how to fulfil their obligations to the strangers who have come reside among them. They are reminded of the transitory nature of human existence.

David is a persuasive leader, and the people bring their freewill offerings for the building of the Temple, out of recognition that everything comes from God and so is returned to God. 'For all things come from you, and of your own have we given you' (verse 14). It's a phrase often recited in the liturgies of the church. David is expressing gratitude to God for the abundance that the nation is enjoying, and beseeching God to continue this blessing.

There's an element of bargaining running through this that sits uneasily – a suggestion in David's speech that these freewill offerings are in part to encourage God to continue blessing the people and the nation. Surely the blessings of abundance and hope are blessings to be sought for all people, not only those who are able to make generous or extravagant gifts?

† 'The blessing of water and light and air, The blessing of earth and its beauty And the time to discover God's world of joy; This blessing be given us all' (Shirley Erena Murray in *Hope is Our Song*, New Zealand Hymnbook Trust). Give thanks today for the blessings you have received.

For further thought
• Consider whether your offerings are indeed freely given, or whether there are strings attached to your donations of time or money or expertise.

Saturday 25 March
Earthed and in harmony

Colossians 1:15–23

He is the image of the invisible God, the firstborn of all creation. (verse 15)

The writers of the Bible, unlike many of us today, were intimately connected with their food and the agricultural year. God was closely involved in rain, wind, storm, and earth – the annual cycle of planting and harvest. All life was interconnected; a poor harvest threatened all.

The word humility comes from the same root as the word for earth. It's a word that has sometimes been distorted in Christian tradition to mean something like self-abasement. Humility as a virtue is still viewed with suspicion by many. Yet in its connection with earthiness and groundedness it could be reclaimed as a positive value.

There's a sense in which the writer of the letter to the Colossians, in describing Christ as the firstborn of all creation, is describing earthiness and connectedness. There are glimpses of that earthiness, that continuity with creation, in some of the parables Jesus told.

As followers in the way of Jesus, we are to keep our feet on the ground, be earthed, to be in harmony with all creation, not for our own gain, but for the benefit of all living things.

If we build strong communities in Christ, humble and earthed, we will break down the selfishness and greed that is the root cause of all that endangers our planet.

† 'Spirit of hope in the Christ who renews us, lighten our winter of anguish with spring; Washed with the showers of loving forgiveness, Warmed by the rays of the love that you bring' (Bill Bennett in *Faith Forever Singing*, New Zealand Hymnbook Trust). Pray for the growth of strong communities, earthed, humble, honest and visionary.

For further thought

• What effect might the UN sustainable development goals have on your community, your country?

At-one-ment
At one with self

Notes based on the New Revised Standard Version by **Jennifer Smith**

Jennifer Smith is a Methodist minister serving in west London. She is originally from Boston, Massachusetts in the USA, but has lived in the United Kingdom since 1993. Before coming into the ministry, Jennifer was a teacher and university lecturer in history and politics; she has also taught and worked over a number of years in the Methodist Church of Nigeria. She is deeply committed to nurturing Christian disciples in multi-ethnic and multi-faith communities, and is surprised daily by unexpected beauty in her urban setting.

Sunday March 26
Spirit-led

Luke 4:1–13

Jesus, full of the Holy Spirit, returned from the Jordan and was led by the Spirit into the wilderness, where for forty days he was tempted by the devil. (verses 1 and 2)

In an average week I get up to a dozen offers for products and processes to cure me of all sorts of ailments and bad feelings. From stress and sore shoulders to wrinkles and regular bowels, there is a cream, pill or treatment that will restore my life to a perfect equilibrium, promising 'inner harmony'.

Where toxic stress, grief or other maladies can be eased they should be. But there are temptations just as real as Jesus faced in the wilderness in the quick-fix, no-pain culture, where it counsels us to go around the wilderness that can accompany bad feeling. Sadness is a normal reaction to grief. Restlessness is a normal part of faith. Anger or hurt are normal reactions to harm. Jesus in the wilderness dealt with these and clarified who he was, and who he was not.

Being 'at one with self' in Christian terms is an ongoing process and is less about perfection than about truth, humour, forgiveness and, most of all, knowing that God loves us just as we are. This week's readings invite us to consider what being at one with self means, as part of being at one with God and the world.

† O Lord, draw me into your embrace. Knit me together in grace and strength, that I may live to your praise and glory.

Monday 27 March
The ease of self-deception

1 John 1:5–10

If we say we have no sin, we deceive ourselves, and the truth is not in us. If we confess our sins, he who is faithful and just will forgive us our sins and cleanse us from all unrighteousness. (verses 8 and 9)

I remember a wise schoolmaster at the end of his career giving advice to a student: 'Never lie, it gives you far too much to remember.' The brilliance of this advice lay in undermining the moralising tone with a simple practical truth everyone could recognise.

Most of us agree in most circumstances that lying is a bad thing, and most of us admit to lying regularly, one way or another. Maybe there doesn't feel time to deal with truth, or truth gives way to kindness, or we are afraid of the consequences. Today's reading complicates our picture of truth-telling and deception further. The author does not assume that the person who says she has no sin is lying: the author assumes instead that the person's confession of sin is limited by her self-awareness.

If self-deception is so easy, how can I count on my sense of understanding my own soul? The simple practical truth, according to the scripture, is that our self-awareness is not a fixed point, once-for-all condition. Our internal selves are like landscapes: some parts managed and well-travelled, other parts unexplored, where God yet dwells. As we walk in light, in fellowship, we will be continually cleansed, convicted, renewed. We can go gently with ourselves – not raking over feelings and actions with a fevered brain seeking wrong-doing, but with the gentle curiosity that asks of God, 'What might you show me next?'

† Holy God, strengthen my conscience, soften my defences and show me more of yourself, day by day.

For further thought
• What does your inner landscape look like today? What needs patient attention?

Tuesday 28 March
A thorn in the flesh

2 Corinthians 12:7–10

But he said to me, '… My grace is sufficient for you, for power is made perfect in weakness.' So, I will boast all the more gladly of my weaknesses, so that the power of Christ may dwell in me. (verse 9)

In my house, pruning the roses is a job we put off until the tangled bush is threatening to blind and maim everyone who crosses the threshold. It lurks waiting for the unwary, trailing long creepers down over the doorway just at face, wrist, and ankle level in perfect arrangement to catch someone coming up the pavement at night, or in a hurry fumbling for house keys.

A thorn that catches in the flesh hurts. And often, the yelping dance trying to escape a single thorn wraps the hopping visitor up in half a dozen. So it is with a sympathetic wince that I read of Paul's 'thorn in the flesh' today. Clearly, he is a righteous man entirely committed to the purposes of God. And yet, he admits he is divided against himself in this unnamed sin that seems to defeat his attempts to draw it out. It is a weakness that God has given, he implies, to keep him honest and human. To keep him in touch with the angst of small difficulties, which are so often our undoing. At one with God, Paul accepts that his person is unfinished creation, no less beloved for it. The mix of division and unity in his soul are exactly what allow him to do what he needs to, for God.

† God at work for our well-being, use our weakness as much as our strength to good purpose.

For further thought

• Consider the phrase 'Lead me not into temptation, but deliver me from evil.' What does this prayer mean in your life today?

Wednesday 29 March
Losing heart

2 Corinthians 4:1–12

But we have this treasure in clay jars, so that it may be made clear that this extraordinary power belongs to God and does not come from us. We are afflicted in every way, but not crushed; perplexed, but not driven to despair … (verses 7 and 8)

Twice, in this chapter of 2 Corinthians, Paul declares, 'We do not lose heart' (verses 1 and 16). He does not ask the readers not to lose heart, nor chastise them if they have; he simply declares as fact, 'We do not lose heart.' I have observed in pastoral life that if people in a community feel like heroes under pressure, they behave like heroes. They do not lose heart. Their resilience becomes a testimony that is a far more arresting statement of the gospel than a smooth-running, successful church.

If, however, people experiencing the same affliction or perplexity feel blamed or beaten, made to feel at fault, they do lose heart. This is followed usually by losing patience with the community and either leaving it themselves or driving others out. This kind of community becomes unattractive, however smoothly things run.

For Paul, 'not losing heart' is both a cause and effect of being entirely given over to the life and death of Christ. There is freedom and a unity of heart in that priority. It is a cause as the one drawn into Christ's grace will be encouraged and upheld by that grace. It is an effect as the one 'strong in heart' will find in the midst of difficulty evidence of God's continuing love and blessing.

So feel tired, feel wrong, feel unsure. Lament to God at the way of things. But do not lose heart, we are renewed day by day.

† Holy God, make me an encouragement to others, as you encourage me.

For further thought
• Where might you today encourage someone who is under pressure?

Thursday 30 March
The call to integrity

March

At-one-ment – Jennifer Smith

Ephesians 4:17–32

Put away from you all bitterness and wrath and anger and wrangling and slander, together with all malice, and be kind to one another, tenderhearted, forgiving one another as God in Christ has forgiven you. (verses 31 and 32)

I remember my father saying that 'an expert is the one who has made the most mistakes in a particular field'. Sometimes the most authentic promise we can make to each other is to make new and different mistakes: that is, not to keep repeating behaviours or patterns that harm us, while acknowledging that we may not get the next attempt perfect either. We should say it with a twinkle in the eye, of course!

The freedom to grow, to 'make new mistakes', is one that needs more than mere tolerance from our companions. In families, in schools and workplaces, in churches, we need to tell the truth while genuinely protecting each other from our shared sins of wrath, wrangling and gossipy slander. This takes the kind of tender-hearted kindness spoken of in today's reading.

Perhaps someone has spoken out of turn, or without full understanding – perhaps it is a stubborn person, perhaps it is an angry person. Perhaps today it is me, having sent an email response I didn't need to, or hitting 'reply all' by mistake. We should address the sources of harm in our communities and circles: the scripture says, 'be angry, but do not sin' (verse 26). This is not about being passive. However, neither is it about being hard-hearted where it is in our power not to be. When we have the chance to cover someone else's bitterness, wrath, wrangling or slander, what a freeing thing to take it.

† Forgive me my trespasses, as I forgive those who trespass against me. Give me a tender heart and true compassion.

For further thought

• How have digital forms of communication and social media changed the way we communicate, in relation to this teaching? Share your views on our Facebook group today.

Friday 31 March
Living by the Spirit

Galatians 5:16–26

By contrast, the fruit of the Spirit is love, joy, peace, patience, kindness, generosity, faithfulness, gentleness, and self-control. There is no law against such things. (verse 22)

It is all too easy to treat the 'fruit of the Spirit' as a list of the rules of engagement in Christian life, what a Christian *should* be or do. Woe betide if I can only achieve six of the nine in any given week! And what to make of an 8-week series in my churches a few years ago, taking a different fruit each week for its theme but leaving self-control off the end because the minister miscounted?

Of course, this is not what the fruit of the Spirit are about at all: they are not a new law to keep, an ever narrowing gateway to holiness or test to pass to get into the kingdom. They are offered as cairns or way-markers, signs of a person who is settled in themselves, in the Holy Spirit. The person at one with herself or himself will show these fruit. A community at one with itself, in the Spirit will show these themes in its patterns of communication, planning, review and self-evaluation.

When do you notice these characteristics in your life? What triggered such wonderful fruit in you, what nurtured it? Follow that path. That is what the scripture today means: then you will be subject to no law, law is irrelevant.

'Well, that's pretty stupid, isn't it?' said one of my church leaders, before laughing hard for more time than was polite and then giggling at intervals through the rest of the meeting when I confessed the miscounting of weeks, and the absence of self-control.

† Holy Spirit, guide and bless us on our way, bear fruit in our lives today.

For further thought

• Read the list of the fruit of the Spirit carefully, slowly. Is there one you are specially drawn to? Is there one you specially see in someone you love or have loved?

Saturday 1 April
Fool for God

Romans 8:26–27

Likewise the Spirit helps us in our weakness; for we do not know how to pray as we ought, but that very Spirit intercedes with sighs too deep for words. (verse 26)

Some religions or systems of thought teach that the path to inner harmony lies in withdrawing from the world, devaluing and diminishing attachments and needs of the flesh. Christianity teaches exactly the opposite, that being at one with ourselves means being reconciled to our fleshly beings. What was good enough for Jesus Christ is good enough for us: to laugh, live, work, love and to be tired, restless, sad, joyful, hungry and all the rest. We are not meant, nor expected to know all nor to be able to be untouched by the events of our lives. Indeed, we are not meant to survive our lives.

Because we apprehend God without comprehending God's final persons or purpose, Christianity teaches that there will always be a restlessness in our human striving, until we find our rest in God. There will be times when we do not know ourselves, or are overwhelmed and do not know what we want or should hope for. The reassurance of today's reading is that even, especially when we feel divided, God holds our unity. When we do not know what to pray, the Holy Spirit prays in us: we are knit together by God's attention, on our worst days.

Today is also April Fool's Day. Consider how God pokes holes in our arrogance and liberates us from grasping pride and greed, which are idolatry. God likes a holy fool. Knowing that the Spirit will pray in me with sighs too deep for words, gives me confidence to be one.

† Spirit of fools and fishermen, pray deeply in my body today with sighs too deep for words.

For further thought

• Have you noticed any April Fools' media stories or advertisements today? What makes them funny? How does God use humour?

Readings in Matthew (2)
Jesus – the last days

Notes based on the New International Version by **Simei Monteiro**

Simei Monteiro is a Brazilian poet and composer. She worked as Worship Consultant at the World Council of Churches in Geneva, Switzerland. She is interested in worship and the arts, and her book, *The Song of Life* (ASTE/IEPG, 1991), explores the relationship between hymnody and theology. As a retired missionary from the United Methodist Church, USA, she lives in Curitiba, Brazil, with her husband the Revd Jairo Monteiro. They have two daughters and three grandchildren.

Sunday 2 April
The plot

Matthew 26:1–5

Then the chief priests and the elders of the people assembled in the palace of the high priest, whose name was Caiaphas, and they schemed to arrest Jesus secretly and kill him. (verses 3–4)

Reflecting on Jesus' last days, perhaps we can ask ourselves where we are in the history. Of course with Jesus! We don't want to be part of a schemed plan to kill someone. This would be terrible and immoral! Nevertheless, we know that there are schemes of death in our world today. In some particular situation people cannot see clearly nor understand the different sides of their own history. People living along the Amazon riverbank are now uprooted because of huge hydroelectric plants. They are losing their ancestral habitats. No more river or fish or trees; and they are still waiting for the promised houses. We are called to be on the side of all these victims of plots; not only persecuted Christians, but also those who suffer all kinds of discrimination. Even nature is under a hidden scheme of destruction. What kind of plots do we face nowadays? Which powers are trying to destroy our lives? Reflecting on Jesus' history is a way we can decide to participate in our world history and not to be part of any hidden scheme against God's children or against God's creation.

† Divine shelter, give us courage to act in your name in any situation we are facing. Help us to discern your will in our times.

Monday 3 April
Beautiful and memorable things

Matthew 26:6–16

Aware of this, Jesus said to them, 'Why are you bothering this woman? She has done a beautiful thing to me' … 'Truly I tell you, wherever this gospel is preached throughout the world, what she has done will also be told, in memory of her.' (verses 10 and 13)

There is no price for beautiful things done to others. A valuable gift is never the same as an expensive one. My father was dying in Brazil and I was working in Geneva. The same day I got the bad news, a good friend came and told me not to worry. Then she arranged the tickets so I could go home and find my father still alive.

Jesus came to the house of Simon, who was probably healed by him, to enjoy the friendship and the food around a common table. They were there to celebrate together memorable things! When the woman came and humbly poured the perfume over Jesus' head, she was criticised. The disciples' criticism had a clear intention to diminish her and her action. Probably they thought: What is this woman doing here? Does she want to show up and why? Jesus was able not only to accept her ointment but also give a real meaning to it. She made such a beautiful thing! There was no waste of money or time!

Because of Jesus' death, we received the gift of eternal life. The strength of a community is rooted in the memories and experiences of good living. Remembrance of God's blessings poured on us is something we cannot erase from our lives. It is pleasant to remember the gifts of gentleness and love we have received from others: dear ones or even from unknown persons. 'What she has done will also be told, in memory of her.' These are the words I desire to be remembered for.

† O Jesus! What amazing memories we have from you and the beautiful things you did in our favour. Help us to be faithful witnesses of your love and enjoy the good perfume you exhale.

For further thought
- What beautiful things done to you can you remember? For what memories would you like to be remembered?

Tuesday 4 April
A real waste!

Matthew 26:17–25

When evening came, Jesus was reclining at the table with the Twelve. And while they were eating, he said, 'Truly I tell you, one of you will betray me.'
(verses 20–21)

In the Bethany scene, the disciples judged the ointment Jesus received from the woman a waste of money and a lost opportunity to do good to the poor.

Reflecting on Judas' betrayal we feel uncomfortable and probably have asked ourselves: Why did he do this? How could he betray his friend Jesus? There are easy answers: Judas was possessed by evil; he was a thief and only wanted money; it was determined in God's plan and we cannot really consider him guilty of his action. Perhaps he felt betrayed by Jesus since he was expecting a revolutionary Messiah.

Again, the issue here is about value. Not monetary value, but true value. The money received for Jesus' life over Judas' was miserable. This was the real waste! Judas did not gain anything. He lost all: his life, his dignity, his friends and Jesus' confidence. In the end, Judas has betrayed himself: his dreams and his wholeness.

Anyone could, like Judas, be trapped by his or her own desire of please others, be carried away by revolutionary fervour or by his or her own greed. The temptation is there for all, and we can hear people saying that 'each person has a price'! We cannot hate Judas for what he did because we are all human beings and we have our own weaknesses. We know that temptation seduces with promises very attractive in principle, but it is completely vain and futile in the end.

† O Holy One, O Whole One! Keep me holy, keep me whole, don't let my being be dissociated and lost. Keep me sharp and sound, so that I may resist all temptations.

For further thought
• How would you judge your physical and spiritual 'wholeness'? What help might you need?

Readings in Matthew (2) – Simei Monteiro

Wednesday 5 April
Sharing bread and wine

Matthew 26:26–35

Jesus took bread, and when he had given thanks, he broke it and gave it to his disciples, saying, 'Take and eat; this is my body.' Then he took a cup, … he gave it to them, saying, 'Drink from it, all of you. This is my blood …' (verses 26b and 27)

Jesus called his disciples not only to eat the last supper with him, but also to enjoy communion, a holy communion. It was not offered to the holy ones, but prepared by the Holy One. Like the memorable and meaningful touch in Bethany, here the action is all about tasting meaningfully. In ancient times, bread and wine were essential elements for living. The bread is our daily bread as we say in the Lord's Prayer. Likewise, wine was used as a balm to cleanse and heal wounds. In Portuguese, the verb *comer* (to eat) carries in itself the meaning of 'eat with someone'. The word comes from Latin: *com+edere* which means 'eat with someone' or 'eat accompanied by someone'. It is similar to the word *companion*, which means 'the one who eats bread with us'. Unfortunately, we see many people struggling against one another just for some bread and a little wine. The bread of life is the bread for survival, not the bread hidden in storage, the manna that perishes if not shared. For a loaf of bread and a little wine, we see people denying God's image in the neighbour. People around the world are longing to have their wounds cleansed and healed with the balm of love. Unfortunately, there is a great amount of stored bread and wine stolen from those who are in need. Jesus calls all of us not to be part of our private *fiesta* in our churches but to set free the stolen bread and wine of God's grace for all human beings!

† O Bread of Life! Enlarge the tent of our hearts; turn our different tables into a single one where your children can celebrate in peace and joy the fullness of life.

For further thought
• Are we able to act when, touched by the Holy Spirit, we feel moved with deep, inner sympathy for our neighbours?

Thursday 6 April
The possible and the impossible

Matthew 26:36–46

'My Father, if it is possible, may this cup be taken from me. Yet not as I will, but as you will.' ... He went away a second time and prayed, 'My Father, if it is not possible for this cup to be taken away unless I drink it, may your will be done.' (verses 39 and 42)

As human beings it is also difficult to accept our lack of power over the impossible. We always think: 'There must be a way out of this or that situation.' An imminent death because of cancer or other illness; a broken relationship. Like Jesus, we sometimes plead: 'O God! Please take this cup away from me'! We are surrounded by possibilities and impossibilities even believing in God for whom nothing is impossible! Yet it is much harder to dare to say 'Yet not as I will, but as you will.'

How can we accept the inevitable? Why limit the use of any and all power to change the situation? Sometimes it is possible to use a mighty power and violence! Human history is always a history of defeat and salvation. The only comfort is given when we accept our own history and leave our life in the hands of God. Acceptance of suffering and death is part of our humanity, and we need to be prepared, for in the words of St Paul: 'If we live, we live for the Lord; and if we die, we die for the Lord. So, whether we live or die, we belong to the Lord' (Romans 14:8). Like the humble seed, when our end is close, we must withdraw our human pride and give ourselves to the heart of our Mother Earth trusting that in Jesus, the cup of ignominy and death drunk for us becomes the cup of our salvation. The seeds of hope are brought from the dead grain. All made possible by the love of God!

† 'God grant me the serenity to accept the things I cannot change; courage to change the things I can; and wisdom to know the difference.' (Reinhold Niebuhr)

For further thought

• How do you deal with the impossible? Are these words of Charles Wesley – 'All things are possible to love' – meaningful to you?

Readings in Matthew (2) – Simei Monteiro

Left behind

Matthew 26:47–56

'... But this has all taken place that the writings of the prophets might be fulfilled.' Then all the disciples deserted him and fled. (verse 56)

Jesus, at this crucial point in the story, was deserted by his disciples. They fled because of fear and disappointment – or were they just scared for their lives? We don't know exactly, but certainly this was not the 'happy end' they were dreaming about. Perhaps they did not understand when Jesus said they would be scandalised. Scandalised by the powerless leader, their Master, the Messiah, the 'Son of God', now arrested! How could they see Jesus beyond their own expectations?

Like Jesus, sometimes we feel completely abandoned by our friends and even by our family. Getting old is sometimes a way of being forgotten and in loneliness. Then we seek comfort and peace in God's shelter.

We have street children in Brazil, and their situation breaks my heart. According to the Brazilian government, there are about 25 000 of them, living on the streets. Some of them are even children younger than 7 years old. We cannot accept this scandal, but actually we feel so powerless to bring an end to this problem or, even worse, we have finally got used of seeing them around. Is this not a way of deserting and fleeing them?

This is also a real situation in our world today. Like Jesus, millions of persons, not only children but also pregnant women, old people and disabled people longing for shelter, food and comfort are abandoned on the roads. Can we see Jesus in their faces? Can we see Jesus abandoned in them? Can we expand our pessimistic vision of them and see in them the risen Christ?

† God, our Father and Mother! We give you thanks for your presence in our lives. Help us to help those facing abandon and loneliness so they may feel comforted by your love!

For further thought

• Have you ever felt abandoned? What feelings were in your heart? How did you keep your faith in God and in the humanity?

Saturday 8 April
At peace in face of death

Matthew 26:57–68

Then the high priest stood up and said to Jesus, 'Are you not going to answer? What is this testimony that these men are bringing against you?' But Jesus remained silent. ... 'What do you think?' 'He is worthy of death,' they answered. (verses 63 and 66)

Jesus keeping silent before his accusers is mysterious. His silence tells them that although they have power, there was another kind of power in Jesus' decision to fulfil God's purpose. Jesus was not there as someone with power and glory, but as a man alone and abandoned. There is no confrontation of powers but humble obedience. Jesus was there for the love of humanity.

Recently I was very moved to watch some published videos about the execution of contemporary Christian martyrs by extremists. I saw a group of them in a kind of cage, slowly sinking into death. They seemed be silent or perhaps murmuring a prayer. I saw Jesus' sufferings in them but was also disturbed by their strange and amazing silence. This is an extraordinary witnessing of faithfulness. Silence is a strong tool when we stand before a judge or before an execution. Being calm and peaceful before our accusers is a way to say much more than words.

'Be faithful, even to the point of death, and I will give you life as your victor's crown' (Revelation 2:10b). 'Even to the point of death' does not merely mean 'until your life ends,' but 'even if fidelity involves death'. We really do not know what could happen to Christians in the rest of the world, in the future. Are we ready to confess our faith in Jesus Christ – even to face martyrdom?

† God of Peace! Give us the faith of our martyrs to face these uncertain times. Give us the courage to witness your love, even when we are threatened by dangers of death.

For further thought

• Mountains are moving into the midst of the sea, but we will still confess your name, and our silence affirms hope.

April

Readings in Matthew (2) – Simei Monteiro

Readings in Matthew (2)
Jesus – the last hours

Notes based on the New King James Version by **Delroy Hall**

Delroy Hall is a bishop in the Church of God of Prophecy, UK, and currently sits on the Bible Doctrine and Polity Committee at the church's international offices in Cleveland, Tennessee. He is an academic and a trained counsellor with over 20 years' experience in various institutions. Delroy enjoys teaching and training, which he says energises him. In 2015 he completed his first sprint triathlon, and he is now training to take part in an Olympic triathlon in 2016. He is married to Paulette and is the proud father of twin young women.

Sunday 9 April
'So he went out and wept bitterly'

Matthew 26:69–75

And Peter remembered the word of Jesus who had said to him, 'Before the rooster crows, you will deny Me three times.' So he went out and wept bitterly. (verses 74–75)

Some years ago a pastor said that people make various statements in testimony services about how much they will do for the Lord, 'come what may'. But when *may* comes, it is a different story. It is easy to make promises when we are not standing in the heat of a trial.

After the meal, Peter is alone and on three occasions he is confronted by people enquiring whether he knows Jesus. Peter repeatedly denies his involvement, but then, a cock crowing pierces his consciousness and jolts him into remembering Jesus' words. His cover is blown and he weeps bitterly.

God gave Peter three opportunities to own up, but he did not. I wonder what would have happened had Peter told the truth immediately. Similarly, I wonder how life might be for us if we own up immediately instead of holding back, hoping things will disappear. Jesus is not with us in person today, but his words have a way of speaking to us when we least expect it.

Is there something you are denying? To escape the pain of weeping bitterly, it is better for us to confess straightaway before we are found out and are made to confess through some unexpected means.

† Father, it is hard to tell the truth in the first instance. Telling lies has instant results, but painful consequences. Help me to tell the truth so I can live freely with you.

Monday 10 April
It is your responsibility

Matthew 27:1–10

'I have sinned by betraying innocent blood.' And they said, 'What is that to us? You see to it!' (verse 4)

Jesus has yet to appear on the earthly stage of salvation to play his final role, but in his absence events are gathering pace.

Today, as yesterday, another of Jesus' disciples finds himself in turmoil. Judas betrays Jesus for thirty pieces of silver and now he wants to end it all. Choked with feelings of guilt, Judas wants to return the money, but the deed has been done and there is no turning back.

There have been times in my life when I wish I could turn the clock back, but I cannot. Maybe you have done something wrong, and like Judas, you cannot forgive yourself and want to end it all. Hold on, you do not need to do that! Consider these two things. First, maybe you cannot forgive yourself. Find someone you trust who is able to help you walk out of your emotional straitjacket. Second, Jesus' forgiveness is much greater than your sin.

I recall working with a woman who had planned to take her life, but remembered she had an appointment with a medical specialist. The woman met the doctor who sensed that something was wrong and got her the help she desperately needed. I met the woman a few months after she had planned to end it all. She said that life seemed surreal, as she was not meant to be here. She survived, and she was a non-believer. How much more is it possible to live beyond our mistakes with the help of our Lord Jesus?

† Lord, when I sin, there are always consequences I must face. Help me to forgive myself and to embrace the greatness of your forgiveness.

For further thought

• If you are finding it hard to forgive yourself, seek professional help or ask someone whom you trust to help you find inner peace and freedom.

Tuesday 11 April
Bowing under pressure

Matthew 27:11–26

Now Jesus stood before the governor. And the governor asked Him, saying, 'Are you the King of the Jews?' Jesus said to him, 'It is as you say.' (verse 11)

Finally, Jesus enters the stage to play the closing scenes of his life, but the story has various perspectives: Pilate the governor, the chief priests and elders, Pilate's wife, Barabbas and the crowd.

Pilate plays an interesting role. He is a leader who has the power and authority to make important decisions. He acknowledges Jesus' innocence, but absolves himself of his responsibilities. Many times in his ministry Jesus was the only voice that spoke for the marginalised, and now again he stands alone.

As believers we know the scriptures must be fulfilled regarding Jesus, but have we not had similar experiences? How many times have you as a leader, manager, supervisor or someone in authority bowed under pressure and left someone feeling vulnerable? I have as a pastor. We often face such challenges, even though they may not be on Pilate's scale.

We all face challenges in which it is easier to keep silent than to speak out. Pilate chose his own path. What will yours be?

† Father, serving you is often difficult. At times we must face the pressure of the crowd, but in those moments grant us your strength and grace to do what is right.

For further thought

• If you are in a responsible role, how can you prepare yourself for those times of pressure in having to make unpopular, but necessary decisions?

Wednesday 12 April
The theology of being there

Matthew 27:27–31

Then the soldiers of the governor took Jesus into the Praetorium and gathered the whole garrison around Him. And they stripped Him and put a scarlet robe on Him. (verses 27–28)

These four verses capture the isolation, alienation, intimidation, humiliation, shame, mockery and physical assault suffered by Jesus in the presence of his antagonists.

In moments of such aloneness, the presence of a friendly face is a source of comfort. Some time ago I visited a friend in hospital. We had been studying for our doctorates when at the age of 33 years she developed breast cancer and battled with it gallantly for 4 years. Before she died, I received a generic text stating that my friend was not taking any visitors. Her family were unaware of the special bond we had developed over the years of study. I took courage and went to visit her, unsure of her reception. I went to the hospital and, poking my head around the door, she was awake and beckoned me in. We sat for an hour, mainly in silence. She was tired, and I did not want to tire her any further. Before leaving I prayed with her and as I left she thanked me for coming and said, 'It is nice having someone's presence with you.' Three days later she died, never finishing or submitting her thesis.

Do you know someone who feels isolated, alone, ashamed or humiliated? If so, can you spend some time with them? You might not need to say much, just being is helpful. Your presence is their gift. Jesus knew what it was to be alone and he identifies with us in our aloneness.

† Dear Father and friend, you are acquainted with being alone. Help me to be an extension of your presence for those who are alone by simply there for those when they are in need.

For further thought
• When has someone helped you by simply turning up?

Thursday 13 April
Help from the most unlikely places

Matthew 27:32–44

Now as they came out, they found a man of Cyrene, Simon by name. Him they compelled to bear His cross. (verse 32)

The closing scenes are now upon us. We see Jesus alone, surrounded with people who mean him no good. Yet that is not the end of the story.

Scholars tell us that those who were about to be crucified had to carry their own cross as a part of their suffering and humiliation process. The instrument of torture was very heavy, but when it became too much to carry the Roman soldiers would grab someone from the crowd to help the condemned carry his burden to the place of crucifixion.

Simon of Cyrene, an African, many miles from home, was grabbed from the crowd and forced to carry the cross of death for our Lord and Master. Simon is coerced into joining the violent throng of the innocent.

One wonders what must have gone through Simon's mind as he bore the heavy cross. He would have been aware that the man whom they were going to crucify was innocent, but somehow under such a traumatic ordeal Jesus still exuded grace. Seeing such grace, I wonder how this chance moment in his life touched him. Later, this same Simon became an influential convert in Antioch.

How do we act when we see the innocent being victimised? Despite our tendency to run away, we need to prepare ourselves to walk the path of shame with the condemned or suffering human being. Maybe, like Simon, you are overlooked and considered to have little significance, but in such an epic and tragic moment you are unexpectedly thrust into doing something important.

† Father, Simon of Cyrene helped Jesus when he needed it most. Who do I know at this moment that needs help the most? Prepare me to accompany them on their road of despair …

For further thought

• What might you need to do to prepare yourself in readiness to help a struggling human being when you least expect it?

Friday 14 April
Alone, but not forgotten

Matthew 27:45–56

Now from the sixth hour until the ninth hour there was darkness over all the land. And about the ninth hour Jesus cried out with a loud voice, saying, 'Eli, Eli, lama sabachthani?' that is, 'My God, My God, why have You forsaken Me?' (verses 46)

Crucifixion day has arrived, Jesus is now secured, nailed to the cross, and he cries out with a loud voice, 'My God, My God, why have you forsaken me?' The continuous feelings of isolation and human despair have reached their zenith. Jesus is alone, occupying a holy space on the cross; the innocent one, the one whose whole being rocks under the weight and depth of human sin and suffering. But hold on a minute. He dies, but his death evokes a reaction in the spiritual, natural and the geological framework of the world. This was no ordinary death, because it demonstrated his power.

Reflecting on these verses reminds me of those moments when we feel we have been forsaken or abandoned by God. Reading these scriptures only takes a few moments, but our painful experiences can seem to continue for an eternity. But look, when we have our Good Friday experiences we are seldom aware of all the positives that can later take place. Oftentimes events are taking place without our knowledge. When in despair we are surprised when we receive an unexpected phone call that offers hope. We receive something that we did not bargain for. We may feel all alone, but God is working silently on our behalf. On many occasions we have to have tough experiences before good comes.

Let us continue to trust the One who has called. While we are experiencing death, new life can be around the corner.

† Father, things are so hard at the moment. As I try to live in obedience help me to trust you, especially at those moments when I do not see things working out for me.

For further thought

- What could you do to strengthen your faith in God especially when things seem dismal? Are there tools God has provided that you can use?

Whom God blesses, no man can curse

April

Readings in Matthew (2) – Delroy Hall

Matthew 27:57–66

Pilate said to them, 'You have a guard; go your way, make it as secure as you know how.' So they went and made the tomb secure, sealing the stone and setting the guard. (verses 65–66)

These verses are laden with words that express maximum security. Observe the following: 'You have a guard; make it secure as you know how', 'make the tomb secure', 'sealing the stone', 'setting the guard'. Wow! Fort Knox in the time of Jesus. What or who can get out of that?

There is a Caribbean aphorism which says, 'Who God blesses, no man can curse.' Such words are uttered to offer encouragement to the one who is doing their best to live life to the best of their knowledge and ability, but whose plans are hindered by people or difficult circumstances.

Pilate was adamant that Jesus' body would not be tampered with. He made sure of that, but you and I both know the end, don't we?

Maybe you are reading this knowing some folks are against you. People are continually blocking your path and trying to hinder you in various ways. They have gathered friends together, have conspired against you and, for the moment, it seems as though they have the upper hand and they have won, but 'seems' is the right word and only for this moment.

Be not discouraged. Keep doing well. Take a lesson from nature: green plants bend towards the warmth and energy of the sunlight, and in doing so they grow, flower and yield their fruit and beauty for all to see. Similarly, when we are obedient to God, regardless of the circumstances, God will bend towards your obedience and bless you, naturally.

† I am living in a hostile environment where people are against me. Despite what is happening help me to be obedient. As I obey you I trust you will naturally bend in blessing my life.

For further thought

• Life is full of trouble of which there is no escape. What do you need in order to help you soar above your difficulties?

'Do not be afraid'
Angels

Notes based on the New Revised Standard Version by **Kate Hughes**

Kate Hughes worked for the church in Southern Africa for 14 years. Since her return to the UK she has worked as a freelance book editor, initially specialising in theology but more recently widening her work (and her mind) to include books on gardening, dog training, climate change, sociology and gender studies. She lives in a small council estate in Coventry with Ruby, her Cavalier King Charles Spaniel, is involved in her local community and preaches regularly at her local Anglican church.

Sunday 16 April (Easter Day)
He is risen!

Matthew 28:1–10

The angel said to the women, 'Do not be afraid; I know that you are looking for Jesus who was crucified. He is not here; for he has been raised, as he said. Come, see the place where he lay.' (verses 5–6)

'Do not be afraid' is a frequent phrase in both the Old and New Testaments. It is said by angels, by God, by Jesus. Fear of the unknown, of the future, of change, of the unexpected can prevent people from hearing God's voice, from allowing themselves to be changed or to move in new directions. So the reassurance 'Do not be afraid' is an important opening sentence in God's conversations with human beings.

This week, as well as reading the last, Easter verses of Matthew's Gospel, we look at God's use of angels as messengers, today with the best message of all: 'He has been raised!' However, the women who had gone to the tomb did not find the appearance of an angel entirely reassuring – it was with fear as well as great joy (verse 8) that they ran off to tell the disciples. They needed the added reassurance of the risen Jesus himself, who also said to them 'Do not be afraid'.

† Risen Lord, the idea of resurrection is difficult to grasp. May we truly know that it is a cause for great joy, never for fear.

Hush it up! Hush it up!

Matthew 28:11–15

After the priests had assembled with the elders, they devised a plan to give a large sum of money to the soldiers, telling them, 'You must say, "His disciples came by night and stole him away while we were asleep."' (verses 12–13)

The Jewish authorities didn't even stop to ask if what the soldiers told them might be a cause for great joy. They went straight into panic mode. They thought they had got rid of the troublesome Galilean preacher, and now here he was, making life difficult for them again. Matthew says that some of those who had been guarding the tomb of Jesus 'went into the city and told the chief priests everything that had happened' (verse 11). Everything? What, from the soldiers' point of view, actually had happened? The noise of the angel rolling the stone from the entrance to the tomb sounded like an earthquake – so perhaps the soldiers heard the rumble of an earth tremor. They saw something like lightning and something 'white as snow' (28:3), which could have been an angel. But there was no 'Do not fear' for them, the angel spoke only to the women who had come to the tomb. So the guards were left with a memory of an earth tremor, a heavy stone that apparently rolled away on its own, a dazzling light, some women coming and then leaving, and, as they discovered, an empty tomb.

If that was what the soldiers reported to the chief priests, no wonder they had to concoct a story to satisfy the governor Pontius Pilate and give the guards a pay-off to keep them quiet. Human beings need to hear God's 'Do not fear' and respond to it; otherwise they can tangle themselves in lies and deception.

† Lord, when we are tempted to fear or panic, help us to keep calm and hear your 'Do not fear'.

For further thought
• How important is the empty tomb to belief in the resurrection?

Tuesday 18 April
'I am with you always'

Matthew 28:16–20

Remember: I am with you always, to the end of the age. (part of verse 20)

The contrast could not be greater. Matthew 26:56: 'All the disciples deserted him and fled.' Matthew 28:19: 'Go therefore and make disciples of all nations.' One going was in terror, leaving Jesus to face his enemies alone. The other going was to be a confident setting out to share the good news of God's resurrection of Jesus. The words 'Do not be afraid' do not occur in today's passage, but the resurrection of Jesus turned his disciples from fearful men who abandoned their Master into bold men who marched out to share their good news 'in Jerusalem, in all Judea and Samaria, and to the ends of the earth' (Acts 1:8). In the resurrection God says the ultimate 'Do not be afraid' to all who have faith in him. Whatever happens to us or to those we love, we have no need to fear. If God can overcome death and raise Jesus, he can see us through our problems, struggles and darkness. These will not necessarily be easier or more comfortable – the crucifixion came before the resurrection – but we can refuse to carry the additional burden of fear because the resurrection tells us that we don't need it. We can leave this part of our load in the empty tomb. As St Paul says in his letter to the Romans (8:39), there is nothing in all creation that 'will be able to separate us from the love of God in Christ Jesus our Lord', love shown above all in the death and resurrection of Jesus; love that says 'Do not be afraid'.

† Lord, may the resurrection of Jesus always be to me your way of saying 'Do not be afraid'.

For further thought

• Does the fact of the resurrection of Jesus make a difference in your life?

'Do not be afraid' – Kate Hughes

Wednesday 19 April
Encounter in the sanctuary

Luke 1:5–14

The angel said to him, 'Do not be afraid, Zechariah, for your prayer has been heard. Your wife Elizabeth will bear you a son, and you will name him John.' (verse 13)

Having thought about the need for God's reassuring 'Do not be afraid' at the end of the story, we now look at some of the angels who appear as God's messengers at the beginning of the story of Jesus. These events were quite enough to terrify those who received God's angelic messengers, so they needed the reassuring 'Do not be afraid'.

Zechariah was a priest. He took his turn by lot in offering incense in the sanctuary of the Temple. You would have thought that he, of all people, might expect to hear from God, or see an angel in the Lord's sanctuary. The people who were there for the offering of incense were praying outside – surely a perfect situation for the activity of God. And an angel does indeed appear to Zechariah, with a message from God that should have made him happy and excited – he and Elizabeth were going to have a son, the child they had longed for.

And how does Zechariah respond to this wonderful message from God? He doesn't believe a word of it! How do I know you really are an angel? What proof can you give me? Elizabeth and I are too old to have a child! When God says, through his angelic messenger, 'Do not be afraid', he is saying 'Trust me! What is going to happen to you and Elizabeth will be OK.' But it was too much for Zechariah. In his dumbness he will have time to think more deeply about not being afraid, about trusting God, about what was to come.

† Lord of the Resurrection and the Life, open my ears to hear what you want to say, and give me the faith to act on it.

For further thought

• In what unexpected ways might God be speaking to you this Easter week?

110

God's favour

Luke 1:26–35

The angel said to her, 'Do not be afraid, Mary, for you have found favour with God.' (verse 30)

The first verse of today's reading tells us that the angel that came to Mary had a name: it was the Archangel Gabriel, the important angel often used by God to bring messages to people. So what follows is important.

However, Mary must have wondered whether having 'found favour with God' was entirely a good thing. No wonder she was initially perplexed. There she was, a virgin, probably a teenager, living in her parents' home, engaged to be married to a man of impeccable lineage ('the house of David', verse 27). And here comes this angel, announcing news that would turn her well-ordered life upside down: she would have a baby that was not her future husband's. Her fiancé might well disown her, her parents might turn her out in shame, there would be gossip.

But Gabriel takes time to reassure Mary. Yes, the message is daunting. But what is going to happen to Mary is very special. This will be no ordinary baby, but God's son, with an incredible future before him. So Mary can be assured of God's favour, God's continuing care for his son and his human mother. Perhaps fortunately, at this stage Mary could have no idea of the extent to which she and her son would need God's care, but she evidently found Gabriel's words reassuring. She asks only one question about the practicalities (verse 34) and then is able to say 'Here am I, the servant of the Lord; let it be with me according to your word' (verse 38), and the angel leaves her, his task completed.

† Thank you, Living Lord, for Mary's acceptance of the message the angel brought. Thank you that your favour rests on all your people.

For further thought
• What would Mary's joy have felt like this week of Jesus' resurrection?

April

'Do not be afraid' – Kate Hughes

Friday 21 April
Sorting out the mess

Matthew 1:18–25

An angel of the Lord appeared to him in a dream and said, 'Joseph, son of David, do not be afraid to take Mary as your wife, for the child conceived in her is from the Holy Spirit.' (part of verse 20)

What a nice man Joseph must have been! Faced with the fact that his fiancée was pregnant and knowing that he was not the father, he was planning to do his best for her – not making a fuss, not exposing Mary to public shame as unfaithful to him, but just quietly breaking off the engagement and perhaps persuading her parents to continue to give her and her baby a home. Presuming that Joseph really cared about Mary, this must have been a painful thing to do, but he was a righteous man, and he did what he felt was right. Having sorted the disaster out as well as he could, he had no trouble sleeping at night. And it was while he slept that an angel appeared to him in a dream.

The angel tells Joseph to change his plans. Joseph saw no way but to break off his engagement to Mary, but now God is saying that Mary's pregnancy is all part of his plan, that the baby will be special, that it is God who is in charge and responsible for the pregnancy. It must have sounded pretty weird to Joseph, but he is a complete contrast to Zechariah, the priest in the Temple we read about on Monday. Zechariah didn't believe what the angel was saying to him about the birth of another baby. Joseph accepts what he hears in his dream and quietly puts away his own plans: 'When Joseph awoke from sleep, he did as the angel of the Lord commanded him' (verse 24).

† Risen Lord, when we hear, in one way or another, what you are saying to us, help us, simply and without fuss or fear, to do what you ask of us.

For further thought

• Have you ever changed a plan because, on reflection or through circumstances, God seemed to be asking you to do something different?

Saturday 22 April
Good news of great joy

Luke 2:8–20

They were terrified. But the angel said to them, 'Do not be afraid; for see – I am bringing you good news of great joy.' (parts of verses 9 and 10)

Not just an angel but the glory of the Lord appeared to these shepherds, sitting with their sheep on the dark hillside outside Bethlehem. No wonder they were terrified. And as people whose occupation put them on the edges of society, they must have been puzzled as well. Why all this glory for them? Why were they being invited to visit this special baby? But when the angelic choir had departed, the shepherds didn't hesitate. Leaving their sheep to the care of God (and possibly a dog), they went running into Bethlehem, found Mary, Joseph and the baby, and blurted out what they had heard and seen.

Mary treasured everything they said (verse 19) and their words gave her plenty to think about. What the shepherds brought to the little family, once they had accepted the angel's 'Do not be afraid', was excitement and joy. Mary and Joseph had had a long journey to Bethlehem, which could not have been very comfortable for a woman in the last stages of pregnancy; and then they ended up in a stable, with the manger acting as a cradle for the new baby. But the shepherds turned the event into a party – angels and choirs and excitement and happiness, just because this baby really was special. The shepherds took their joy back to the fields with them; Mary treasured the event in her heart.

† Lord, the birth of Jesus, like his resurrection, is an event through which you say to us 'Do not be afraid', for his name is Immanuel, God with us for ever. Alleluia!

For further thought

• Have you had events with God in your life that you continue to treasure and ponder in your heart?

'Do not be afraid' – Kate Hughes

'Do not be afraid'
God

Notes based on the New Revised Standard Version by **Stephen Willey**

Stephen Willey is a Methodist minister who has been involved in mission to the economic world for several years. His work has included chaplaincy at CIBA Chemicals and the NEC Group; he also established the West Midlands' regional anti-trafficking network, which has been developed to challenge exploitation and modern-day slavery. Currently Stephen serves three churches in Birmingham, England of which two are in areas of multiple deprivation. Stephen is committed to seeing people's potential fulfilled inside and outside the church. This includes those who are vulnerable or living in difficult circumstances.

Sunday 23 April
Being found out – being intimately known

Genesis 3:8–13

But the Lord God called to the man, and said to him, 'Where are you?' He said, 'I heard the sound of you in the garden, and I was afraid, because I was naked; and I hid myself.' (verses 9–10)

I was sitting in my junior school assembly hall, red-faced. The head was talking about me. 'If anyone knows who started this, tell me now – put up your hand.' My hand remained within folded arms and I longed to escape. I had been playing, quite innocently, when Christopher and I discovered that there was a certain area of the playground where there was an updraft. The wind lifted everything that blew there and sent it high into the sky. We tried a leaf, a feather and then a piece of paper. We showed our friends and they showed their friends. When the whistle blew at the end of playtime the playground was alive with children ripping pages from exercise books and watching them fly away. Little did we know that the litter was landing in a still corner right outside the head's study.

The consequences of our actions can get out of hand – beyond anything we thought possible. This was true for Eve and Adam. The implications of eating the apple were not at first obvious, but when God entered the garden their hearts told them that things had changed, and they felt the fear of being known. A sober and honest place in which to begin exploration of God in relation to stories of fear, and God's abiding presence in the midst of it!

† When things get out of my control, grant that I may not be afraid to be fully known and loved by you.

Finding a new perspective

Genesis 15:1–6

The Lord brought Abram outside and said, 'Look towards heaven and count the stars, if you are able to count them.' Then he said to him, 'So shall your descendants be.' And he believed the Lord; and the Lord reckoned it to him as righteousness. (verses 5–6)

In the early spring, we were climbing Snowdon, the highest mountain in Wales. At first a cool drizzle fell, but by the time we were three-quarters of the way up it was hailing and snow covered the ground. My teenage daughter sat on a rock, clearly afraid. 'Do you want to go down?' I asked. 'No.' she said. Do you want to climb to the top? 'No.' 'Do you want to stay here?' I smiled. 'No.' She flashed her eyes at me, 'I'm scared and tired, but I think I'd regret going back down.' She stood and began climbing up an icy slope.

When we got to the top I knelt, numb-fingered, to tighten my shoelaces which were stiff with frost. 'What did we go through that for?' I wondered, but then, as I straightened up, the cloud broke and I felt the sun on my back. I looked north and there was a view of hills and distant sea. The world had changed in an instant: the white-out replaced by golds and greens and blues. This vision lasted all of 15 seconds and then was gone. The wind picked up, snow fell and all was white and dangerous once more. But in that moment, I had not felt afraid – there was a bigger world which was beautiful and held great promise. Something greater than I could imagine had been obscured by the fog surrounding us.

Abram was asked to look towards heaven and count the stars. He looked, and his perspective and future were changed for ever.

† God of mountains and stars, open my heart to your wonder and wake in my heart the faith you have in my future, so that I might see and be comforted.

For further thought

• When have I become aware that the world is bigger and more wonderful than my fears? How can I share those experiences with others?

Fear of an imagined future

Exodus 14:10–14

In great fear the Israelites cried out to the Lord. They said to Moses, 'Was it because there were no graves in Egypt that you have taken us away to die in the wilderness? What have you done to us, bringing us out of Egypt?' (verses 10b–11)

I was talking to Jeff, under threat of redundancy for the third time in as many years. The worry of not being able to pay his mortgage was compounded by distress that, if he wasn't made redundant, someone in his department would be. Jeff criticised the management for the insecurity of his work and seemed close to tears of frustration. But then, quite unexpectedly, he relaxed. 'You know,' he said, 'in my experience of times like this, it is not insecurity or money worries that are most important. It is your friends. With friends around you who love you, you can get through it.'

Isaiah writes that even if it were possible for a mother to forget her baby, God would never forget Israel. When we worry about a possible future which distracts or even terrifies us, blame can seem easier than trust. The Israelites blame Moses for an imagined future which seems worse even than the slavery of Egypt, but Moses remains firm, trusting in the power of God to save the people. So it is possible to take courage and, even if we do not have Jeff's experience, remember Moses who trusted the One always present at our side. With God who loves us, we are not abandoned.

† Risen Christ, may we be in communion with you at all times. May your love, at the heart of communion, be shared with those around us, bringing comfort, especially where fear has dwelt.

For further thought

• When we are afraid of the future, how do we experience the love that God, and the Christian community, have for us?

Wednesday 26 April
When courage fails

Exodus 20:18–21

The people were afraid and trembled and stood at a distance, and said to Moses, 'You speak to us, and we will listen; but do not let God speak to us, or we will die.' (verses 18b–19)

I had taken a short cut, several times, though a farmer's wheat field which my friends had said was a footpath. Suddenly, one day, the farmer was there, waiting for us. We started to run and he shouted at us to come back. 'If you don't come back, there'll be trouble,' he threatened. My friends looked at each other, terrified. For some reason, that day I turned. 'I'll go.' I said, and as they ran away. Somewhere within, I think I wanted to be reconciled with this farmer whom I was afraid of and whom I knew I had offended.

When I got to him, the farmer looked surprised I had returned. 'What are you doing paddling around in my field?' He spoke in a quiet voice which contrasted with his earlier tone. I looked at him. He was big man but seemed gentle, even kind. 'I thought it was a path,' I said, lamely. 'No, it isn't a path. You're damaging my crop,' he said. 'I'm sorry,' I said. 'Well, go on then,' he said, pointing across the field, in the direction my friends had gone. 'And don't do it again!'

Moses went into the presence of God when the people were too afraid. They had seen the mountain tremble with God's presence, and they trembled too. They were so afraid of God that they needed Moses to go for them. This Moses did, and his courage and love for the people and God, enabled the Israelites to continue their journey to the Promised Land.

† Risen Christ, you faced crucifixion and death when your friends were trembling and afraid. Open up a way for us to follow even if we are filled with fear.

For further thought

• When have we been courageous and stood in a place which has encouraged others to be reconciled in some way?

Thursday 27 April
Chosen and afraid!

Isaiah 41:8–10

You whom I took from the ends of the earth, and called from its farthest corners, saying to you, 'You are my servant, I have chosen you and not cast you off'; do not fear, for I am with you, do not be afraid, for I am your God. (verses 9–10a)

To be chosen, as we are, by God, offers us reassurance that we are, indeed, called to be none other than ourselves. Yet that reassurance is often counterbalanced by a sense of fear. Christians may talk of their feelings of exhilaration when they have felt God's calling – but many also speak of the fear they feel when they are called. Especially when called into challenging or uncertain places.

It was 10 years from my first sense of calling until I finally offered myself for ordained ministry. I think my slowness was partly because I was afraid of losing myself in church life, though I now believe the call was simply to be myself in the life of the church. Several years on, although I still have fears when I start a new phase of ministry, I find that focusing on God reassures me.

Dietrich Bonhoeffer's poem 'Who am I?' explores his dilemma. Is he the weak, terrified man he experiences himself to be, or the brave person he appears to be to his warders? Bonhoeffer concludes that, whoever he is, he is God's.

God chose Isaiah, the Israelites, Moses, Bonhoeffer, and each of us, from earth's farthest corners, to be servants and not to be afraid. God's call is discovered not in fear or even in being distracted from fear, but in focusing on God, the source of our being.

† God, your love extends to the ends of the earth. Strengthen and uphold me as I discover myself in response to your call.

For further thought

- How is God calling you now? Does that make you feel afraid? Beyond fear, how is it possible to focus more on God?

April

'Do not be afraid' – Stephen Willey

Rivers will one day flow

Isaiah 44:1–8

Thus says the Lord who made you, who formed you in the womb and will help you: Do not fear, O Jacob my servant, Jeshurun whom I have chosen. For I will pour water on the thirsty land, and streams on the dry ground. (verses 2–3a)

My baby was smiling and so was I, his health check over. All that was left was an MMR vaccination. He'd been playing happily in the surgery with his toys and was on his mother's lap, safe and content – or so it seemed. A nice woman spoke gently to him and then she pierced his upper arm with a needle. His face creased with shock and a deep sense of injustice. How could this be possible? The unexpected pain! His eyes opened wide. His body stiffened. Then the tears and the wailing started. Betrayed by the ones who should love him best?

My perspective was different. I knew he needed to be protected, I knew he would recover and that the pain would be short-lived. I knew that he would forget that needle in the arm and that it was ultimately for his own good. Nevertheless, the pain and the tears were real and, yes, my stomach tightened too. I saw his face!

In Isaiah, the dry ground – the thirsty land – is part of everyday experience, but the water which will come is, at first, only seen in the words of the prophet. At such times prophets' voices can give comfort and hope. Even in the driest place, Isaiah says, rivers will one day flow; God does not give up on us; the One who formed us promises to help us. Even in the places of greatest pain and sorrow, it is possible for healing to come.

† Risen Christ, you knew pain and felt the shock of abandonment on the cross, yet you are the source of our salvation. In times of drought encourage us to discover the well-springs of hope.

For further thought

• Are there places in life that you are not willing to trust to God's blessing – dry places which you fear will never become green again?

'Do not be afraid' – Stephen Willey

April

119

Speech lessons

Ezekiel 2:1–7

Do not be afraid of their words, and do not be dismayed at their looks, for they are a rebellious house. You shall speak my words to them, whether they hear or refuse to hear. (verses 6b–7)

A friend and colleague died recently. He was a wonderfully clear-sighted person with a prophetic voice. He spoke about life and hope, often reminding his listeners of the need for peace and how weapons of mass destruction were contrary to God's desire. Though my friend had several health concerns, he was not distracted by them but kept challenging people to live out the gospel.

My friend didn't have all the answers, but he asked important questions about issues of justice which challenged the powerful and influential people he came across. He had a voice which was rarely silent when he saw that an issue needed to be addressed.

In John's Gospel, the baptiser comes as a voice crying in the wilderness, preaching a message of repentance, challenging perceptions and talking of the One to come. Yet he was not the Word, though he was witnessing to the Word. The Word, we know to be Jesus – the Word through which we have life.

My friend will be remembered for daring to believe that the world can be transformed. He was not silenced by the fear of being thought irrelevant or just not being heard. On the contrary, like Ezekiel, he used his wisdom and wit to speak out even when the ears of others seemed closed. I believe his voice has encouraged me to be a little more of a prophet too.

† Holy Spirit, show me God's desire for the world I live in. Grant me courage and wisdom to share what I have discovered, even if my voice is unheeded or I am disregarded.

For further thought

• Is there an area in your community where something seems to be wrong? How might it be possible to challenge the situation?

'Do not be afraid'
Jesus

Notes based on the New International Version (UK) by **Deseta Davis**

Deseta Davis serves as associate pastor of a Pentecostal church. She also works as a tutor in the Centre for Black Ministries and Leadership at the Queen's Foundation in Birmingham, where she is able to bring the study of theology to a range of people who may never have considered such study. She also works very closely with a local prison chaplaincy team, helping to bring hope to those who are incarcerated. Married to Charles, Deseta has two grown-up children and a beautiful granddaughter.

Sunday 30 April
With Christ in the vessel … smile at the storm

Matthew 8:18–27

He replied, 'You of little faith, why are you so afraid?' Then he got up and rebuked the winds and the waves, and it was completely calm. (verse 26)

Fear is a natural emotion that we all experience which can overwhelm us at times. But this week Jesus constantly says, 'Do not be afraid'.

A couple of years ago I sailed across the Atlantic. Everything was calm until we hit the Bay of Biscay. The ocean became so bad that quite a few of the crew were ill with sea sickness and could not carry out their duties. I remember one day when fear started to rise within me as the ship tossed to and fro. Taking deep breaths, I spoke to myself, not allowing the fear to envelop me.

Sometimes our lives are like this. One moment everything is calm, then suddenly it's a storm. We can become so overwhelmed with fear that we fail to hear Jesus' voice – 'do not be afraid'.

Jesus, having rebuked the disciples for their fear also rebuked the issue that made them afraid. The storm 'listened' to the voice of Jesus; may we in our fear listen also.

There is an old song that my parents used to sing when life dealt them a blow: 'With Christ in the vessel we can smile at the storm.' No need to be afraid.

† Fearless God, help us to hear your voice in our time of fear and accept your peace when we are overwhelmed.

His eye is on the sparrow

Matthew 10:24–31

Are not two sparrows sold for a penny? Yet not one of them will fall to the ground outside your Father's care. And even the very hairs of your head are all numbered. So don't be afraid; you are worth more than many sparrows. (verses 29–31)

The story is told of Mrs Doolittle who had been bedridden for 20 years. Her husband was a disabled wheelchair user. They lived happy Christian lives bringing inspiration to all who knew them. When asked the secret of their hopefulness, Mrs Doolittle replied 'His eye is on the sparrow and I know He watches me'. The famous hymn we now sing was born out of that experience.

Sparrows were one of the smallest birds, very common and cheap. They were used by the poor people for sacrifice as they could not afford the sheep or goats. Yet God cares for them, as insignificant as they may seem.

In today's text, Jesus was sending the disciples out on their mission journey. He told them not to be afraid of the way they would be treated, for as much as God took care of the sparrows he would take care of them.

Today's ambassadors claim diplomatic immunity within the foreign country where they abide, but we as Jesus' ambassadors to this 'fallen' world cannot claim diplomatic immunity in this life. Jesus said 'I am sending you out as sheep among wolves' (Matthew 10:16); you may feel insignificant, but your immunity is with me, I am your protector. God cares for the little sparrow – not one falls to the ground outside of his care, therefore, do not be afraid for you are more than many sparrows. As his eye is on the sparrow, so he watches over you.

† Caring God, thank you for caring about the seemingly insignificant people or things in life, please help me to care for them too.

For further thought

• Think of some of the people or things that may be deemed insignificant – how do you think you could show care to them?

Fight or flight

> **Matthew 14:22–33**
>
> *But Jesus immediately said to them: 'Take courage! It is I. Don't be afraid.'*
> *'Lord, if it's you,' Peter replied, 'tell me to come to you on the water.'*
> *'Come,' he said. Then Peter got down out of the boat, walked on the*
> *water and came toward Jesus. (verses 27–29)*

I am horrendously afraid of spiders. When I see one, I do one of two things. I either run for my life or (if I have shoes on) I jump up and down on it until there is no sign of life … then I run for dear life dusting myself off as I go, feeling as if the spider is crawling up and down on me.

The fight-or-flight syndrome really took hold of the disciples in this story. The flight syndrome had them crying out in fear of a 'ghost' but after Jesus said 'Do not be afraid', Peter's fight syndrome took over – 'If it's you, tell me to come'.

Peter faced his fears and walked on the water to Jesus. We sometimes condemn Peter as one who 'speaks before he thinks', but Peter was the only one who got out of the boat and walked to Jesus on the water. All the other disciples heard Jesus say, 'It is I', but they took the flight option and continued sitting in the boat, still afraid. Although Jesus eventually rebuked him, Peter stepped out in faith.

In our time of fear, like Peter we sometimes need to step out in faith. We need to keep our eyes on Jesus and not on the circumstances that may be around us. Although seemingly far away at times, Jesus is always with us and if we start to sink he will stretch his hand to catch us, even in our doubt and fear.

† Loving God, help me to face my fears remembering that you are with me always.

For further thought

- Do something that really scares you. Think about how you react to the fear. What else could you do to help you face your fears?

May

'Do not be afraid' – Deseta Davis

Wednesday 3 May
God and the small stuff

Luke 12:22–34

Consider how the wild flowers grow. They do not labour or spin. Yet I tell you, not even Solomon in all his splendour was dressed like one of these. If that is how God clothes the grass of the field … how much more will he clothe you? (part of verses 27–28)

The famous book *Don't Sweat the Small Stuff* talks about simple ways to keep the little things from taking over your life. It is a simple book that is a collection of strategies to avoid struggle and helps you to put things into perspective. As human beings we can become overly concerned about our everyday life and what will happen. We are encouraged in this book to live in the moment and not to 'sweat' it.

Yet Jesus already told us many years ago not to 'sweat' it. 'Do not worry for your heavenly father feeds the ravens, the fields are clothed with lilies at the hands of your Father and God knows you have need of food and clothing. Do not be afraid, it's God's pleasure to give you the kingdom.'

God looks at the seemingly 'little' things in our lives and tells us not to worry or be afraid. Jesus came to earth in our likeness and suffered hunger, had no place to lay his head, had no money and ate with people who were willing to feed him. Yet Jesus knew his Father would take care of him even to the end of his life.

Some of us may live in affluence and yet we still worry about the 'little' things; others, living in poverty, may not know where the next meal is coming from, but God tells us that he cares about these things. He encourages us not to 'sweat' the small stuff but seek his kingdom. As God is already in the seemingly small things, there's no need to worry!

† Gracious God, thank you for caring about the things that worry me, as small as they may be. Help me to seek your kingdom and trust you to work it out.

For further thought
• Some people do not have a meal or anywhere to live today. Check for organisations on the Internet and see what you can do to help.

Thursday 4 May
The true social media?

John 14:25–31

But the Advocate, the Holy Spirit, whom the Father will send in my name, will teach you all things and will remind you of everything I have said to you. (verse 26)

Before the age of technology, when my elders emigrated back to the Caribbean, we would have a 'send off' service, where we would wish them the best, sing songs and have a 'sad' celebration, hoping they would remember us and we would remember them. In those days, flying was very expensive and once a person left, it was unlikely that you would see them again. In today's technological world we can now check up on social media and know what each other is doing from one minute to the next, even on the other side of the world.

In today's text Jesus tells his disciples he was about to depart the scene. The last 3 years of their lives have been immersed with Jesus; they have eaten, slept and walked together, and now Jesus was about to leave. Imagine their fear and sadness. However, Jesus was sending them an advocate, the Holy Spirit – the true social media that would maintain contact with Jesus and bring everything back to remembrance.

There are times in all our lives when friends and family leave, whether emigrating or through bereavement. Fear is one of the emotions that is evident at such a time. Technological social media is not always the answer, but we can be that social media to support a person and help them to keep contact or remember what their loved one has left behind. Through God we can be the peace that encourages them not to be afraid.

† God of comfort, help us to be the true friend that will support someone who may be hurting through the loss of a loved one at this time.

For further thought
• How can you use social media to help someone going through bereavement?

Friday 5 May
He touched me

Revelation 1:9–18

When I saw him, I fell at his feet as though dead. Then he placed his right hand on me and said: 'Do not be afraid. I am the First and the Last. I am the Living One; I was dead, and … I am alive for ever and ever!' (part of verses 17–18)

I remember going to a garden party with the queen of the United Kingdom at Buckingham Palace. When the queen and her entourage came, I could not get near her. There was a barrier between the people and the queen; no one could touch her and we could only watch as she passed us into the special tent erected for her and her family. Quite rightly so … and yet in this text the one who was like the Son of Man, the immortal, touched the mortal.

I wonder today, whether we would touch someone who was deemed as below us, those people on the edges of society who may be afraid of where they have found themselves. A couple of weeks ago, I visited an organisation whose staff get up early every Saturday morning and cook breakfast and lunch for the homeless. When I got there at 8.30am those who were homeless were already standing outside, waiting for the door to open. There were so many homeless people, including families with children. I helped in the kitchen cooking and serving until I was very tired, but felt that this was really where God was; touching the untouchable!

Many people on the fringes of society are afraid. They fear to ask for help sometimes, they are afraid of what people will think of them. What are we saying to them? Are we telling them to keep their distance or are we saying 'do not be afraid, I will help?'

† Living One, touch me that I might live and praise you, and bring your healing touch to others.

For further thought

• What can you do to touch the lives of the homeless and others on the margins of society?

Faithful to the point of death

Revelation 2:8–11

Do not be afraid of what you are about to suffer. I tell you, the devil will put some of you in prison to test you, and you will suffer persecution for ten days. Be faithful, even to the point of death, and I will give you life as your victor's crown. (verse 10)

During the time of slavery, the enslaved Africans knew their lives could be taken at any time. They were tortured, beaten and punished and treated like property. Yet many held out and believed that if this temporal life was taken, they would have an eternal body made by God himself and not by human hands (2 Corinthians 5:1). Many stood up to the point of death and died with the belief that one day victory would arise and the slave trade would be over.

There are many people today who suffer persecution due to their Christian beliefs. Many have given and are still giving their lives for their faith. 'Open Doors', an organisation that serves persecuted Christians, says 'Persecuted Christians are not just people who are prepared to die; they are people who have learned how to live, and to enter their world is to learn more of what it means to live like Jesus.'

The thought of persecution is a very fearful prospect. Many might find it easier to give up the faith rather than suffer, but Hebrews 12:2 tells us to 'Fix our eyes on Jesus, the pioneer and perfecter of faith. For the joy set before him he endured the cross, scorning its shame, and sat down at the right hand of the throne of God.' The one who was dead but is now alive tells us not to be afraid, to remain faithful unto death. We are assured of a great reward which is that the second death will have no power over us.

† Loving God, please bring comfort to all who are suffering persecution with the assurance that they have a great reward. Turn the hearts of the persecutors towards love and peace.

For further thought

• Check www.opendoorsuk.org online and see how you can help support persecuted Christians.

May

'Do not be afraid' – Deseta Davis

Exodus 16–40
Journeying to the holy mountain

Notes based on the New King James Version by **Bola Iduoze**

Bola Iduoze originally trained as an accountant and has worked in various industries with a specific interest in corporate and personal financial management. She is the author of *52 Little Things That Make a Big Difference 1 & 2* and blogs weekly at www.inspirationwithpb.com. Bola is a teacher of God's word and enjoys helping people discover and deploy their potential in the marketplace and in their spiritual life. Bola assists her husband in pastoring at Gateway Chapel, Kent, UK (www.gatewaychapel.org.uk). Bola and Eddie Iduoze have two children.

Sunday 7 May
Come and take as you need

Exodus 16:1–18

This is the thing which The Lord has commanded; let every man gather it according to each one's need, one Omer for each person, according to the number of persons, let every man take for those who are in his tent. (verse 16)

I grew up in West Africa, in a city called Ibadan in Nigeria, as the second of six children. I was not from an affluent family, but my parents had just enough to take care of us. My mum had a policy when it came to our meal times. She prepared the food and all of us had the chance to dish our meals. We were allowed to eat only as much as we needed. My mum would warn us about dishing too much and then having to waste food, because we also had people around us who could not afford to eat. It was a big no-no in my home to dish more than you could eat.

God's children complained to God about needing a meal, and God answered them and sent them a meal with instructions. Every man was meant to gather according to each one's need. God made provision for all and everyone was allowed to come and take as much as they required. As we come to God today, we need to take enough grace, provision, spiritual empowerment and many other benefits we require for each day, just as we need. I pray that you will find this empowerment today and every day this week as we explore the Israelites' journey to Sinai.

† Father, give me the grace to come daily to your feet and take the bread of life needed for each day, in Jesus' name.

Monday 8 May
Is the Lord among us or not?

Exodus 17:1–7

So he called the name of the place Massah and Meribah, because of the contention of the children of Israel and because they tempted the Lord saying, is the Lord among us or not? (verse 7)

A few decades ago, my husband Eddie got a clear call from God to migrate to Cyprus from Nigeria. We were newlyweds, and we prayed for confirmation from God. It was very obvious that was God's will, and Eddie proceeded to Cyprus. On his arrival, life was tough and the situation he encountered was contrary to his plans. Things were so difficult we had to check again that we were in the right place at the right time, because our situation did not correlate with what we had expected from God. A comfortable life, at least commensurate with where we were in our homeland, would have been much more in line with our expectation.

The children of Israel set out on their journey from the Desert of Sin according to the commandment of the Lord and, as they proceeded on the journey, they ran into a problem: there was a scarcity of something they needed for survival. They were in the wilderness and lacked water. They were so concerned that they complained against their leader and then against God. Their need made them forget their past experience and their future promise.

There are times in our lives that God allows us go through some situations that will test our heart and trust in God's ability to provide for us. Remember, God is still with you even in the tough times.

† Lord, help me to put my trust in your leading and your ability to provide for me in difficult situations.

For further thought

• When was the last time you found hope and help in a hopeless place?

Tuesday 9 May
Victory from the mountaintop

Exodus 17:8–16

And Moses said to Joshua, 'Choose you some men and go out, fight with Amalek. Tomorrow I will stand on top of the hill with the rod of God in my hand'. (verse 9)

My best friend as a teenager had the benefit of an older sister who was a believer, and a very wise one. One day she asked me a question: 'When you grow up, if your husband was elected the president of our country, Nigeria, what would you like your major role to be?' Our First Lady at that time was very glamorous and fashionable. Every young lady wanted to dress like her. So as expected, I said that I'd like to be a fashionable First Lady; but my friend said she would spend 95 per cent of her time on the mountaintop unseen, while the action was happening elsewhere.

My friend's words came to mind when I read this scripture today. Moses was happy to stay on the mountaintop, not in the midst of the action, but in the place of prayers where he lifted up his rod, the authority God gave to him. The Bible says that as long as Moses lifted the rod, Joshua and the Israelites won the battle. As he was getting exhausted, some other people around him came over to lift his hands up on the mountaintop. The mountaintop action determined the results in the valley.

Today many of us think we need to be at the scene of all events, whereas we just need to take a few steps back and stay longer at the mountaintop; then God will give us the victory we require in the valley of life.

† Lord, please give me the grace to go to the mountaintop and dwell there while you are working around me to give me victory.

For further thought

• Who around you might lift your weary arms when your strength is failing? Give thanks for them today.

Wednesday 10 May
Share your testimony

Exodus 18:1–12

And Jethro said, 'Blessed be the Lord who has delivered you out of the hand of the Egyptians and out of the hand of Pharaoh, and who has delivered the people from under the hand of Egyptians. Now I know that the Lord is greater than all the gods.' (verses 10–11)

Jethro came from afar to visit Moses on the journey to the Promised Land. On arrival, Moses reported what God has done for the Israelites from the beginning of their journey up to the point of the visitation. The report was so encouraging that Jethro, who was not even part of them and their journey, was able to make a declaration that blesses God and acknowledges that God is greater than the Egyptians and their gods.

I remembered this when friends came to visit a few years ago. As we were sharing dinner, my husband started sharing what God had been doing in our lives and how God had protected us and provided for us as we came into a new land without support. After sharing our testimonies, the couple glorified God and left our home full of faith. They mentioned the fact that they were believing God would provide money for a missionary trip, and our testimony blessed them so much that their faith had been boosted and they could now believe God for the funding. A few weeks later, they called us to share their own testimony with us of how an anonymous person blessed them with the exact amount they required for the trip.

Sharing God's faithfulness and works in our lives is one of the responsibilities of a believer. As others hear your testimony, they can equally testify about God and experience God. So as we go around today, let us share our testimonies with others!

† Father, help me to be a true mouthpiece for you in all I do, and continue to share the testimonies of your goodness.

For further thought

• What testimony, spoken or unspoken, has helped guide you in your faith?

Exodus 16–40 – Bola Iduoze

Do not wear yourself out

Exodus 18:13–27

So Moses' father-in-law said to him, 'The thing that you do is not good. Both you and these people who are with you will surely wear yourselves out. For this thing is too much for you; you are not able to perform it by yourself.' (verses 17–18)

God gives us assignments to fulfil in life. The call of God upon our lives is God calling us to come and assist him in fulfilling his work here on earth. This call, however, is not meant to wear us out or weigh us down.

Moses was fulfilling what he was called by God to do. But even though he had a call, he needed wisdom to manage the assignment God called him to do. It took a man of wisdom to come and teach him how to manage his time and assignment well. Jethro observed Moses' schedule and realised that it was neither sustainable nor healthy for Moses or the people. The system was wearing them all out, yet Moses never knew how to do things differently.

God, however, had mercy on Moses and the people and sent a man of wisdom, who had the wisdom to divide the people and the task into manageable parts, even though there is no record that he had managed this same number of people in the past. This advice became a major managerial principle that still guides many today.

God can call a person to do an assignment, but that person might need to acknowledge that he cannot do the assignment by himself. There is a place for looking around for the 'destiny helpers' that God has assigned and prepared to assist us in carrying out the divine instruction. The God who gave the assignment to Moses had prepared the helpers for Moses. You have a helper; so ask for help!

† Father thank you for choosing me to do an assignment for you. I ask for grace to identify the people you have called to assist me.

For further thought

• In your time of need, who might be nearby and willing to help?

Friday 12 May
Preparation for the visitation

Exodus 19:9–25

Then the Lord said to Moses, 'Go to the people and consecrate them today, tomorrow and let them wash their clothes. And let them be ready for the third day. For on the third day the Lord will come down upon Mount Sinai in the sight of all the people.' (verses 10–11)

Years ago, my parents moved to a new development in a very remote part of Ibadan, in Oyo State in Nigeria. My siblings and I hated the new place, but my parents were determined to make us settle in the area. We started attending a local church, as directed by my then unchurched parents. One by one, every member of my home found Jesus and started living for Christ and serving the Lord in our local church and community.

For me, one of the highlights of our being part of the church was my local pastor's visitation. My pastor made it a point of duty to visit his parish members during the Christmas week and, for my parents, that was a big deal. The six of us children would sweep and wash the courtyard, wipe the living room floor, furniture and the windows – all the places the pastor would walk through. My mum would make delicacies out of pounded yam, Egusi soup for the children made with melon seeds and dried fish, and a special Jollof rice dish, prepared with tomato and chicken.

With that visitation at the back of my mind, I understand to some extent the whole issue of how the children of Israel were commanded to consecrate themselves in preparation for the visitation of God in their midst! Many of us put in huge effort when we think someone special is coming to visit with us; how much more our God, the creator of the universe? We as Christians have the responsibility of preparing our vessels and keeping them holy for God's dwelling.

† Father, I ask for the grace to remember that I am your vessel and to keep myself pure and holy for you always.

For further thought
• What in our world and in your community would need preparing for a visitation from God?

May

Exodus 16–40 – Bola Iduoze

Saturday 13 May
Look up and not around

Exodus 20:1–17

You shalt not covet your neighbour's house, thou shalt not covet thy neighbour's wife, nor his male servant, nor his female servant, nor his ox, nor his donkey, nor anything that is your neighbour's. (verse 17)

I have always known the saying, 'The grass is always greener on the other side.' Thinking about this saying recently, I was having a chat with a young lady about her childhood years. She mentioned to me something that I could relate with: always wishing you owned the neighbour's house, cars, wealth and so on. Growing up with this wish and thoughts, and the modern-day media propaganda on what a perfect life should look like, lures many people into working against what God has said to us. God gave a straightforward instruction that we should not desire our neighbours' house, wife, servants, assets or anything else that belongs to our neighbours.

We sometimes glamorise this wrong desire with names that make the actions seem acceptable. We try to justify our actions by speaking of having a 'vision' of what we desire, or using what our neighbour has as a 'benchmark' for where we want to get to or be in life. Wanting what belongs to our neighbours will inevitably lead to us breaking God's commandments.

Cain and Abel went before the Lord and both gave a sacrifice to the Lord; one was accepted and the other was not. Because Cain's was not accepted and his brother's was, Cain became jealous and eventually murderous. God actually warned Cain before he committed the crime of murder to show him that the state of his heart towards his brother, or neighbour was wrong. Quit looking at others; instead look to God!

† Father, I receive grace to look up and not around; to desire what you have for me and not what others have.

For further thought
• Where in your life do you need to look to God today?

Exodus 16–40
Revelation at Mount Sinai

Notes based on the New Revised Standard Version by **Ann Conway-Jones**

Ann Conway-Jones is a freelance theologian who teaches, preaches and writes. She worships at Old Church, Smethwick, UK. Her academic interests include early Jewish–Christian relations and the biblical interpretations of early mystics. She is an honorary research fellow at the University of Birmingham and associate tutor at the Queens Foundation and Woodbrooke Quaker Studies Centre. She is actively involved in Jewish–Christian relations and has been elected joint honorary secretary of the Council of Christians and Jews. Her older son is a student; the younger one still lives at home.

Sunday 14 May
The covenant ceremony

May

Exodus 24:1–11

Then Moses and Aaron, Nadab, and Abihu, and seventy of the elders of Israel went up, and they saw the God of Israel. Under his feet there was something like a pavement of sapphire stone, like the very heaven for clearness. (verses 9–10)

Exodus 16–40 – Ann Conway-Jones

The covenant between God and Israel was sealed by a ritual which, with its use of blood, seems alien and distasteful. But this was clearly a solemn occasion, establishing a legal contract, akin to a wedding ceremony. Moses and the elders were then invited up Mount Sinai, where 'they saw the God of Israel' – an extraordinary statement, given that elsewhere God states, 'no one shall see me and live' (Exodus 33:20). The translators behind the Greek Septuagint (the scriptures read by the early church) amended it to 'they saw the place, there where the God of Israel stood'. That mountaintop experience, that closeness to heaven, was a one-off event, but became the wellspring of an enduring relationship. This week we will read of Moses receiving instructions for the tabernacle. That portable structure enabled the relationship to be sustained through the vicissitudes to come. Hymns sung in the Jerusalem Temple, the tabernacle's successor, are recorded in the book of Psalms. Each day I will provide a brief extract – you may like to meditate on it, or find the rest of the psalm for use in your prayers. Psalms, like the covenant ceremony, originate from a distant context, but their imagery still resonates.

† The Lord is gracious and merciful. He provides food for those who fear him; he is ever mindful of his covenant. (Psalm 111:4b–5)

Moses enters the cloud

Exodus 24:12–18

Then Moses went up on the mountain, and the cloud covered the mountain. The glory of the Lord settled on Mount Sinai, and the cloud covered it for six days; on the seventh day he called to Moses out of the cloud. (verses 15–16)

Moses is now alone at the top of Mount Sinai, enveloped by a cloud, sometimes described as 'thick darkness' (Exodus 20:21). One way of understanding this cloud is as protection against the blinding radiance of God's glory. The cloud prevents people from seeing God, because to do so would entail certain death (Exodus 33:20); the full reality of the divine is more than human beings can bear. The symbolism of this cloud has proved inspirational, especially to mystics. Gregory of Nyssa, a fourth-century Christian bishop, wrote in his book *Life of Moses*, 'In this is the true knowledge of what is sought, and in this is the seeing which consists in not seeing, that what is sought transcends all knowledge, cut off on all sides by incomprehensibility, as by a kind of darkness'. The closer we get to God, the less we understand; and we need to relinquish any hope of grasping God with the mind. An anonymous fourteenth-century English priest wrote a book entitled *The Cloud of Unknowing*. He instructs his readers in contemplative prayer, telling them to forget all created things and concentrate on God alone. They will discover that there is only darkness between themselves and God. But they are not to give up; they are to put all thoughts aside, reconcile themselves to waiting, and continue to 'smite upon that thick cloud of unknowing with a sharp dart of longing love' (chapter 6).

† He bowed the heavens, and came down; thick darkness was under his feet. … He made darkness his covering around him, his canopy thick clouds dark with water. (Psalm 18:9, 11)

For further thought

- Accept the times of uncertainty in your life. Trust that God is present in the cloud.

The pattern of the tabernacle

Exodus 25:1–9

Have the Israelites make me a sanctuary, so that I may dwell among them.
In accordance with all that I show you concerning the pattern of the
tabernacle and of all its furniture, so you shall make it. (verses 8–9)

Enveloped within the cloud, Moses is given detailed instructions for the building of the tabernacle. This was to be the place which symbolised God's presence among the Israelite people. Although the construction of the tabernacle was a co-operative enterprise, to which all contributed, it was not intended as a communal gathering place, unlike a modern church or synagogue. Once the glory of God had filled the tent (Exodus 40:34), it became, as it were, a portable Mount Sinai – the meeting point of heaven and earth. As such it was a sacred site, the source of an intense holiness, radiating life and blessing. God tells Moses that he will be shown a 'pattern', a blueprint. Later interpreters understood this not as a set of architectural drawings, or a scale model, but as a vision of the heavenly temple. Moses was believed to have glimpsed God's celestial dwelling, the site of angel worship, of which God's earthly dwelling was to be a copy. So Hebrews talks of 'the greater and more perfect tent (not made with hands, that is, not of this creation)' (9:11), saying that when Christ became its high priest, 'he entered into heaven itself, now to appear in the presence of God on our behalf' (9:24). John's Gospel takes inspiration from the earthly tabernacle to describe the incarnation: 'And the Word became flesh and tabernacled among us, and we have seen his glory' (1:14). There is a paradox at the heart of both the tabernacle and the incarnation, for how can a building or a human body contain the uncontainable God?

† O send out your light and your truth; let them lead me; let them bring me to your holy hill and to your dwelling. (Psalm 43:3)

For further thought

• Look into the night sky as did ancient peoples, for whom physical and spiritual heavens merged, and for whom stars were a celestial host praising God.

May

Exodus 16–40 – Ann Conway-Jones

Wednesday 17 May
The Ark of the Covenant

Exodus 25:10–22

In the ark you shall put the covenant that I shall give you. There I will meet with you, and from above the mercy seat, from between the two cherubim that are on the ark of the covenant, I will deliver to you all my commands for the Israelites. (part of verses 21 and 22)

The instructions for the tabernacle move from inner to outer. The first item to be described, therefore, is the most important: the Ark of the Covenant. This was a gold-plated wooden chest in which would be placed the 'testimony': probably the stone tablets engraved with the Ten Commandments (Deuteronomy 10:5). A 'cubit' is the distance from the end of the middle finger to the elbow, say about 40 cm, making the Ark in this account around $100 \times 60 \times 60$ cm. In the ancient Near East, when covenants were enacted between kings and their vassals, the treaty was often kept in the king's footstool or deposited at the feet of the image of the deity in a temple. And the Ark is indeed referred to as a footstool (1 Chronicles 28:2). God promises to speak to Moses from the space between the cherubim that are fitted to its lid, the mercy seat. This accords with the phrase 'enthroned upon the cherubim', which recurs several times in the Bible (see 1 Samuel 4:4, 2 Kings 19:15). It seems that the cherubim were imagined as bearers of God's throne and guardians of the covenant treaty. Their wings symbolised God's mobility. But descriptions of the cherubim are inconsistent: did they have one face and two wings as here (and 1 Kings 6:24–27), or four faces and four wings (Ezekiel 10:20–21)? Such inconsistency warns us against taking these descriptions too literally. Cherubim are an attempt to give visual expression to beliefs about God's simultaneous immanence and transcendence. Nothing about the divine can be pinned down.

† The Lord is king; let the peoples tremble! He sits enthroned upon the cherubim; let the earth quake! (Psalm 99:1)

For further thought

• How does God speak to you? Maybe it is through the Bible, music or the wise words of friends.

The veil before the holy of holies

May

Exodus 16–40 – Ann Conway-Jones

Exodus 26:31–35

You shall make a curtain of blue, purple, and crimson yarns, and of fine twisted linen ... You shall hang the curtain under the clasps, and bring the ark of the covenant in there, within the curtain; and the curtain shall separate for you the holy place from the most holy. (part of verses 31 and 33)

A veil divides the tabernacle tent into two: the holy place and the holy of holies. This is reminiscent of the dome or firmament, which, according to Genesis 1:7, divides the waters below from the waters above. So one way of interpreting the tabernacle symbolism is to see the holy place as the earth, and the holy of holies as heaven: the dwelling place of God, inaccessible to human beings. First-century Jewish interpreters (Philo in Alexandria and Josephus in Rome) talk of the four colours of the veil as representing the four elements of matter in Greek science: blue for air, purple for water, crimson for fire and white linen for earth. Early Christians took that association into their understanding of the incarnation: in Hebrews 10:20 the veil stands for Jesus' flesh. A legend in the second-century *Infancy Gospel of James* turns this into story form: it relates how Mary was spinning purple and crimson threads for a new Temple veil when the angel appeared and she became pregnant. And, according to Mark 15:38, when Jesus died, the veil of the Temple was torn in two: his flesh was ripped, but he opened up a new pathway into the presence of God. In the tabernacle that presence was symbolised by the Ark; but since it would have been pitch black inside the holy of holies, nothing could be seen. For God is not an object to be described and analysed. At the heart of faith is a mystery: a sacred empty space.

† Rise up, O Lord, and go to your resting place, you and the ark of your might. (Psalm 132:8)

For further thought

• Where do you feel the presence of God most strongly? Consider creating a space in your home conducive to prayer.

Friday 19 May
Priestly garments

Exodus 28:1–12, 31–38

You shall make sacred vestments for the glorious adornment of your brother Aaron. … These are the vestments that they shall make: a breastpiece, an ephod, a robe, a checkered tunic, a turban, and a sash. (verse 2 and part of verse 4)

Exodus 28 gives a detailed description of elaborate garments which Aaron, Moses' brother, was to wear in his capacity as high priest. Not all the details are now comprehensible. The design of the ephod, for example, is unclear. Its breastpiece was probably a pouch of some sort, containing the Urim and Thummim – a device for determining the will of God. The names of the twelve tribes of Israel were to be engraved on the two stones adorning the shoulder-pieces of the ephod. And twelve gemstones, each representing a tribe, were to be set into the breastpiece. This indicates that when wearing these garments Aaron represented the people as a whole. Later interpreters saw the vestments as symbolic of the entire cosmos. Philo, a first-century Alexandrian Jew, said that the blue robe was an image of the air, the two shoulder-piece stones symbolised the sun and moon, and the twelve breastpiece gems represented the signs of the zodiac. All this finery is in sharp contrast to the plain linen garments which Aaron was to wear for his yearly entrance into the holy of holies on Yom Kippur (the Day of Atonement) – see Leviticus 16:4. Then he was stripped of his representative function and entered 'naked' into the presence of God. There are times when we carry duties and responsibilities, we have status, and are obliged to play a role; and there are times to stand before God stripped of all pretensions.

† Let your priests be clothed with righteousness, and let your faithful shout for joy. (Psalm 132:9)

For further thought

• What liturgical garments do the ministers in your church wear? What do they symbolise for you?

Saturday 20 May
The daily sacrifices

Exodus 29:38–46

Now this is what you shall offer on the altar: two lambs a year old regularly each day. One lamb you shall offer in the morning, and the other lamb you shall offer in the evening. (verses 38–39)

The description of sacrifices, perhaps more than anything else, reminds us that the Bible originates from a distant time. Throughout the ancient world people sacrificed animals: performing the slaughter in a holy place was a way of giving thanks for the provision of meat, and of returning the life of the animals involved to the god being worshipped. Jesus took sacrifice for granted (see Matthew 5:23–24). When he and his disciples celebrated the Passover, the centrepiece of the meal will have been a lamb sacrificed in the Temple that afternoon. But since the destruction of the Jerusalem Temple by the Romans in 70ce, Jews and Christians have no longer offered animal sacrifices. 'Sacrifice' has been reinterpreted as prayer and praise ('the fruit of lips' – Hebrews 13:15) or righteous deeds. Paul instructs the Romans to 'present your bodies as a living sacrifice, holy and acceptable to God' (Romans 12:1). In Christianity, sacrificial language has also been transferred to Jesus' death on the cross, and its commemoration in the Eucharist. However, what we might recognise as familiar in today's verses from Exodus is the daily rhythm of worship. Many churches, and many individuals, have patterns of morning and evening prayer. In the morning we give thanks that we have been brought safely to the beginning of a new day; and in the evening we pray to be defended from all the perils and dangers of the night. This regular rhythm of prayer binds our lives to the God who dwells among us.

† Offer right sacrifices, and put your trust in the Lord. (Psalm 4:5)

For further thought

• What is your daily pattern of prayer? Do not force an impossible discipline upon yourself, but use the God-given opportunities amidst your daily routines.

May

Exodus 16–40 – Ann Conway-Jones

Exodus 16–40
Relationship broken and restored

Notes based on the New International Version (UK) by **Mark Woods**

See Mark's biography on p. 15.

Sunday 21 May
The God who won't settle for being second best

Exodus 32:1–14

When the people saw that Moses was so long in coming down from the mountain, they gathered round Aaron and said, 'Come, make us gods who will go before us. As for this fellow Moses who brought us up out of Egypt, we don't know what has happened to him.' (verse 1)

The underlying theme of the book of Exodus is the forging of the Hebrews into a nation united by their uncompromising allegiance to a jealous God. At times his demand for absolute commitment looks fierce. He will allow no rivals. The rest of the Old Testament story is the painful tale of God's faithfulness in the face of his people's repeated betrayals.

It begins here, with the creation of the golden calf. Without Moses' reassuring presence, the people are adrift. To fill the spiritual vacuum, they create an imaginary god. They pour their resources and their energy into a fantasy. God will not share their loyalty with a childish invention.

In his condemnation of their golden calf, God is calling them to a higher and more demanding spirituality. It would be very convenient if we could make our own gods, who asked nothing of us. But there is only one God, who asks everything and gives everything.

Alongside his demand for absolute commitment is his loving mercy. He threatens to destroy Israel and fulfil his promises through Moses alone, but relents when Moses pleads for his people. Even in these early chapters of the divine story, we see that God is love.

† God, we're sorry that we still try to replace you with other things that aren't real. Forgive us our blindness and lack of faith.

Monday 22 May
When people let you down

Exodus 32:15–24

When Moses approached the camp and saw the calf and the dancing, his anger burned and he threw the tablets out of his hands, breaking them to pieces at the foot of the mountain. And he took the calf the people had made and burned it in the fire. (verse 20)

The disappointment we feel when people let us down can be crushing. Moses had been to the top of the mountain. He'd met with God and wanted others to share the wonderful treasure he'd been given. He descends to find that the people had turned their back on their deliverer and put their trust in a worthless idol. No wonder he was angry. And the wretched excuse offered by his brother Aaron, whom he ought to have been able to trust to keep the faith, must have disappointed him even more ('I threw the gold into the fire and out came this calf', indeed!).

Our response when people fail us is often anger. Sometimes it's justified. In Moses' case it drove him to a decision that was not his to make. He decided that the Hebrews were not worthy of the gift of God, the commandments, and destroyed them.

At one level this looks like a child taking his ball away because the other team committed a foul. But it reminds us of the destructiveness of anger and of what happens when we allow ourselves to judge people as unworthy of forgiveness and beyond the grace of God.

Later in the story God implicitly rebukes Moses by giving him a replacement for the stone tablets he broke. There is always room for redemption.

† God, we're angry and grieved when other people disappoint us, but we disappoint others too. Help us to be patient and understanding, even when we're right to feel hurt.

For further thought

• Do we react too harshly to other people's failures? How can we learn patience and grace?

May

Exodus 16–40 – Mark Woods

Tuesday 23 May
Glimpses of God sometimes have to be enough

Exodus 33:12–23

When my glory passes by, I will put you in a cleft in the rock and cover you with my hand until I have passed by. Then I will remove my hand and you will see my back; but my face must not be seen. (verses 22–23)

Moses is a man deeply conscious of his inadequacy for the task God has given him. He can only do it if God goes with him. The passage speaks of the 'presence' of God and the 'goodness' of God almost as though they were separate from God's essential being. It is a way of emphasising his holiness and 'otherness'. It's the same with his promise to hide Moses in the cleft of a rock and let him see his back: God is only knowable to the extent that he chooses to reveal himself.

Christians believe that when Jesus was born, God incarnated himself – literally 'enfleshed' himself. His disciples saw his face. In her novel about the mediaeval scholar Peter Abelard, Helen Waddell suggests the metaphor of a great tree that's felled. We see the rings at the point it's cut down, but the tree is like that all the way through. So it is with Christ, she says.

But the story in Exodus also speaks to us of the limitations of our walk with God day by day. Moses wanted clarity. He wanted everyone to know that God was with the Hebrews and asked God to put the matter beyond doubt. However, the revelation is partial, because 'no one can see my face and live'.

We might want to see God's face, but usually we have to be content with a glimpse of him now and again.

† God, sometimes I wish I could see more of you. I don't understand what you want of me. I pray for clearer sight, and the patience to bear it when I only see glimpses.

For further thought
• Is it true that Jesus is a cross-section of God? If so, what do we learn about the nature of God from him?

Wednesday 24 May
The unworthy but chosen people of God

Exodus 34:1–10

Then the Lord said: 'I am making a covenant with you. Before all your people I will do wonders never before done in any nation in all the world. The people you live among will see how awesome is the work that I, the Lord, will do for you.' (verse 10)

This part of the story reflects a solemn moment of covenant-making. We are taken behind the scenes in the moment God adopts the Hebrew nation as his own people. It begins with a moment of grace, as God renews his gift of the commandments. This time Moses is alone. The stress is on the otherness and the intimacy of this meeting with God.

God 'proclaimed his name, the Lord': Yahweh, 'I am' (verse 5). But while this tells us about his nature – he is not like anything other than himself – it doesn't tell us about his character. God is compassionate, gracious, patient, loving and forgiving, Moses is told. He is also just, and the absoluteness of his justice is expressed in words that seem startlingly harsh.

Moses accepts the bargain. He says to God that his people are 'stiff-necked', wicked and sinful, but asks God to 'take us as your inheritance'. God's response is, 'I am making a covenant with you.' He will 'do wonders' with them.

And the point is that he is taking the Israelites with his eyes wide open. He knows they will let him down. But a covenant is different from a contract. A contract is broken if one party fails to fulfil it. A covenant endures.

God knew us before he chose us. We will often let him down, but that's allowed for. His covenant with us is eternal.

† God, thank you that you know me as I am, and that you still chose me. Help me to respond to your grace with gratitude, your love with loyalty and your forgiveness with service.

For further thought

• Can you imagine knowing someone's faults as intimately as God knows ours, and still committing ourselves to them in an unbreakable covenant?

May

Exodus 16–40 – Mark Woods

Thursday 25 May
Reflecting the glory of the living God

Exodus 34:29–35

When Moses came down from Mount Sinai with the two tablets of the covenant law in his hands, he was not aware that his face was radiant because he had spoken with the Lord. When Aaron and all the Israelites saw Moses, his face was radiant, and they were afraid to come near him. (verses 29–30)

Moses' face shone when he had been with God, on the mountain and when he approached God in the tent of meeting, the place set aside for worship. It is a way of saying that something of the glory of God hung about him. He was inwardly transformed and the experience showed outwardly. He veiled his face while it was still radiant because those who saw him were seeing the afterglow of God's own glory – and 'no one can see my face and live'. When he went into the tabernacle, he removed the veil because there is no hiding from God.

The apostle Paul expresses this perfectly when he says: 'And we all, who with unveiled faces contemplate the Lord's glory, are being transformed into his image with ever-increasing glory, which comes from the Lord, who is the Spirit' (2 Corinthians 3:18). In being granted the privilege of knowing Christ, we are allowed into the holy of holies. We take on the likeness of Christ as Moses took on the likeness of God.

The people around Moses were afraid to come near him because of his transformation. There is a sense in which we too are made different, sometimes uncomfortably so, by ours. If we are really being changed into the likeness of Christ, our behaviour, our values and our character will change too. For some of those around us, this may feel like a rebuke. It isn't personal; we are just being true to Christ.

† God, may my worship of you transform me from the inside out. I pray that people will see less of me and more of your son Jesus in all I do.

For further thought

- How can I reflect more of the character of Jesus in the life I live day by day? Am I getting better at it?

Friday 26 May
We cannot forget that beauty: meeting God in worship

Exodus 35:30 – 36:8
The people continued to bring freewill offerings morning after morning. So all the skilled workers who were doing all the work on the sanctuary left what they were doing and said to Moses, 'The people are bringing more than enough for doing the work the Lord commanded to be done.' (verses 3–5)

The Hebrews were nomadic pastoralists, but they were not savages. They had skilled artists and craftspeople and Moses commissioned them to create a beautiful place for the worship of God. Those who were not skilled in the work could give, and their generosity was such that Moses had to order them to stop.

Their work and giving was the overflow of their faith and gratitude. It showed itself in the creation of a beautiful structure.

Christian churches are often lovely buildings. But they are not art for art's sake. Our investment in them says something about our dedication to the God who is worshipped in them. They point beyond themselves to him.

When Vladimir the Great (980–1015) was seeking a new religion for his kingdom of Kiev, he sent ambassadors to Constantinople where they were invited to worship in the great church of Hagia Sophia. They reported back to him: 'We knew not whether we were in heaven or on earth. For on earth there is no such splendour or such beauty, and we are at a loss how to describe it. We know only that God dwells there among men, and their service is fairer than the ceremonies of other nations. For we cannot forget that beauty.'

Christian worship, whether in great cathedrals or draughty school halls, should create a longing for God. Beauty is a signpost to him.

† God, thank you for all beautiful things made by human hands. Help me, too, to give you my best, and let all I do be a signpost to you.

For further thought
• How can I use my gifts and skills in the service of God? Am I willing to give him everything I have?

All the way my Saviour leads me

Exodus 40:34–38

Then the cloud covered the tent of meeting, and the glory of the Lord filled the tabernacle. Moses could not enter the tent of meeting because the cloud had settled on it, and the glory of the Lord filled the tabernacle. (verses 34–35)

The cloud that covers the tabernacle, which is lit by fire at night, is a sign of God's presence with the Hebrews. We have met it before: Exodus 13:21–22 tells us that the Israelites were led through the wilderness by a pillar of fire by day and a pillar of cloud by night.

Here, though, God seems to be associating himself with a particular place. The Israelites have created a place where his presence is focused. It is the forerunner of the Temple built by Solomon and the second Temple begun after the Jews returned from exile under Cyrus (Ezra 3).

Linking the presence of God to a place is a natural, human thing to do. It can enrich our experience of him. Sacred places become full of memories. They become places where we expect to meet with God, and so we do.

But just as the Jews have had to learn to do without tabernacle or Temple, all God's people need to remember that God 'does not dwell in temples made with hands' (Acts 7:48). We are sustained in our discipleship not by buildings but by community. As Paul says to the Corinthians, 'Don't you know that you yourselves are God's temple and that God's Spirit lives among you?' (1 Corinthians 3:16).

The Israelites saw the pillars of fire and cloud and it told them God was with them. But he is with us whether we see them or not.

† God, thank you for the gift of special places. Thank you too that we don't need them, because you are with us everywhere. Help me to find you in people, not just in buildings.

For further thought

• What special places have helped you in your journey with God? What difference have they made in my life?

Longing to belong
Belonging to God

Notes based on the New International Version (UK) by **John Birch**

Based in South Wales, John Birch is a Methodist local preacher and writes prayers, worship resources and Bible studies which are available on faithandworship.com. He is constantly amazed at where in the world these resources are being used and how God has used and blessed lives through them. Some of the prayers have been adapted for use within both choral and more contemporary worship settings. John has four published books including *The Act of Prayer*, a collection of over 700 lectionary-based prayers, and in his spare time loves walking the beautiful Welsh coastline.

Sunday 28 May
A sense of belonging

Psalm 24

The earth is the Lord's, and everything in it, the world, and all who live in it;
for he founded it on the seas and established it on the waters. (verses 1–2)

I am fortunate in having easy access to the rugged and varied coastline of South Wales. Walking its coastal footpaths my wife and I have discovered hidden gems in both the landscape and the wildlife that inhabits it, and enjoyed the wonderful peace that this can bring at the end of a busy week.

The wilder places of our world offer us something else that can be difficult to experience within the bustle of a city. Standing on the coastline with the roar of the ocean before you, seabirds above and wind in your hair it is possible to feel 'at one' – truly belonging to this world that we call home!

This feeling of 'belonging' reflects the words of the psalmist who sees everything and everybody connected with each other via the God who created all things. This sense of belonging can have a profound effect on the way we look at the world and those who live upon it. We should not be isolated individuals grabbing what we can, but working together to care for what has been given us, and for the common good of all with whom we share this planet!

† Creator God, help us to see beauty not only in the landscape but in the people who surround us, and within that beauty appreciate your love for all creation.

Monday 29 May
Letting go, trusting God

Job 12:7–25

But ask the animals, and they will teach you, or the birds in the sky, and they will tell you; or speak to the earth, and it will teach you, or let the fish in the sea inform you. Which of all these does not know that the hand of the Lord has done this? In his hand is the life of every creature and the breath of all mankind. (verses 7–10)

We live on the seasonal migratory routes of several bird species. As well as the familiar garden varieties which we welcome each spring and bid farewell to in autumn there are large flocks of geese and ducks following the coastline. They rest a while in the nearby estuary before continuing on their way or staying around for the winter months. As one species goes, another arrives.

Migration is about escaping extremes of weather and finding food, which are the basics of life, really! The mechanism is not fully understood. I think about it in much the way I do my laptop or smartphone: I know very little about what goes on inside but continue to be surprised by what they can do!

Those flocks of birds that pass overhead don't need complex satellite navigation, maps or tourist guides to find their way; it is hardwired into them. In a sense it is a matter of trust once they open their wings and take to the sky.

I remember someone saying that within each of us is a God-shaped hole into which we try and push far too much, and fail. If we simply asked God to enter in, fill and guide us, then our lives might make more sense. We don't need to know the mechanism by which that works, but rest in the knowledge that generations of Christians have made that same step of faith and found real purpose and direction in their lives. Ask the birds, they know!

† Lord, help us to look to you for direction in our lives, and trust that you will always be with us, and protect us, wherever we might go.

For further thought

- Are there things that stop you from letting go like those birds, and trusting God as guide?

Called to service

> ## Exodus 19:1–6
>
> *Now if you obey me fully and keep my covenant, then out of all nations you will be my treasured possession. Although the whole earth is mine, you will be for me a kingdom of priests and a holy nation. (part of verses 5–6)*

A few years ago I researched my family tree. Sadly, I didn't find any famous, or indeed infamous, people among my ancestors. But it was actually quite a humbling experience because I discovered generations of the family were farm workers struggling to raise families on the low wages, poor diet and fluctuating harvests of the nineteenth century. Some did seek their fortunes elsewhere but appeared sadly to find not wealth but further misery.

I have much to be grateful for from those ancestors struggling to bring up families in often very difficult circumstances. It is because of their strength and hard work that I am here!

Spiritually we can look back at a group of ordinary people in the Old Testament who were chosen by God to be the means through whom the whole world would eventually be given the opportunity of belonging to the family of God. These people were not perfect, and they struggled with life and faith, but from them came the ones who followed Jesus Christ, wrote the words we find in our New Testament and became the church of which we are a part.

We are now called to become that holy nation, and we are also called to ministry and service. Being a Christian means I belong to a worldwide fellowship of believers, and I am called to use my God-given gifts to help build up the church to which I belong, serve the community in my local area, and live a life that is pleasing to God.

† Gracious God, who called a people to be your own, and now calls us your children, guide us as we seek to serve you, minister to the needs of others, and build up your church.

For further thought

• Have you considered what your area of ministry might be within your church, bearing in mind the gifts and talents that you have?

May

Longing to belong – John Birch

Wednesday 31 May
Called to speak out

Numbers 11:24–30

A young man ran and told Moses, 'Eldad and Medad are prophesying in the camp.' Joshua, son of Nun, who had been Moses' aide since youth, spoke up and said, 'Moses, my lord, stop them!' But Moses replied, 'Are you jealous for my sake? I wish that all the Lord's people were prophets and that the Lord would put his Spirit on them!' (verses 27–29)

I have been in meetings where people have sat around a table and struggled to get a discussion going because no one wanted to be seen taking the lead. I have also been part of a gathering where the most unlikely participant has contributed something very profound and had a real impact on the outcome of that discussion – because they were passionate about a particular subject.

I wonder how often decisions are made in families, churches, business or even government where someone sitting around a table has longed to shout, 'No!' or 'It won't work!' and ended up saying nothing for fear of upsetting others or being seen as a troublemaker?

It's very difficult to look back in hindsight and think 'I knew that would go wrong!' if you were not willing to put your head above the parapet and say so at the time!

So when you are in a church meeting and the discussion has got around to mission and outreach, and you just feel you've got to say something because you're pretty sure this has come from God … are you likely to find a willingness to consider what you might say, or will it be greeted by grumbling and hostility?

Moses was so pleased that God was empowering people by his Spirit within the camp who were unafraid to stand up, speak out and share God's word with the people.

Maybe that is a lesson for some of our churches!

† Lord, by your Spirit empower your people with the courage to stand up and speak your word in due season, that your will might be done.

For further thought

• How many times have you stayed silent and then afterwards regretted not saying anything?

Thursday 1 June
Staying close, keeping focused

Psalm 42

My soul thirsts for God, for the living God. When can I go and meet with God? My tears have been my food day and night, while people say to me all day long, 'Where is your God?' (verses 2–3)

The strength of relationships within families and friends can change over time for many reasons. Circumstances might move us apart both physically and emotionally, and the very things that kept us close at one moment in time may change as we grow older until we find we have simply drifted apart.

It would be nice to think our relationship with God was on a firmer footing, but even those with strong faith have times where they are unable to feel that familiar presence or hear the comforting voice of God. Prayer becomes difficult, almost a one-sided conversation, and a sense of desperation such as that of the psalmist can begin to develop. We begin to wonder if God has abandoned us!

And the world is always taunting us with that question, 'Where is your God?'

Where is God to be found? My experience has been that it is never God who distances himself from us, but the reverse. Sometimes my busyness and failure to make time regularly in the week to read my Bible and pray means that I can find myself spiritually adrift, searching for the life jacket!

But God is also to be found within worship and the lives of those who share fellowship with us, as well as in the world through the love shown by so many towards those in need – the homeless, the sick, refugees, the vulnerable and lonely – because such love expressed in serving others can point us once again to its source, the God of love.

† You are never far from us, Lord. Help us to see your love through the beauty of this world, the truth of your Word and the love and compassion that we see expressed through the lives of others.

For further thought

- Where do you 'find' God within your everyday life, and could anything be changed to make it easier to discern God's presence and purpose?

June

Longing to belong – John Birch

Getting to know the family

Isaiah 56:1–8

These foreigners I will bring to my holy mountain and give them joy in my house of prayer. Their burnt offerings and sacrifices will be accepted on my altar; for my house will be called a house of prayer for all nations. (verse 7)

We often complain about the direction this world is going in, but one positive movement in the UK has been that towards a more inclusive society. Political parties and board rooms are gradually achieving a more even gender and cultural balance, the church continues to address the role of women, private clubs that were once the domain of men now open their doors to all, and for youngsters the same is true within, for example, the Scouting movement.

In the increasingly multicultural society we live in there is a growing belief that better integration and a sense of belonging are vitally important. There are encouraging reports of people from many faith backgrounds sharing their own faith stories and joining together to promote greater understanding within communities.

So it should come as no surprise to find the prophet Isaiah telling the people of Israel that although they might consider themselves God's special people, and keep themselves apart from others, this is not how God intends it to be!

Through this one people will come one person, Jesus Christ, who will open the door to all, with the only entry requirement a desire to enter into a relationship with God and belong to an inclusive and worldwide family, worshipping and serving God in the places they live and wherever they are sent.

We are not there yet. The world still has those who consider themselves to be outsiders – they need to hear the good news that there is a welcome waiting for them inside!

† Remind us, Lord, as we walk through the streets where we live, to bring all those people we pass to you in prayer, for they are all precious in your eyes.

For further thought

• What could you do to better understand the people who live and work around you, from whatever culture or background they might come?

Saturday 3 June
A blessing for all

Joel 2:23–32

And afterward, I will pour out my Spirit on all people. Your sons and daughters will prophesy, your old men will dream dreams, your young men will see visions. Even on my servants, both men and women, I will pour out my Spirit in those days. (verses 28–29)

When circumstances conspire to make life a struggle do you find yourself saying, as I sometimes do, 'Hopefully, things can only get better'?

The Jews had a hope that things would get better as they looked from the present age, which was considered to be a mess, towards the age to come when God would intervene and establish a new covenant and kingdom where his people could live in peace and plenty. We see Jesus as opening the gates to this new kingdom, and on one amazing Pentecost morning it seemed as though the Holy Spirit, through whom God spoke to the people in the past, was now empowering ordinary people in new ways – the young, the old, men and women, slave and free, all being used by God in the building of this new kingdom on earth.

Once again it's the inclusiveness of life in God's kingdom that Joel emphasises, and which our churches need to be mindful of. So we should rejoice when anyone within our fellowship shares what they think God is saying, or displays a spiritual gifting, whether they have been ordained or not – God is no respecter of age, status or title when it comes to pouring out his Spirit!

And when we despair of life and talk about things only getting better, we are actually a part of that 'getting better' as we seek to serve God and each other by sharing the load, showing compassion, encouraging and being a blessing as we are blessed!

† Empowering God, help us to hear your Spirit's voice and take hold of the vision that you have for us, as individuals and within our places of worship.

For further thought

• How inclusive is your church, and what could be done to encourage all members to exercise the gifts that God has given them?

June

Longing to belong – John Birch

Longing to belong
One in the Spirit

Notes based on the New Revised Standard Version by **Katie Miller**

Katie Miller is an Ordained Pioneer Minister in the Church of England working in Speke, Liverpool. She previously worked for a number of years as a lay Pioneer Minister in an area of social housing in the west of Norwich, UK. She is trained as a palaeoceanographer (climate scientist) and has lectured in environmental sciences. Katie also writes poetry and plays and has worked as a theatre director in Canada, the United States and the UK. She is married to Bill and they have three grown children.

Sunday 4 June (Pentecost)
Poured out

Acts 2:1–21

In the last days it will be, God declares, that I will pour out my Spirit upon all flesh. (verse 17)

This week we continue our Pentecost theme of God's empowering love for all by exploring our being 'one in the Spirit'. We will see how belonging to God through the work of his Spirit is for every tribe and tongue, all of creation, all ages, the weak and the strong; and for ever. By his Spirit God makes we who were not a people into his people.

The promise in today's reading is that God will pour out his Spirit on all flesh, not just the flesh we like, or agree with, or which looks like us, or thinks like us. This is such an encouragement, that God's work is not restricted by our understanding or experience or sense of who we feel belongs. And there is a further promise in this passage; that everyone who calls on the name of the Lord will be saved – everyone. Here is the heart of the wonderful promise of the coming of the Holy Spirit and the birth of the church; that God is making us one in him. He is making a people from all the nations and peoples of the earth.

† Lord, open my eyes this week to see all the people you are calling to be part of your family, and to see you at work, pouring out your Spirit on all flesh and saving all who call on your name.

Monday 5 June
Creation groans

Romans 8:18–25

We know that the whole creation has been groaning in labour pains until now; and not only the creation, but we ourselves, who have the first fruits of the Spirit, groan inwardly while we wait for adoption, the redemption of our bodies. (verses 22–23)

As we consider what it means to be one in the Spirit, today's reading reminds us that this unity is not just about a unity between the peoples of the earth, but between humanity and creation itself. The full redemption of humanity will be the full redemption of creation. As I write we are experiencing a glorious autumn. The colours are some of the brightest I have ever seen; flame reds, coppers and bright yellows. In this very urban setting of Liverpool the colour comes as a shock to the eye, especially as we look upwards and see the leaves contrasted against a bright blue sky. Looking down, I see a single daisy has forced its way through our reseeded lawn.

It is easy to forget in our city landscape that God's plan for redemption and unity is for all creation. Perhaps even more challenging to us, however, is the reminder in this reading that our physical bodies with be redeemed also along with all creation. When we so easily identify ourselves by all that is *other* than our physical bodies, may God help us to see the wholeness he brings to *all* that we are: body, mind and spirit. We ourselves are made one by his Spirit.

† Lord, open our eyes to your work in all creation. Give us the humility to see that we are simply part of your glorious plan for all you have made.

For further thought
• Take time to give thanks for God's creation as you experience it around you today. Give thanks also for your own physical being.

Tuesday 6 June
God's breath

> ### Psalm 33
>
> *By the word of the Lord the heavens were made, and all their host by the breath of his mouth. (verse 6)*

This psalm is such a glorious explosion of praise. And what does it tell us? That the Lord is upright and faithful, righteous and just; that the earth is full of his steadfast love. But importantly the psalm also tells us that all things are created by his word and breath. We are reminded here of the account of creation in Genesis where God spoke all things into being and his breath, his Spirit, swept over the face of the waters. As we consider what it means to be one in the Spirit we are reminded that it is this same Spirit that was present at creation who makes us one. When being one in the Spirit feels too difficult with brothers and sisters we find it very hard to love, or with whom we profoundly disagree (I am fairly confident this is not simply my own experience), we can remember that it is this same creative Spirit of God who gives this unity. It is not our hard work, effort or even good intentions. Our relationships can feel as dark and formless as the world of Genesis before God speaks. It is God's creative Spirit, his breath, that broods over us and makes us one.

† Lord, help us to submit to the work of your Spirit in those relationships where we find it hard to be one.

For further thought

- Which relationships do you need to especially hand over to God for the work of his loving Spirit?

Longing to belong – Katie Miller

Wednesday 7 June
One in giving, one in receiving

Mark 10:13–16

Let the little children come to me; do not stop them; for it is to such as these that the kingdom of God belongs. Truly I tell you, whoever does not receive the kingdom of God as a little child will never enter it. (verses 14–15)

Jesus reminds us here that we are one in the Spirit with those of all ages. Children are not to be excluded. They are welcome and belong also. In fact, they are to be an example to us of how to receive the kingdom of God. I was recently at a church weekend away where there were, as is not uncommon, activities for the children. At the end of the weekend, at the final service, the children sang for us and showed some of the activities with which they had been involved. Everyone was delighted and appreciative of their input. None of this is unusual. However, after this the adults were then invited to hold out their hands so that the children could pray for them. Praying simple prayers for those who wished to be involved, the children circulated the group blessing and praying for all those holding out their hands. It felt like a profound reversal of roles to allow the children to bless us. I was reminded that being one in the Spirit with others means allowing all to both give and receive. We are not truly one when one group is only ever giving and another only ever receiving.

† Lord, break us out of our understanding of who is giving and who is receiving. Allow us all to be those who give and receive as you make us one by your Spirit.

For further thought

• Who are we inviting alongside us, whom we only allow to receive from us? Try and find a way to allow them to give.

Longing to belong – Katie Miller

Many dwelling places

John 14:1–7

In my Father's house there are many dwelling-places. If it were not so, would I have told you that I go to prepare a place for you? And if I go and prepare a place for you, I will come again and will take you to myself, so that where I am, there you may be also. (verses 2–3)

As a family we have recently moved over 250 miles across the country. This has caused some confusion as to our use of the word 'home'. We find that we have had to add extra words to this simple term such as 'old home', 'new home' or in some cases 'real home' in order to be understood by each other. At other times, we have been reduced to using the specific address to which we are referring in order to communicate at all.

The very good news of our belonging and being one in the Spirit that we find in today's reading is that it is a thing of permanence and for eternity, not just for here and now but forever. Jesus himself is going to prepare a place for us, and not only that he will come again and take us to be with him. And where is this home? Fundamentally it is with Jesus. We may have different understandings of our heavenly home, but at its core it is to be with him: 'so where I am, there you may be also'. We are one in finding our true home, our eternal home in him.

† Lord, help us to see that we are one in having our hope and our eternal home with you.

For further thought

• Do you see those around you as those with whom you share an eternal hope and home?

June

Longing to belong – Katie Miller

Welcome one another

Romans 15:1–16

We who are strong ought to put up with the failings of the weak, and not to please ourselves. Each of us must please our neighbour for the good purpose of building up the neighbour. (verses 1–2)

'We're all in this together.' This slogan may remind us of a political campaign or simply start us singing. Our reading today reminds us that our being one in the Spirit means that we are to look out for one another, not only to think of ourselves but build up each other. 'Weak' and 'strong' are difficult terms. It is probably true that at different times and in different circumstances each one of us can be the weak or the strong, even as Paul understands it here. But the overwhelming message of this reading is not that we decide which side we are on, but that we prefer one another. If we are to be one in the Spirit, then we are one, weak and strong.

We live in a part of the city that it would be easy to consider as inhabited by the weak. Certainly in terms of economic power and influence, we are not the strong. Our church is relatively small and many people in our community have complex problems. It would be easy for me to conclude here, therefore, that we must be welcomed as the weak, which is certainly true. However, I am challenged coming from a community that is seen as weak to remember to welcome the strong. Not to be resentful or judgemental towards those who have power but to ask God to help me to embrace and welcome them as we are one in the Spirit.

† Lord, in weakness and in strength help us to be welcoming to all.

For further thought

• Whom am I closing my heart to because I perceive them to be weak or strong?

June

Longing to belong – Katie Miller

Saturday 10 June
God's own people

1 Peter 2:1–10

Once you were not a people, but now you are God's people. (verse 10)

Many of us live in societies where the prevailing culture encourages individuality. We must have the thing we want in the way we want and if the group does not meet our needs, we will elect to leave the group. We may then seek out a group that better meets our needs or indeed chose not to be part of a group at all. This is not God's way.

Instead, God chooses a people. God makes us a people who were not a people. God choses to reveal how he wants us to live through our corporate life as his people made one in the Spirit. God reveals himself to the world through our corporate life with him. We have explored this week how this unity is the work of God's Spirit and is for every tribe and tongue, all ages, the weak and the strong. The church is a people that only God could have put together, that only makes any sense because of God. I am thankful for all the people I would never have met but for their being my brothers and sisters in Christ: for all that they teach me, and for all the ways they show me something of God.

† Lord, we give you thanks for all those with whom you have made us one in the Spirit.

For further thought

• Today, give thanks for the gift of unity in the spirit with others around the world by posting 'one' on our Facebook page.

The creativity of the Trinity

Notes based on the New International Version (UK) by **Peter Langerman**

 Peter Langerman lives and works as a pastor in a Presbyterian church in Durbanville, Cape Town. He is married to Sally and they have three daughters. Peter is passionate about the dynamic rule and reign of God and how we see that breaking out among us. He believes that we are all invited to be part of God's mission to transform the world through love, and that the most potent and powerful agent for the transformation of local communities is the local church living out faithfulness to God.

Sunday 11 June (Trinity)
A loving and creative community

Genesis 1:1–5

In the beginning God created the heavens and the earth. Now the earth was formless and empty, darkness was over the surface of the deep, and the Spirit of God was hovering over the waters. And God said, 'Let there be light,' and there was light. (verses 1–3)

Right at the beginning, the created order came into being out of a community. At the core of our belief, at the centre of our worship, there is a community of persons: three, yet one; one, yet three. And before we get caught up in trying to understand the nature of the Trinity, let's acknowledge how marvellous it is to affirm that our God is a loving, creative family. Just as new life comes out of a loving family, so it is out of the love that the Father, the Son and the Holy Spirit share with one another that the creation is born. There is much speculation about the origin of all things. We maintain the origin of creation is love. God the Father creates, God the Spirit broods over the waters, and God the Word speaks the formless into shape and the empty to fullness. Somewhere between the fourth and eighth centuries, the church coined a term to describe the way in which the persons of the Trinity relate to one another: perichoresis, to dance around. Continuous movement, grounded in love; what a beautiful way to describe our God!

† Father, Son and Holy Spirit, thank you for being a creative, loving, gracious and welcoming community.

Monday 12 June
Can these dry bones live?

Ezekiel 37:1–14

Then he said to me, 'Prophesy to the breath; prophesy, son of man, and say to it, "This is what the Sovereign Lord says: Come, breath, from the four winds and breathe into these slain, that they may live."' (verse 9)

In much the same way as the creation came from a situation of chaos and disorder, so Ezekiel finds himself in among chaos and disorder. The Northern Kingdom of Samaria has been overrun by the Assyrians and the people taken away into captivity. The Southern Kingdom of Judah has been overrun by the Babylonians, the people exiled and the Temple destroyed. Is there any hope left? Many times we can feel ourselves slipping into a sense of despair as we look around us, so we can identify with what the people of Israel must have felt: no hope, no future, no promise and no way in which to change their circumstances. Suddenly, in the midst of this awful reality, God gives Ezekiel a vision of dry bones coming together. Skeletons are covered with muscles, tendons and skin. Cadavers are filled with breath and rise up as an army. Ezekiel did not think such an outcome was possible, but God wanted Ezekiel – and us – to know that things that seem impossible to us are possible with God. The amazing thing about this passage is not so much that the bleached bones came to life, but that Ezekiel, a human being like you and me, was so instrumental in making this happen. At creation it was God who spoke, but here it a created one, a son of Adam who speaks to the breath, the wind, the Spirit and causes new life to rise up.

† Pray for those situations in your life that seem to be like a valley of dry bones.

For further thought

• As you reflect on those dry bones, consider how God might be calling you to speak life and hope into situations of death and despair today.

Born free

John 3:1–17

For God so loved the world that he gave his one and only Son, that whoever believes in him shall not perish but have eternal life. For God did not send his Son into the world to condemn the world, but to save the world through him. (verses 16–17)

This is such a well-known scripture that even people who are not churchgoers might even have heard it and may even be able to quote it off by heart. The context, however, of these verses is a question put to Jesus by a Jewish religious leader. The reasons why this leader came to Jesus by night and why he chose to speak to Jesus alone are not revealed to us, but he certainly gets more than he anticipated out of the late-night discussion. Jesus tells him that there is only one way in which any person can enter the realm of God's gracious rule and reign (the kingdom of God) and that is by being born again. This phrase has been so used and abused in recent years that it has become almost a cliché, but Jesus explains that 'born again' means to be born of the Spirit, to be born from above. Just as we are born into the physical world by physical birth, so we need to be born into the realm of the rule and reign of God by being born of the Holy Spirit. Nicodemus is confused by this, but Jesus explains that spiritual birth comes through faith in the Son of God. He is the one sent by the Father because of the Father's love for the world. Just as creation was a loving act of the Triune God, so recreation, rebirth is an act of the Triune God.

† In simple conversation with God, express your faith in the Son, give thanks for the love of the Father and the work of the Spirit in your own words.

For further thought

- How would you explain the process by which a person is born of the Spirit to someone who asked you?

Wednesday 14 June
Deeply enmeshed

Psalm 104:24–35

When you send your Spirit, they are created, and you renew the face of the ground … I will sing to the Lord all my life; I will sing praise to my God as long as I live. (verses 30 and 33)

We are very privileged to be able to spend time at the house of a very special family in our congregation some 200 km from our home – far away from the pressures of daily life, cell phones and even electricity. The house is next to a lagoon, and sweeping up from the lagoon are some impressive mountains. We have been fortunate to have been there at different times of the year, and no matter what time we are there, it is simply beautiful to sit on a chair and watch the changing colours of the sky at sunset reflected on the sides of the mountain and on the still waters of the lagoon. There are all sorts of birds and some small animals there and, especially at sunset, it is amazing to see and hear all the wildlife making their way back to their roosts for the night. Often when I am there, and it is very quiet in that beautiful place, I can feel the presence of God simply enjoying the beauty and tranquillity with me. The God who in community created everything does not leave creation up to its own devices. Rather, God is integrally involved in this topsy-turvy world where great beauty and great tragedy exist side by side. Having created the universe, God does not retreat off somewhere to leave the creation up to its own devices. Rather God continues to be deeply enmeshed in the life and struggles of creation. Such is our confession.

† Give thanks for places of beauty and tranquillity that speak so powerfully of the presence of God.

For further thought

• Next time you are in a quiet, beautiful space, be attentive to the presence of God simply being there with you and taking delight, with you, in the beauty.

Thursday 15 June
The Lord's Prayer

John 17:20–26

My prayer is not for them alone. I pray also for those who will believe in me through their message, that all of them may be one, Father, just as you are in me and I am in you. May they also be in us so that the world may believe that you have sent me. (verses 20–21)

What we call the Lord's Prayer should actually be called the disciples' prayer; it was the prayer given to the disciples by Jesus in response to their request, 'Lord, teach us to pray.' The prayer that Jesus prayed is today's reading in John 17, and it is remarkable prayer. In the prayer, Jesus prays for the disciples and he prays for those who will come to faith in him because of the disciples – in short, Jesus prays for us. He prays that we might be one, that we might reflect the essential unity that exists between Father, Son and Holy Spirit. Although the Father, Son and Spirit are distinct persons with distinct roles in the great economy of salvation, they are one God. The Father-creator, the Son-redeemer and the Spirit-sanctifier, are, despite their diversity, one. This is what Jesus prays for us. We are all different, we are all unique, yet, we share a common humanity and, as believers, we are part of the same family. Jesus says an amazing thing about our unity. He asks that we may be one in order that the world may know that the Father loves the world. Our unity speaks far more loudly than our words. Our unity as the body of Christ becomes a witness to the love which God has for the world. Our disunity becomes evidence of our disobedience and makes this prayer of Jesus, as yet, unanswered.

† Take time to pray for a church other than your own in your area. Pray for the priest/ pastor/minister, the leaders and congregation.

For further thought

• Think about something that you could do to build unity in your area: a joint lunch, or a project (looking after a local school), or a ministry (feeding the hungry) and ask God to help you.

June

The creativity of the Trinity – Peter Langerman

Friday 16 June
Shared life

2 Corinthians 13:11–end

May the grace of the Lord Jesus Christ, and the love of God, and the fellowship of the Holy Spirit be with you all. (verse 14)

There is a beautiful Greek word that expresses the kind of relationship that exists between the persons of the Trinity and should exist between us as well: *koinonia*. Sometimes translated fellowship, the word actually means 'shared life', and it points to the kind of relationship we are called to have with other pilgrims on this journey of faith.

In our congregation we have a programme called 'Keeping Koinonia'. It is a celebration of the gift of hospitality, the goal of which is for people to share a meal and to build deeper relationships; where friend or stranger can experience the hospitality of Christ. At each gathering, participants pray this prayer as a grace before the meal: 'Dear God, we live in a world where there are so many who go to bed hungry each night, and we recognise that we are very privileged to be able to share this meal. In a world where so many people do not know the love and compassion of family and friends, we thank you for the opportunity to be together. Be present with us to that we may we share together with joyful hearts.' God calls us to live with an unveiled face; to live openly, authentically and honestly with others; to be willing to be vulnerable with them and to trust them with our most intimate concerns. This is part of the work of the Holy Spirit who enables us to walk in the freedom of communion and deep relationship with our brothers and sisters in Christ.

† Give thanks for those people with whom you are privileged to share koinonia, those people with whom you are blessed to share your life.

For further thought
• Perhaps you're facing a challenge in your walk of faith. Is there someone with whom you can share your concerns, someone who can pray with you?

Saturday 17 June
The great commission:
walk the talk, talk the walk

Matthew 28:16–20

All authority in heaven and on earth has been given to me. Therefore go and make disciples of all nations, baptizing them in the name of the Father and of the Son and of the Holy Spirit, and teaching them to obey everything I have commanded you. (part of verses 18–20)

Christians are known for their words, but do our deeds correspond to our actions?

Yesterday, 16 June, is such an important day in the history of our country, South Africa. On this day, in 1976, students in the townships took to the streets to protest being taught in Afrikaans, which for many of them was a third or even a fourth language. A young learner, Hector Peterson, became the first casualty on that day, but, sadly, there would be many more casualties in the weeks and months that lay ahead. Many people were imprisoned and there was a crackdown on the work of those organisations that opposed the apartheid government, the National Party. Over the next number of years the protest begun by students became a national movement that brought down apartheid and led our country into the democratic era. Many Christians, as individuals and as part of civil society, were part of that opposition movement, making their opposition known against the system of racial injustice not only in their words, but also through their actions. Jesus sends his disciples out and in the process they change from disciples (learners or apprentices) into apostles (those who have been sent). We say in the creed that the church is 'one, holy, catholic and apostolic'. We too have been sent to bear witness to the good news in the name of the Triune God by word and deed. Let's be willing to do that with courage and determination and, like the students of 1976, we too may change the world!

† Pray for situations of injustice and especially for the persecuted Christians all over the world.

For further thought

• Think about your own community: are there any issues of injustice about which you might be able to raise awareness, and perhaps, mobilise support?

The creativity of the Trinity – Peter Langerman

Isaiah 1–39
Whom shall I send?

Notes based on the New Revised Standard Version by **Catherine Williams**

 Catherine Williams is an Anglican priest working in discernment and selection for the Ministry Division of the Archbishops' Council in the Church of England. Her role is to facilitate the processes by which new clergy are selected to train for the ordained ministry. Catherine lives in the English town of Tewkesbury and works in London. She is married to Paul, also a priest, and they have two adult children. Catherine is also an experienced spiritual director. In her spare time, she enjoys singing, theatre, cinema, and reading and writing poetry.

Sunday 18 June
Hollow worship

Isaiah 1:1–8, 11–17

... cease to do evil, learn to do good; seek justice, rescue the oppressed, defend the orphan, plead for the widow. (part of verses 16–17)

Today we begin a three-week exploration of First Isaiah, leading us through the people of God's faltering relationship with the Lord, the prophet Isaiah's emphatic efforts to turn them around and the subsequent Assyrian siege of Jerusalem. During the reigns of the kings of Judah from Uzziah to Hezekiah, the prophet Isaiah relays the word of the Lord to the people. Chapter 1 sets the scene. Though the Lord has been like a parent to his children, the people have rebelled and gone astray. They are behaving like teenagers – desperate to break away and experiment, with the result that they are on a path of self-destruction. This dangerous and harmful behaviour extends to the whole community and even to the land.

Such turning away from the goodness, holiness and provision of the Lord leads to hollow worship. The people of God observe worship and keep the feasts and festivals, but their observance doesn't extend to a change of behaviour. Worship that does not transform the life of the believer, challenging injustice, and making a difference to those who are oppressed and on the margins of society is empty of meaning. God has had enough of such charades!

† Lord God, may our encounter with you flood our whole being, so that our worship, words, thoughts and actions may transform our world.

Monday 19 June
No more war!

Isaiah 2:1–5

They shall beat their swords into ploughshares, and their spears into pruning hooks; nation shall not lift up sword against nation, neither shall they learn war anymore. (verse 4)

In today's reading, Isaiah presents a vision to the people of a bright future in which the Lord's house will be exalted and everyone will be drawn to it. People will encourage one another to return to the Lord, and they will be eager to learn God's ways and walk in his paths. Isaiah calls the house of Jacob to walk in God's light so that all the nations will follow and obtain God's blessing. A new order of religious and international harmony will be established, with Israel's repentance as the catalyst.

In this time of restoration, when all have their eyes fixed on God, peace will reign and all arguments, disputes and conflicts will cease. War will be no more. In these verses, which are echoed in Micah 4, weapons of destruction will become the tools that cultivate the land, helping to feed and nurture the next generations.

Sadly, humanity is addicted to conflict and to the brutality and oppression of others. Tragically since the Second World War there have only been 26 days when a major war hasn't raged somewhere on the planet. This is a horrifying statistic, and one which brings great shame on humanity. Peace doesn't just happen. It is not an absence of war but an active seeking after harmony and justice, which begins with repentance, a fresh turning to God and a disciplined focus on the light of the Lord and his ways.

† Lord God, give us a fresh vision of the unity you long for. Help your church to draw all people to you.

For further thought

- In what ways can you turn negative words, thoughts and actions into peaceful interactions that enable others to flourish?

June

Isaiah 1–39 – Catherine Williams

Tuesday 20 June
Sackcloth and shame

Isaiah 3:16 – 4:1

… instead of a rich robe, a binding of sackcloth; instead of beauty, shame.
(from verse 24)

Having given the vision of how the world might be, Isaiah now turns his attention to how it actually is. A time is coming when all the finery and wealth of Israel will be stripped away. The Lord picks out the daughters of Zion for special mention; they are acting as if they believe they are beyond judgement. A picture is painted of excess, both in manner and dress. Isaiah lists in great detail the finery of these women – they have the very best of everything, and they know it. The prophet declares that they are skating on thin ice. All the fripperies and fineries will be no more. The daughters of Zion will be covered in scabs, naked, bald and stinking. Their beauty will be turned to shame and they will fight over the few men who are left after the conflicts that are coming.

This is a bold passage and one that makes the reader uncomfortable. There are parts of our world where wealth and excess are commonplace and the where the norm of the culture is to have the best and most up to date of commodities. Fashion and beauty are huge industries and taken for granted by many in our societies, as is the respectability that often attaches itself to wealth. Here is a reminder that God has little regard for outward show. God looks on the heart and takes note of inward finery; love, faith, hope, goodness and a right relationship with God are what truly matters.

† Lord God, help me to remember that outward show means little to you. May my walk with you lead to the inner finery that you long to see.

For further thought

• Give away something of which you are particularly fond.

Wednesday 21 June
Shelter and shade

Isaiah 4:2–6

... over all the glory there will be a canopy. It will serve as a pavilion, a shade by day from the heat, and a refuge and a shelter from the storm and rain. (verses 5–6)

Warnings of doom and judgement alternate in First Isaiah with visions of restoration and renewal. While humiliation is coming for the women of Jerusalem and obliteration for the men, once the dust settles those who are left will be washed clean and made holy. From the ashes will rise a restored creation. The branch of the Lord will be beautiful and fruitful, and the people will once again see God's glory.

Following judgement and cleansing, Jerusalem will know again the Lord's ongoing protection and care. As in the liberation from Egypt recorded in Exodus, so God will be a tangible presence in cloud, smoke and flame. There will be shade in the daytime and shelter at night. God's people will be safe and secure, set apart for God and ready for flourishing.

The 'Branch of the Lord' is a term used many times in the Old Testament to refer to the coming Messiah. It denotes new growth, life and fruitfulness emerging from the leftovers and reaching out into the world, while remaining connected to God, the source. Jesus identifies with this metaphor in his teaching on the True Vine in John 15, encouraging his disciples to remain in the vine while allowing themselves to be pruned and tended by God, in order for new growth to emerge. While this can be a painful process, we are assured of God's shelter and shade as we are tested and refined, enabling us to grow more into the likeness of Christ.

† Lord God, thank you for providing shelter and shade, in which we can rest and feel secure, even when life is challenging.

For further thought

- Read John 15:1–11. Where does the Lord need to prune you in order for new growth to emerge?

Isaiah 1–39 – Catherine Williams

Heartbroken

Isaiah 5:1–7

What more was there to do for my vineyard that I have not done in it? When I expected it to yield grapes, why did it yield wild grapes? (verse 4)

Have you ever spent a long time or much effort choosing or making a present for someone you love, only to have them take little notice of it, take it back to the shop or not bother to thank you? It's not a pleasant experience. You wonder what you've done wrong, or why you wasted so much time and care over it. You might be sad or confused, angry or humiliated. You might think twice before you give such a gift again.

In today's sad love song from the Lord we hear all these heartbroken reactions as his gifts and love tokens are rejected. Continuing the theme of the vine we explored yesterday, the Lord sings of his vineyard, Israel, and his planting Judah. He has given Israel every opportunity and advantage to flourish but instead of bearing good fruit, stinking fruit has been produced. Instead of righteousness and justice, violence and weeping reign. The Lord decides to take away the protection and special attention from his people. He will allow them to go to waste since his time, love and affection has been squandered and ignored.

We know that this is not the end of the story, and that God continues to nurture and protect his people, wooing them back into faithful relationship with him through the monumental gift of his son Jesus. While our love is often weak and temporary, God's love is eternal and should call forth from us gratitude, faithfulness and transformation.

† Lord God, thank you for your many love-gifts, and especially the gift of Jesus Christ. Help me to respond with renewed love and thankfulness.

For further thought

• List God's gifts to you and your community. How does your life reflect your gratitude?

Friday 23 June
I'll go!

Isaiah 6:1–13

Then I heard the voice of the Lord saying, 'Whom shall I send, and who will go for us?' And I said, 'Here am I; send me!' (verse 8)

Today's reading takes us back to the moment of Isaiah's submission to God, and his subsequent calling and commissioning. In the Temple he experiences an extraordinary vision of the holiness and sovereignty of the Lord, which brings him to a significant point of repentance. Isaiah realises both his own unworthiness and that of his people. Once his lips are cleansed and his sin forgiven in a sacramental act, Isaiah is set free to hear the Lord calling and is eager to be sent out in service. The extraordinary vision has inspired him to give his all.

However, God's calling turns out to be very difficult indeed. The Lord warns Isaiah that the people will listen but not understand him, and will refuse continually to turn back to God. 'How long, O Lord?' he asks, and receives the answer that not until almost everything is destroyed and all the people gone will new life come. It's a devastating commission for God's eager new prophet.

In our Christian discipleship we, too, are forgiven through the power of the cross and empowered by the Holy Spirit to worship and serve God. Our initial calling, often inspired by a strong experience of God, sees us fired up and ready to go wherever God sends us. Though a great privilege, serving the living God can be very demanding and at times we can't see how the future can possibly work out for good. Faith in the power of Christ to bring new life, and a deep commitment to worship will keep hope alive amidst the challenges and demands of discipleship.

† Lord God, grant your church a fresh vision of your holiness. May we each be made right with you, and inspired to worship and to serve.

For further thought

- What strategies do you have in place to help keep your vocation alive when faced with the demanding challenges of lifelong service to God?

Isaiah 1–39 – Catherine Williams

Saturday 24 June
Stand firm!

Isaiah 7:1–17

If you do not stand firm in faith, you shall not stand at all. (verse 9)

In our passage today Isaiah and his son go out to meet King Ahaz after a foreign attack against Jerusalem. The king is inspecting the city's water supply which needs to be robust to withstand possible siege. Ahaz is very anxious and trying to work out the best possible alliances to make. Isaiah goes with the message that he need not fear but must remain firm in his faith if all is to go well. Ahaz is to ask for a sign from the Lord – but he fears to put God to the test, even though he is the king and heir to the house of David.

It is a strange sign that the Lord gives. A young woman will have a son who will be called 'God with us' through whom God will bring restoration. We are not told who this child is, but by the time he is weaned prosperity will return. Ahaz rejects the God who is with him and for him, he is unable to trust God and stand firm in his faith. Disaster looms!

The strange sign for Ahaz, has become for Christians a prophecy of the birth of Jesus. God does indeed bring restoration through the gift of his son with us and for us. We, too, like Ahaz are called to remain steadfast in our faith and to trust God to fulfil his promises even when all seems broken and hopeless. In extraordinary and astonishing ways God is working to bring good from even the most challenging situations. Our calling is to stand firm and to trust!

† Lord God, help me trust even when the way ahead seems fraught with danger. Give me courage to remain firm in my faith.

For further thought
- Lend your strength to someone who is finding it hard to trust God, so that together you can stand firm in faith.

Isaiah 1–39
The people who walked in darkness

Notes based on the New International Version (UK) by **Jane Gonzalez**

Jane Gonzalez is a Roman Catholic laywoman from Hertfordshire, recently retired from paid employment. She is about to start a professional doctorate in Pastoral Theology, looking at collaborative ministry. She has a keen interest in studying scripture, is a visiting preacher at a local Anglican Church and occasionally pops up on local radio reviewing the Sunday papers. Hopefully retirement will allow her to spend more time in Spain and to achieve her ambition of walking the Camino de Santiago. And also to do more gardening and sewing – although she wonders now how she ever found the time to go to work!

Sunday 25 June
A lamp for my feet

Isaiah 9:2–7

The people walking in darkness have seen a great light; on those living in the land of deep darkness a light has dawned. (verse 2)

This week's readings come from Isaiah – a prophet for all seasons. Gregory of Nyssa, one of the early church writers, called him 'the fifth evangelist' because his words and his themes are brought to perfect fulfilment in the person of Jesus. Isaiah preaches salvation through a steadfast and enduring faith in God's love and mercy. Consolation and final vindication are promised to those who trust, even in the face of great trials, that God will never abandon them.

At times, although we have faith, life's burdens threaten to overwhelm us. The light of Christ received at baptism seems faint; the darkness – our sinfulness, the myriad problems that confront us daily, the indifference or hostility that we face in being Christians in a secular world – may seem impenetrable. We are walking and living in darkness.

Isaiah's words encourage us not to give up. His oracles of joy, comfort, admonition and exhortation are as relevant now as when he spoke seven centuries before the birth of Christ. We need to allow them to be 'alive and active', as letter to the Hebrews puts it, so that we may be beacons of light, illuminating our path and that of those we meet.

† Father, increase my faith. Help me always to see that your loving hand and guiding light are never absent from any situation or struggle.

Monday 26 June
Deceptive appearances

Isaiah 11:1–10

He will not judge by what he sees with his eyes, or decide by what he hears with his ears; but with righteousness he will judge the needy, with justice he will give decisions for the poor of the earth. (verses 3 and 4)

We have not long returned from an eight-week holiday in Spain – one of the joys of retirement! We spend our summers in the region of La Mancha, south of Madrid. One of our favourite outings is to a viewing place high in the hills where you can see the immense flat plain spread out for miles – a fertile expanse of vines and olive groves. The plains of Spain are high and the climate extreme – intense heat and sun in the summer; cold winters often with snow and freezing temperatures.

So, in winter, the landscape presents a different, often rather bleak picture. The olive trees, harvested in January, seem dormant; the vines appear black and stunted. It is hard to imagine that they will ever produce a shoot or a leaf, never mind grapes. Amazingly, they do. Once they take off in summer, within a very short while they are green and growing and productive. Appearances can deceive.

I suppose it all boils down to how we look and perceive. It is so easy to look without actually seeing what is going on. Isaiah exhorts us here to look beyond the obvious, and beyond our own desires and needs. To see with the heart and with the wisdom of the Holy Spirit. How can we start to achieve harmony and peace in our homes and our world? By looking anew at situations, seeing life where things look dead, freshness in what appears tired and mundane. By fostering, through the sad and bad times, real Christian resurrection hope.

† Father, increase my hope. Help me to see with the eyes of faith beyond the merely obvious and to the heart of things.

For further thought

• Read and reflect on Mark 4:26–29, The parable of the growing seed. Where is God working – maybe unnoticed – in your life?

Tuesday 27 June
Without mercy, where is goodness?

Isaiah 12:1–6

In that day you will say: 'I will praise you, Lord. Although you were angry with me, your anger has turned away and you have comforted me. Surely God is my salvation; I will trust and not be afraid.' (from verses 1 and 2)

At the start of Advent 2015, Pope Francis initiated a Year of Mercy in the Roman Catholic Church. Mercy is a key theme of his pontificate and during the year last November he asked believers (of all denominations, not just Catholics!) to reflect more deeply on the mercy of God and how we can make it known to our world. The papal churches and cathedrals opened their 'Holy Doors' – normally sealed – so that people could enter through them: a symbolic entering into the merciful embrace of God. His intention was to show that the church wants to reach out to a needy world in compassion and friendship. He sees mercy as a way of living out our faith.

We are often keener on the concept of justice (vengeance?), especially when we have been hurt or damaged by someone. As Christians we are commanded by Jesus to forgive and to love, to be merciful as the Father is merciful, but hurts run deep and we would rather nurse our anger or ask God to vent his anger on those who have done us wrong.

St Thomas Aquinas tells us that God's response to everything is always mercy. This is not to undervalue legitimate justice or to condone wrongs. It is a choice God makes in love. His anger is the justifiable response to human sinfulness but he always opts for mercy. That is how great our God is – and why the prophet sings out in praise.

† Merciful Father, I thank you for your loving kindness. Help me to respond with grace and generosity to those who hurt me.

For further thought

• Small kindnesses show God's mercy to the world. Reflect on Micah 6:8. What would it mean to your relationships to really love mercy?

June

Isaiah 1–39 – Jane Gonzalez

Wednesday 28 June
Fear and faith

Isaiah 14:3–20

How you have fallen from heaven, morning star, son of the dawn! You have been cast down to the earth, you who once laid low the nations! … All the kings of the nations lie in state, each in his own tomb. (verses 12 and 18)

One of my favourite subjects at school was history. Our inspirational teachers taught us the relevance of the past to the present and future. Although the worldview and culture of a particular era might appear alien or different, human nature in all its complexity is not. Certainly our capacity for self-delusion and arrogance have not changed during the passage of the centuries. Nor has our inability to learn lessons from the past. We only have to turn on the television to see the results – war and conflict and rivalry among nations. It can be difficult to believe that the evils presented so graphically to us will ever be defeated.

Isaiah, speaking many centuries ago, proclaims an oracle against the superpower of his day, Babylon. Babylon's star is in the ascendant, but this star will fall; the higher they climb, the harder they fall, as the saying goes. There is a stark warning for all who think that power or celebrity or money will last for ever. Thousand-year Reichs come and go. It is never inevitable that evil will prevail, although we may fear it will.

Fear is the great enemy of faith because it paralyses us and makes us doubt. There's an urban myth that 'Do not be afraid' occurs 365 times in the Bible, once for each day. I haven't counted but some people have and it's far fewer! However, we seem to need reminding not to fear on a daily basis.

Isaiah encourages peoples, past and present, to keep the faith. To cast out fear, and dare to believe …

† Lord, I believe, help my unbelief! Take my fears away and guide me according to your ways, your wisdom.

For further thought

- He is not afraid of bad news; his heart is firm trusting in the Lord (Psalm 112:7). Look at a newspaper, local or national. Look for the good news and give thanks.

Thursday 29 June
A green and pleasant land?

Isaiah 24:1–16

The earth dries up and withers, the world languishes and withers, the heavens languish with the earth. The earth is defiled by its people; they have disobeyed the laws, violated the statutes and broken the everlasting covenant. (verses 4 and 5)

I recently went flying with a friend. He has had a pilot's licence for many years but needs to put in so many hours in the air in order to keep it. He worships at my church and when he hires a plane he loves to share the experience, so invites fellow parishioners to come along. It was a short trip, flying at 1000 feet or so – well away from the big aircraft. We were blessed with perfect visibility and could literally see for miles. As far as wind farms off the coast; London and its skyline shimmering in the sunshine; the river Thames snaking its way through the countryside. And of course, the patchwork of fields, green and brown, dotted with trees. It truly was, as the poet Blake said, a green and pleasant land.

Yet we know that in many places in the world this is not the case. The world is experiencing severe drought in many places with the subsequent problem of lower crop yield, bush and forest fires and polluted water supplies. The earth 'drying up and withering …'

The causes are many and complex but it cannot be denied that God's fragile and beautiful creation is threatened and human irresponsibility is part of the problem. Isaiah's exhortations bear reflection: the covenant asks us to have a due regard to our relationships, to love our neighbour. This surely must include our relationship with nature, with sister earth, one of the new poor whom we are called upon to love, care for and treat with justice.

† Father, teach me to love the world you have created as you love it. To tend, nurture and to reverence the work of your hands.

For further thought

- Read *The Canticle of the Sun* by St Francis of Assisi. How can you live more simply and in greater harmony with creation? Do you have the courage to change?

June

Isaiah 1–39 – Jane Gonzalez

Friday 30 June
Bless us, O Lord, and these thy gifts ...

Isaiah 25:1–9

On this mountain the Lord Almighty will prepare a feast of rich food for all peoples, a banquet of aged wine – the best of meats and the finest of wines. On this mountain he will destroy the shroud that enfolds all peoples, the sheet that covers all nations ... (verses 6 and 7)

It is a sad fact of life, I think, that we are often too busy nowadays to stop and share the simple pleasure of a meal. Families and individuals rush from one appointment to the next and food is often grabbed when we can. Older people bemoan the demise of the family meal. Yet, most of us relish the opportunity to go out for meals or to have our friends and family over to eat. In our own family, we try to sit down together at least twice a week – to take time to catch up with what we're doing, to laugh together and listen to each other.

Meals were central to the ministry of Jesus. The meals he shared with rich or poor were the context for healing and grace. His table fellowship was the place where he fed many hungers. It wasn't just food on offer at table but forgiveness, acceptance, love and welcome. There was hospitality for all. All invited, all welcome.

Isaiah comforts his listeners with the image of a banquet. It suggests lavishness and abundance. An occasion when the wine will never run out! There may be hardship and trials but the reward at the end is great. (It's no wonder that this passage is so often used at funerals.) God's mercy and healing are without limit. Whatever our circumstances, this message and invitation are for us as well. For those of us privileged to eat and drink in safety, perhaps a fitting response would be to emulate Jesus – to offer hospitality and friendship to all.

† Father, the world is hungry for your word and your healing. Help me to be channels of both for the people I meet.

For further thought

• Say a grace before and after your meal. Check out Mary's Meals at www.marysmeals.org. What can you do to show your gratitude for God's abundance in your life?

Saturday 1 July
The long and winding road

Isaiah 35:1–10
Strengthen the feeble hands, steady the knees that give way; say to those with fearful hearts, 'Be strong, do not fear …' (verses 3 and 4)

As a family we are very fond of films – the television is mostly used for watching DVDs! One of our favourites is *The Way*. It's a charming, at times sentimental film about Tom, a rather grouchy older man who walks the Camino de Santiago in Northern Spain – the ancient pilgrimage route to the cathedral of Santiago de Compostela. He carries with him the ashes of his son Daniel, killed accidentally while starting the long trek. Tom intends to walk the 500 miles alone, sprinkling Daniel's ashes en route. He wants to be left alone in his grief.

Pilgrimages are seldom undertaken in solitude, however. Like it or not, Tom's path crosses that of others, in particular three people, each with their own pain and neediness as part of the baggage they carry. By the end, the unlikely foursome are companions, in the truest sense of the word, having walked, eaten and shared along the way. Each of them finds grace and redemption through the journey and through each other.

We are all pilgrims on the journey of faith. Sometimes we are full of vigour and can stride out confidently; at other times, the going is tough. It's important for our life/faith journey to remember that we don't all walk at the same pace, and to adjust our speed and curb our impatience if our companions cannot keep up with us or need our support. Who knows what we might learn from them if we but take time to walk alongside them? And how we might need, one day, to lean on them …

† Father, I thank you for those who have walked with me so far. Bless our journeys and teach us to walk in your ways.

For further thought
• Take some time to look back at your own faith journey. Identify the graced moments and the companions who have brought you this far. How can you now help others on the path?

Isaiah 1–39 – Jane Gonzalez

July

Isaiah 1–39
Jerusalem besieged

Notes based on the New Revised Standard Version by **Jules Gomes**

The Revd Canon Dr Jules Gomes is Canon Theologian at the Isle of Man Cathedral and Vicar of the Parish of Castletown and Arbory on the Isle of Man. He earned his doctorate in Old Testament from the University of Cambridge and taught biblical studies at the United Theological College, Bangalore, the London School of Theology and Liverpool Hope University. Formerly a journalist in Bombay, he now contributes to Manx Radio and has written five books. Jules enjoys literature, art, classical and jazz music, target shooting, motorcycling, walking and golf.

Sunday 2 July
When I'm careful but not prayerful

Isaiah 36:1–12

See, you are relying on Egypt, that broken reed of a staff, which will pierce the hand of anyone who leans on it. Such is Pharaoh king of Egypt to all who rely on him. (verse 6)

I long for security and stability. I want to be absolutely certain of a job, a house, a pension and a future. Like an impetuous child I want it now. I hate 'waiting patiently on the Lord' (Psalm 40:1). I don't seek first the kingdom of God. I plan, strategise, network and look for supporters who are rich and powerful. Sooner or later my efforts fail. My supporters let me down. My strategies collapse.

I'm like Hezekiah! He is a good king. He loves God. He rids his land of idolatry. He resists the initial attempts of King Sennacherib of Assyria to bully Judah and extract tribute. But … then … he turns to Egypt for support. He trusts that an alliance with an ancient superpower will save him from a new superpower. Does he not remember that once Egypt was the tyrant from whom God rescued his people? Why is it so difficult for him to trust in that Superpower of the King of Angel Armies, who is greater than all superpowers? Why do I lean on securities that are broken reeds – so flimsy that they could pierce my hand and self-destruct, when I can lean on the Rock of all Ages?

† With shame, I confess, Good Lord, my tendency to trust in chariots and horses; I repent of not seeking you first and above all things.

A cat and mouse game

> **Isaiah 36:13–21**
>
> *Do not let Hezekiah mislead you by saying, The Lord will save us. Has any of the gods of the nations saved their land out of the hand of the king of Assyria? (verse 18)*

A mouse is caught between two cats. Each cat is promising to protect the mouse from the other cat. Which cat does the mouse turn to for help? The answer is obvious. Neither. Egypt has been all-powerful in the past. Assyria is all mighty in the present. Who will rule the future? With whom should King Hezekiah forge an alliance? The mouse needs to turn to someone more powerful than the two cats. And who is that? Yahweh, God of Israel is King of kings! King Sennacherib of Assyria sends the Rabshakeh, his senior military attaché, to talk Hezekiah into surrendering. The Rabshakeh unleashes a diplomatic onslaught. First, he mocks the other cat – Egypt (36:4–6). He is right. Egypt is a broken reed. Assyria has defeated Egypt. Isaiah has warned against alliances with Egypt. It is political and spiritual suicide for Judah to trust in Egypt. Second, he scorns Hezekiah's religious reform (36:7). Hezekiah had eliminated the idolatrous shrines. But to a pagan like the Rabshakeh, that is a bad idea, because God may be offended since his places of worship have been reduced! What is culturally acceptable may be divinely offensive. Third, he injects fear into the populace by speaking in the popular language of Hebrew, not the diplomatic language of Aramaic (36:11–12). Fear is the enemy of faith. Fourth, most insidiously, he ridicules Hezekiah's trust in Yahweh (36:7, 18). He uses a false analogy and compares Yahweh with the gods of the nations. They couldn't deliver their people from Assyria! Is Yahweh greater than other gods? Who really rules the world?

† Almighty God, when I am trapped between impossible choices and face hostility from human and demonic powers, help me to put my trust in you alone, through your Messiah Jesus Christ.

For further thought

• How realistic is faith in God in the world of harsh realpolitik? How does the prophet Isaiah deal with this struggle?

Isaiah 1–39 – Jules Gomes

July

Tuesday 4 July
How faith casts out fear

Isaiah 37:1–20

Isaiah said to them, 'Say to your master, "Thus says the Lord: Do not be afraid because of the words that you have heard, with which the servants of the king of Assyria have reviled me."' (verse 6)

The Rabshakeh has struck fear into God's people through his perverse propaganda. Fear kills faith. How do we respond to a rhetoric that generates fear? First, like Hezekiah, we repent (verses 1–3). Judah's king, officials and priests tear their clothes and cover themselves with sackcloth. They repent of their lack of faith and their succumbing to fear. Second, like Hezekiah, we pray. They ask Isaiah to pray that God will 'rebuke' the Rabshakeh's words that have caused this fear. Hezekiah prays (verses 4, 15–20). Third, they seek a prophetic word from the Lord (verse 6). God's word is the ultimate antidote for fear. God's word creates faith. Faith kills fear. Isaiah speaks God's word commanding, 'Do not be afraid because of the words you have heard' from the Rabshakeh (verse 6). Words are never 'mere' words. This is ironically what the Rabshakeh had told the leaders of Judah (verse 5). But, he cleverly uses 'mere' words to destroy them. Words have the power to do things. This is what the Oxford philosopher J L Austin said in a famous series of lectures that resulted in a significant development in philosophy and linguistics known as speech-act theory. Thus far philosophers had argued that to say something was 'always and simply to state something'. Austin argued that in some cases, 'to say something is to do something'; to say something actually makes something happen. Words have the power to reorder reality. Austin calls this performative speech. Prayer is performative speech. God's word is performative speech. When God's speaks and we pray things happen, and fear takes flight.

† Lord God, I bring before you the many words spoken that create fear in me. Help me to hear your word in scripture and speak your word in prayer and so cast out fear in Jesus' name.

For further thought

• Use a word search on a Bible computer program or concordance to find out how many time the Bible commands us to 'Fear not'!

Wednesday 5 July
The politics of prayer

Isaiah 37:21–35

Then Isaiah the son of Amoz sent to Hezekiah, saying, 'Thus says the Lord, the God of Israel: Because you have prayed to me concerning King Sennacherib of Assyria, this is the word that the Lord has spoken concerning him.' (part of verses 21–22)

Prayer is political. It changes the course of history. It dethrones dictators. It topples tyrants. It provokes God to speak. It provokes God to act. Prayer is performative speech of the most powerful kind. Hezekiah prays for God to act in politics and history. He prays specifically for God to act against Sennacherib and in favour of Judah. Through prayer Hezekiah calls Sennacherib's bluff. Through prayer Hezekiah indicates that he is now trusting in God alone and not in his alliance with Egypt. God's word is in response to Hezekiah's prayer. Conversely, our prayer must be in response to God's word for God reveals his will through his word. God speaks through the prophet Isaiah and clarifies his sovereignty. Sennacherib's conquests have only been made possible because Israel's God has foreordained them for his purposes to bring Israel back to himself. God will defend his city. God will save a remnant and continue to work through them in history. When we work, we work. When we pray, God works. The Bible joins our initiative with God's sovereignty. What if Hezekiah had not prayed? What if Hezekiah had continued to trust in Egypt? What if Hezekiah had allowed himself to be manipulated by the rhetoric of the Rabshakeh? What if Hezekiah had looked around at other nations and seen that Sennacherib had indeed conquered them? What if Hezekiah had not consulted Isaiah? What if Hezekiah had closed his ears to God's word? History would have been written very differently. Do we really believe in the power of prayer to redefine and reorder the twists and turns of history?

† Sovereign Lord, teach us to pray and teach us to trust the performative power of prayer for Jesus' sake.

For further thought

• Who are the most infamous dictators you've spotted in the news this week? Have you considered praying for their downfall?

Thursday 6 July
Does God change his mind?

Isaiah 37:36 – 38:8

Go and say to Hezekiah, Thus says the Lord, the God of your ancestor David: I have heard your prayer, I have seen your tears; I will add fifteen years to your life. (verse 5)

Has Isaiah's prophecy worked or has it failed? After all, his prophecy is not fulfilled and Hezekiah does not die! Isaiah first tells King Hezekiah that is he to die but later tells him that God has extended his life by 15 years. Has God changed his mind? Has the prophet changed his tune? Biblical prophecy is not divine meteorology. It is not fortune-telling. It is not predicting a predetermined future. The pagan prophets of Israel's day were soothsayers. They foretold the future. But biblical prophecy rejected this model. Biblical prophets spoke truth to power. They confronted kings and nations. They challenged public opinion. Biblical prophets did occasionally talk of the future. But they did it only to warn people what would happen if people did not repent. If people repented the future could be radically different. Hezekiah repents as a response to Isaiah's prophecy. Surely that proves his prophecy has worked? Surely the word of the Lord has had a tremendous impact in leading a powerful king to repentance? We misuse God's word when we treat it as a conjurer's hat or a horoscope or use it to merely titillate our desire for esoteric information. God speaks so that we may repent and be transformed. Perhaps a lesson about prophecy is that it is meant to give us a second chance. God is generous with second chances. Hezekiah's name means something like 'The Lord has strengthened me.' Depending on himself and trusting in Egypt, Hezekiah is weak. Repenting and praying and listening to God's word, Hezekiah lives up to his name. He becomes strong and lives another 15 years.

† Almighty God, thank you for giving me so many chances and for being eternally patient with me. I promise to be attentive and responsive to your word in scripture and your Word in Christ Jesus.

For further thought

- What are some of the other instances in the Bible where God changes his mind and when the word of prophecy apparently misfires?

Friday 7 July
The power of lament

Isaiah 38:9–20

Like a swallow or a crane I clamour, I moan like a dove. My eyes are weary with looking upwards. O Lord, I am oppressed; be my security! (verse 14)

'Praise God and keep praising God even when you are in despair.' That's what we're often told. But is the mantra of perpetual praise a pious platitude? Forty of the 150 psalms – nearly one-third of the Psalter – are lament, not praise. In the abyss of agony, when you want to cry, scream and shout at God, does it not seem a bit hypocritical to praise God? Lament is raw prayer. Hezekiah's poem is a psalm of lament. Lamenting before God means that we begin with lament. It doesn't mean we end with lament. There is a remarkable movement from lament to praise. The psalm begins with Hezekiah lamenting at the 'gates of Sheol' (verse 10); it climaxes with him rejoicing with stringed instruments at the 'house of the Lord' (verse 20). It moves from damnation to salvation. Hezekiah goes on mourning that he will 'not see the Lord in the land of the living' (verse 11); he ends by including himself among the 'living' who thank God for his faithfulness (verse 19). At the heart of his psalm is a pair of opposites: God's wrath and images of despair are juxtaposed with God's restoration and images of hope (verse 12–17). It is wrestling with this paradox that turns the psalm on its head and catapults Hezekiah from lament to praise. Unless we plumb the depths of lament, we will never be able to ascend the mountaintops of praise. On the cross Jesus prays a psalm of lament. He screams at God, 'My God, my God, why have you forsaken me?' In an age of feel-good, foot tapping, happy-clappy worship, we have expunged lament from the liturgy. It's time to reclaim the power of lament.

† Lord, when we don't feel like praising you because we think you have abandoned us, help us to lament. And grant that as we lament in tears we will soon rejoice in laughter for Jesus' sake.

For further thought

• How is lamenting different from complaining or moaning?

Isaiah 1–39 – Jules Gomes

July

A wise prophet and a foolish king

Isaiah 38:21 – 39:8

Isaiah said, 'What have they seen in your house?' Hezekiah answered, 'They have seen all that is in my house; there is nothing in my storehouses that I did not show them.' (verse 4)

Wisdom is the ability to make the right choices. It constitutes a major chunk of the biblical witness in the Old Testament. Wisdom literature teaches us how to live life rightly. It warns us of life's pitfalls. The prophets were astute practitioners of wisdom. Isaiah offers a poultice made of figs to Hezekiah for his healing; this is the wisdom of medicine. But Hezekiah rejects wisdom and does something extraordinarily foolish. Apart from holding on to his faith in God, he should have learned the hard lessons of forging alliances with Egypt and believing that Assyria was as powerful as she claimed to be. He now shamelessly succumbs to a subtle bribe offered by Babylon. Babylon is now the rising star – the new potential superpower. In 703BCE, Merodach Baladan, son of the king of Babylon, defeated the Assyrians at Kish. In an act of monumental stupidity, Hezekiah invites the Babylonian envoys, who are very likely spies, to survey his palace treasury. Is he showing off? Is he sucking up to them and trying to get into the good books of his new superpower? His idiotic act has dire consequences. Isaiah warns him that the Babylonians will invade Judah, take the people into exile and ransack its treasures. But Hezekiah has so hardened his heart and fossilised his mind that his response is indifferent. He couldn't care less since it will not happen during his reign! He is concerned only with himself and his short-term goals with no regard for the long-term consequences his actions have had on the people of God!

† Lord, help me to trust in your wisdom and not to lean on my own understanding, believing that you will make my paths straight through Christ, my wisdom.

For further thought

• Have you ever considered reading the book of Proverbs one chapter a day through the month?

Feet
Feet washed and ready

Notes based on the New International Version (UK) by **Jan Sutch Pickard**

See Jan's biography on p. 8.

Sunday 9 July
Setting foot in the Jordan

> ### Joshua 3:9–17
>
> *... as soon as the priests who carried the ark reached the Jordan and their feet touched the water's edge, the water from upstream stopped flowing. It piled up in a heap ... So the people crossed over opposite Jericho. (part of verses 15–16)*

The island of Oronsay, like other places round Britain's coast, is both a tidal island and place of pilgrimage. A mediaeval priory, flocks of birds, wind-blown grass, great peace – to reach these, it's necessary to cross a mile of strand at low tide. With friends, I made that journey barefoot. The tide was still going out and we found ourselves walking sometimes on hard sand, sometimes in squashy mud, sometimes across beds of sharp shells. The water didn't withdraw suddenly, like Jordan in this story. Instead, we let the tide open a path for us in its own time.

Each of us reads the Bible in the place where we put our feet on the ground, taking time, feeling our way. Reading this passage, I remembered living among Palestinian shepherds in the hills above the Jordan valley, looking out over the land to which Joshua and the Israelites crossed carrying the Ark of the covenant, without getting their feet wet.

Standing on land claimed and conquered many times, I wondered how driving people from their land can be God's will. How do Palestinian Christians read this passage? Sometimes reading scripture is like wading through mud, walking on sharp shells.

† Think of, and maybe sing, hymns/spirituals which refer to the crossing of the Jordan, e.g. 'I went down to the river to pray' or 'When I tread the verge of Jordan' in 'Guide me O thou great Jehovah'. Why do you think this story has taken on such spiritual significance?

Following wholeheartedly

Feet – Jan Sutch Pickard

July

Joshua 14:6–15

The land on which your feet have walked will be your inheritance and that of your children forever, because you have followed the Lord my God wholeheartedly. (part of verse 9)

The emphasis of this passage goes beyond the promise of land from which others have been driven out. We are reminded of the way Caleb set foot in this land. He was a spy, one of those sent by Moses to find out the lie of the land. Some of his companions brought back discouraging messages. But Caleb was convinced that this could be the home his wandering people had been seeking, that it could support them with its harvests and that they could settle there with God's help. This was the message he brought back. It carried authority, because he had actually been there (what modern strategists call 'boots on the ground').

It's a war story, of course. From being a courageous spy, Caleb had become part of an invading force and then an army of occupation. Many years later, he came into his 'inheritance' – a tract of hill-country. An inheritance can be an unearned benefit, but Caleb seems to have earned it by following God 'wholeheartedly'. This is still not an easy story: the Anakites, who lived on that land before Caleb and his family ever came there, were driven out.

But what can we learn from the Caleb himself? He didn't come easily or instantly into this inheritance: he was an old man. Forty years had passed. His wholehearted following of God's ways seems to have included a great deal of patience. In the way he was prepared to wait, as in his testimony to Moses about the Promised Land, he was steadfast. Caleb was a man who stood his ground!

† Oh God, help me to be steadfast; help me to follow you wholeheartedly.

For further thought

- Think about this beautiful but underused word 'steadfast' – what might it mean for your own choices and actions? Would they be easy?

Tuesday 11 July
The footsteps of the poor

Isaiah 26:1–7

He humbles those who dwell on high, he lays the lofty city low; he levels it to the ground and casts it down to the dust. Feet trample it down – the feet of the oppressed, the footsteps of the poor. (verses 5–6)

Trampling is a vengeful and violent act (the Old Testament is full of them, done in God's name). If we focus not on the brutality but on 'the feet of the oppressed, the footsteps of the poor' – then we'll notice their vulnerability. These are probably bare feet, like the feet Jesus washed – tired and dusty with walking the roads of the world, feet of those trying hard to follow in God's way.

Trampling is terrifying. Lashing out is one human reaction to oppression. There are other forms of protest, too. In 2009, in central London, you would have seen hundreds of shoes lying in the road. Ordinary British folk, who felt their voices had not been heard, found a non-violent form of protest. To chants of 'Shame on you, have my shoe,' demonstrators threw 1000 shoes down outside the front door of the Prime minister, Gordon Brown, to protest British inaction over the Israeli onslaught on Gaza. 'Shame on you,' they shouted at their leaders.

Their action was inspired by Muntazer al-Zaidi, an Iraqi who, distressed after witnessing the effects of US foreign policy, hurled his shoe at George Bush. 'I say to those who reproach me: do you know how many broken homes that shoe which I threw had entered? How many times it had trodden over the blood of innocent victims? Maybe that shoe was the appropriate response when all values were violated.' Feet can be brutal or vulnerable and shoes signs of shame. We can be oppressors.

† Take off your shoes and hold them as you reflect on when you may have deserved to be told 'Shame on you'? Then look at your bare feet, remembering that Jesus knelt to wash dirty, hurting feet that were trying to walk in God's way.

For further thought
- Hear the oppressed who cry 'Shame on you'. Never ignore the footsteps of the poor.

Feet – Jan Sutch Pickard

July

Wednesday 12 July
Feet that bring good news

Isaiah 52:1–10

How beautiful on the mountains are the feet of those who bring good news, who proclaim peace, who bring good tidings, who proclaim salvation. (part of verse 7)

A friend was celebrating 50 years since ordination. His ministry had taken him to many parts of Britain, and other places, too. He had served as a Mission Partner in Sierra Leone and a volunteer on the Ecumenical Accompaniment Programme in Palestine and Israel. Inspired by his story and these words from Isaiah, I wrote him a poem:

Are your feet beautiful?
Are your feet beautiful, Warren? What a personal question! But it's relevant.
Your feet must be worn by now: not worn-out but well used.
You've trodden stony tracks, bush paths, city streets, mountain heights and dark valleys,
pilgrim ways – your whole life has been a journey.
These feet have carried the word of the gospel to African villages and Black Country chapels …
they have travelled the world. These feet faithfully journeyed with a life-companion, Joan;
they keep pace with friends, sometimes they walk alone …
These feet have carried you, early in the morning, to the grim separation barrier in Bethlehem,
witnessing at the checkpoint, accompanying oppressed and courageous people;
standing your ground on God's kairos.
Worn, wounded, dirty with being down to earth – are your feet beautiful?
These are the feet of one who brings good news, the feet of a disciple.
Jesus knelt to wash them. They are beautiful.

† Thank you, God, for the good news of your love, shared to the ends of the earth and among neighbours. Bless the feet that walk your way, people who proclaim peace, who bring good news.

For further thought

• In what way are your well-worn feet beautiful?

Thursday 13 July
Standing on the highest point

Matthew 4:1–6

Then the devil took him to the holy city and had him stand on the highest point of the Temple. 'If you are the Son of God,' he said, 'throw yourself down. For it is written: "He will command his angels concerning you, and they will lift you up in their hands, so that you will not strike your foot against a stone."' (verses 5–6)

Jerusalem is a holy city and a stony one, too. Massive city walls and buildings old and new are built of pale limestone, which also paves the narrow streets of the Old city, polished by many passing feet. Observant Jews flock to the western wall of the Temple site, to pray hard by the great rough limestone blocks. Other Jewish families bury their dead on the slopes of the Mount of Olives, in graves with stones placed on them as a sign of remembrance. Christians walk the Via Dolorosa, or the stony ground of Gethsemane, under ancient olive trees. They visit the rock-hewn Garden Tomb, near a cliff-face like a skull. Muslims revere the Temple mount as a present day place of worship, in a place where they believe the Prophet set foot. Archaeologists study the stones and some draw political conclusions. Children throw stones at soldiers. Pilgrims come to walk in the steps of Jesus, and to touch the stones with reverence. But the 'living stones' from which the church was built are people who still live in this land that we call 'holy'.

Imagine Jesus fasting in the wilderness, where his fevered dreams lifted him to stand on the pinnacle of the Temple. Here he would have looked out over the whole city – full of the hard reality of stones and the power of human hopes and fears. What would happen if he threw himself down into the midst of all this? Would God save him? Would angels catch him before he landed? Could his dramatic action make a difference?

Jesus told the tempting voices that testing God achieves nothing.

† Pray for the peace of Jerusalem, a holy city and a stony city. Pray for the people of three faiths who belong there, that they may find ways to live together in peace.

For further thought

• Is trusting God different, then? Can we expect that angels will save us from ever stubbing our toes? What do we learn when we do?

Friday 14 July
If your foot causes you to stumble ...

Mark 9:42–50

If anyone causes one of these little ones – those who believe in me – to stumble, it would be better for them if a large millstone were hung around their neck and they were thrown into the sea ... If your foot causes you to stumble, cut it off ... (verses 42 and 45)

What radical surgery, to cut off a clumsy foot – either that or a savage punishment! Or could it be simply a way of saying 'This is something we can do without'?

In a church community I know well, there was a well-meaning member who tended to 'put his foot in it'. He believed so strongly in some things (mostly to do with literal readings of biblical texts) that he hammered home his beliefs in every conversation. He told folk who didn't agree with him that they were going against God and would be punished. He was sure that he was right, and so didn't respect the way that others read the same Bible. Now his neighbours were gentle people, good people who wanted to live in God's way. They became distressed and confused. Their faith was shaken. One by one they stopped coming to church. So the whole congregation lost its way.

I'm struck by the fact that in this Gospel passage the word 'stumble' is used twice: once for the people who are misled when they need help in their faith journey; once for the foot that takes wrong steps, and trips up its owner. How do we get out of such a situation? None of us wants the man who keeps 'putting his foot in it' to have a millstone round his neck and be thrown into the sea. We do want him to understand that other people are also loved children of God, with the ability to understand, find and follow God's way. Otherwise we'll all start to stumble and fall.

† Loving God, you bless us with both convictions and compassion: however strongly I feel about things, help me not to cause others to stumble.

For further thought

• Jesus said: 'Salt is good, but if it loses its saltiness, how can you make it salty again? Have salt among yourselves, and be at peace with each other.'

Saturday 15 July
Surefooted

Habakkuk 3:17–19

The Sovereign Lord is my strength; he makes my feet like the feet of a deer, he enables me to tread on the heights. (verse 19)

Across boulder-strewn plains in Africa, antelopes are running free; on a Scottish mountainside, a red deer stag leads the herd, finding a way swiftly through heather and scree; on rocky hillsides, which shepherds of biblical times knew well, gazelles bound, surefooted.

Deer are creatures of the wild, and they can move safely around their habitat. Their hooves are sensitive to different surfaces, feeling the way among stones, sand, scrub and sheer rock-faces, keeping a balance. Watching deer, we realise how clumsy we humans are.

Children in a playground, running, climbing and balancing – 'on top of the world' – aren't clumsy. But few adults are so fit and agile. More than that, there's the way we live together, stumbling and causing each other to stumble. This can be true of congregations, local communities, nations, when we fail to care for each other or for creation. In the days of the prophet Habakkuk, people were as distressed about failing harvests as we are about global warming now. When fields produced no food and there were no longer sheep in the pen, they took this as a sign of their failure – and sometimes of God's anger with humankind.

The prophet reminded his contemporaries of God's grace. The graceful deer can be a symbol of that, surviving because it is fleet and surefooted, and knows its place in God's creation. The prophet reminds us that we are also recipients of grace. God enables us not only to survive, but to climb mountains, to 'tread on the heights' – to fulfil our potential, becoming fully the beings that God created in love.

† I will rejoice in the Lord; I will be joyful in God my Saviour. The Sovereign Lord is my strength; he makes my feet like the feet of a deer. He enables me to tread on the heights.

For further thought

• What gives you joy? What are your God-given strengths? What does it mean, to you, to 'tread on the heights'?

Feet – Jan Sutch Pickard

July

Feet
Passive Feet

Notes based on the New Revised Standard Version by **Vron Smith**

 Vron Smith has worked as a laywoman in the church for over 20 years. Her ministry has included work with young people in a parish and as a chaplain in school, university and hospice settings. She currently lives and works in a residential spirituality centre in Wales which is run by the Jesuits. Much of the time is spent accompanying others on silent retreats but she also delivers training in spiritual accompaniment both in the UK and further afield in the far East.

Sunday 16 July
Bare feet, bare heart

Exodus 3:1–10

When the Lord saw that he had turned aside to see, God called to him out of the bush, 'Moses, Moses!' And he said, 'Here I am.' Then he said, 'Come no closer! Remove the sandals from your feet, for the place on which you are standing is holy ground.' (verses 4–5)

Have you ever as an adult kicked off your shoes and walked on dew-soaked grass or squelching mud or hot sand? Our feet have more nerve-endings per centimetre than any other part of the body, but more often than not, the only messages being sent by them are about the surrounding socks and shoes. In rare moments when I do stand outside barefooted, feeling the textures of the earth underfoot, I notice sometimes a shift within me, a deep anchoring sense of my own place in a creation made by the incredible Creator.

Moses, too, had that experience of taking off his sandals, invited to stand on the dusty earth where God's presence turned what was common ground into a holy place of encounter. Importantly though, Moses had to turn aside, to become barefoot and then he could hear what God wanted to share.

Moments in life can catch our curiosity. In these coming days, our feet can lead our hearts to stand in all sorts of places. Perhaps through them, we'll encounter God enticing us to look closer, to recognise the moment's holy ground and inviting us to mission.

† God of the curious, lead me to meet you. Show me how to stand bare-hearted before you so that I may hear you voice and respond.

Monday 17 July
Sure feet, sure heart

Psalm 91:1–16

On their hands they will bear you up, so that you will not dash your foot against a stone. You will tread on the lion and the adder, the young lion and the serpent you will trample under foot. (verses 12–13)

The recent tragic Ebola outbreak saw many people choose to risk their lives in order to help others because they had the skills needed and saw the human suffering that could be averted if they offered their service. They made a choice to live in dangerous conditions for the greater good of others.

Today's psalm tells us something about God's care, God for whom the little things like a stubbed toe matter as do the bigger events like terrors of the night or plague. We are told to trust that we will be unharmed. Yet, as we know from experience, there is harm. Some of those serving others in the Ebola crisis lost their lives as well as the many victims. So how can we pray these words sincerely?

There is more to it than simply living life like a person who rashly treads on any wild and dangerous animal because God will offer protection. Discipleship is risky but it's less about thoughtless danger-seeking that tests God and more about when we find ourselves struggling or threatened – whether through mission or circumstance – making a choice to shelter in God. After all, Jesus' death is the ultimate example of these promises of the psalm seemingly failing – and yet we know God raised him up. There lies our hope and reason to trust: God, who cares about all people, does the same for us.

† Help me Lord to trust in you, to seek you as my shelter, to be a disciple in courage and wisdom.

For further thought

• Look at nature around you and see how shelter is offered. If one image stirs your heart, stay with it and speak with God.

Tuesday 18 July
Kissed feet, kissed heart

Luke 7:36–50

You gave me no kiss, but from the time I came in she has not stopped kissing my feet. You did not anoint my head with oil, but she has anointed my feet with ointment. Therefore, I tell you, her sins, which were many, have been forgiven. (part of verses 45–47)

Have you ever had the experience of someone kiss your feet? As babies, our feet maybe were kissed in play; as children, we may have had a foot kissed better after hurting it; as adults we can kiss feet to show love. In some cultures it is a mark of respect, in others it can demonstrate servitude.

Today we see Jesus having his feet kissed – not once or twice but continuously – by a woman who is unfamiliar to him. He shows no embarrassment over her actions, doesn't try to stop her and indeed accepts her actions gracefully and without concern. How unlike Simon the Pharisee who reacts to this seemingly wanton show of love with judgement, both of Jesus and the woman. You can imagine the thoughts running through his head, 'How could he let himself be touched so sensually by this sinful woman? Shame on him! He should be pushing her away.' Yet the woman gives unreservedly; her tears, her expensive ointment, her kisses are all signs of love for Jesus. In contrast Simon offers little – no kiss of welcome, no foot washing, no anointing – these omissions signal his seeming indifference towards Jesus.

In this narrative, we are shown what the kingdom looks like – generosity, forgiveness, acceptance, big-hearted love. We see too what stands in opposition – meanness, judgement, rejection, cool indifference. Let's desire to be extravagant lovers of Jesus, to kiss the kingdom into fullness.

† Jesus, let me know you welcome me as I am, a loved and forgiven sinner, who kisses your feet in love.

For further thought

• Notice today moments where you see the kingdom being kissed into fullness in your life, and give thanks.

Washed feet, washed heart

John 13:1–11

Then he poured water into a basin and began to wash the disciples' feet and to wipe them with the towel that was tied around him. He came to Simon Peter, who said to him, 'Lord, are you going to wash my feet?' (verses 5–6)

'Ugh! You're not touching my feet!' stated some of the teenagers on the Cross Walk. We'd walked all day through mud and rain carrying a cross and that evening we offered foot massage for any weary feet. A brave few decided to see how it would be, watched by the others, and ended up lying blissfully relaxed on their sleeping bags, unwilling to move. The next night a few more had their feet massaged and by the pilgrimage end, it was part of everyone's evening routine. It didn't matter if they had corns or bruised toes or broken blisters or that their feet were smelly. They experienced that those things weren't going to get in the way of love in action.

Peter too doesn't get it. Why would Jesus wash his feet? The other disciples have made no fuss but he resists the gift that is being offered, this service of love from the one who loves him. Then, given the choice between being washed or having no share with Jesus, he over-reacts and says to wash all of him! He wants a big share of Jesus. Peter's head and heart are all over the place because Jesus isn't behaving how he imagined a Messiah would, and only in the experience of letting Jesus love him and serve him would he come to understand. As brothers and sisters there are times we need to receive, to be ministered to in love. Like Peter, that is the challenge and the gift.

† Open me, Lord, to let you serve me through my brothers and sisters; to experience through them your love and to do likewise for others.

For further thought

• What gifts do I receive through the service of others and how might I learn to be generous in receiving?

Feet – Vron Smith

July

201

Righteous feet, righteous heart

Feet – Vron Smith

July

> **Psalm 110:1–7**
>
> *The Lord says to my lord, 'Sit at my right hand until I make your enemies your footstool.' The Lord sends out from Zion your mighty sceptre. Rule in the midst of your foes. (verses 1–2)*

In the British Museum there is a stone-carved Assyrian relief that dates from around 750 years before the birth of Jesus. It shows Pul, the king of Assyria (mentioned in 2 Kings 15) standing with his foot on the neck of his enemy who is sprawled on the ground before him. The enemy's life and death is in the hands, or rather under the foot, of King Pul.

As I consider that picture, and imagine that it was God who put that enemy at my feet for me to use as I willed, it leaves me somewhat disturbed. What God would allow such a thing? Would let me rest my feet on another, even if it were my foe? Even more disturbing, what God shatters heads over the earth? Today's psalm is a somewhat violent song associated with kings of the Old Testament who were seen as the instruments of God, appointed as his representative and who used or abused the power and authority of their position.

In the Gospels of Mark and Luke, Jesus, who quotes the same psalm, is the King, the Lord, who brings in the reign of God. That reign is not one of violence. The enemies of this Lord are not human foes but rather sin and death that are conquered and become his footstool. The sin that Jesus has firmly underfoot includes ours; and for that reason we can lift up our heads.

† Give me wisdom, Lord, to know the freedom of your victory over sin and death and to live it joyfully.

For further thought

- Ponder on how Jesus who is King attracts you to follow and what you desire for the kingdom.

Humble feet, humble heart

James 2:1–9

You take notice of the one wearing the fine clothes and say, 'Have a seat here, please,' while to the one who is poor you say, 'Stand there', or, 'Sit at my feet', have you not made distinctions among yourselves? (verses 3–4)

I used to play a game with the youth club in which I showed a number of pictures of real people with a mix of age, race, gender and dress. Some looked rich, intelligent, successful; others appeared poor and struggling to survive. They then had to imagine the world was about to end and a spacecraft could carry some people to a space station so that the human race might survive. They had to decide who to leave behind. Without much thought, their first choice was nearly always a photo of a man wearing tattered clothes who looked tired, dirty and worn down. Later they discovered that he was actually a medical doctor who had just escaped from his war-torn country. Too late for a seat on the spacecraft.

We make distinctions every day. Whose company do I want to be seen in so that I'm seen to be popular; who would I never go out with because they don't wear designer gear? Judge everything on appearance and you'll get places – and not just any place but the places of honour, so we are led to believe.

But James is clear. Don't make judgements on the basis of looks. Don't treat some differently from others. Don't presume that those who appear better off can have the good places. God has other ideas. God isn't into being fashionable or riches as a means of status; God wants hearts that can be fashioned and that are rich in faith. God chooses the poor.

† God of the humble, let my heart be fashioned by you and my faithfulness be your riches.

For further thought

- Observe people around you and imagine seeing the people you meet through God's eyes. How does that change your response?

Saturday 22 July
Happy feet, happy heart

Acts 3:1–10

'In the name of Jesus Christ of Nazareth, stand up and walk.' And he took him by the right hand and raised him up; and immediately his feet and ankles were made strong. Jumping up, he stood and began to walk. (part of verses 6–8)

It's only when something you take for granted is no longer possible that you realise your dependence. So I learnt when, following a sports injury, I ended up unable to use my left knee or put any weight on that foot. From going where I wanted when I wanted I was reduced to barely hobbling between three rooms on the ground floor of my home. Going upstairs required sitting on the steps levering myself up on my backside. Others had to bring me a drink or food. My world shrank and I remember feeling hugely restricted.

That was for me only a taste of how it must have been for the lame man who relied on other's generosity, day in, day out, both to carry him to the Beautiful Gate and to give him alms. Sadder still, because he was lame and therefore unclean, he was not allowed access to the Temple, the place where God dwelt. God was not accessible to him. How could he ever then be healed? Notice then, when Peter spoke those words, 'In the name of Jesus Christ, stand up and walk', and those ankles and feet were made strong, how it was not only the man who could move but God was on the move as well. God sees our lameness too, the times when we are not free whether in body, mind or heart. If we speak his name, God, who cannot be restricted, can move and make strong.

† God who makes strong, heal what makes me lame so that I may stand firm once more through your love.

For further thought

• If the opportunity arises, spend time with a person who is disabled learning what life is really like for them.

Readings in Matthew (3)
Blessed are ...

Notes based on the New Revised Standard Version by **Lesley G Anderson**

Lesley G Anderson is a minister of the Methodist Church and a past president of the United Theological College of the West Indies, Jamaica. He studied in the UK and the United States and enjoys the arts, music, reading, writing and Scrabble.

Sunday 23 July
Live a life of grace which comes from God!

Matthew 5:1–5
Blessed are the meek, for they will inherit the earth. (verse 5)

The Sermon on the Mount envisions Jesus' crucifixion and begins with the Beatitudes (from the Latin for blessed): Jesus' paradoxical declarations of God's grace. Each declaration begins with the word, blessed (*makarioi*, Greek) which means 'happy'. 'Happiness', however, is not of same spiritual level and quality as 'blessedness', which we cannot earn. To be blessed is to experience God's gift of daily grace.

When we are crushed by economic woes and become poor in spirit due to our poverty and destitution, we can live another day to fight for a better life, and experience blessedness in Christ who declares: 'Blessed are the poor in spirit ...' (verse 3). Further, when we are overwhelmed by sin and death, and drawn to God's throne of grace, there in our grief, God himself will provide us comfort and Christ, who still gives us his peace will declare: 'Blessed are those who mourn ...' (verse 4). Finally, like Christ, the meek are strong. In obedience to his Father, Christ humbly bore his sufferings 'to the point of death' on Calvary's cross (Philippians 2:7–8). He forgives us of sin and thirsting for our salvation declares: 'Blessed are the meek, for they will inherit the earth' (verse 5).

This week we explore together, and hopefully experience together, this daily gift of God.

† O Lord, Jesus Christ, teach us how to humbly live a blessed life of grace, glory and victory.

Monday 24 July
Hungering and thirsting

Matthew 5:6–9

Blessed are those who hunger and thirst for righteousness, for they will be filled. (verse 6)

Millions of persons on every continent are living in physical poverty. There is a hunger for food and a thirst for water. Christ takes these basic human drives and transforms them into spiritual purposes. He sees persons who are hungry for love and others who thirst for the good of others. He sees persons who are poor and spiritually poverty-stricken and who hunger and thirst for righteousness which only God can give them. What hunger means to the hungry and thirst to the thirsty are understood as the continuous spiritual filling of the Christian to completion with the righteousness of Christ. This act is of God, the source and supplier of our spiritual filling, who supplies us now and always! This is truly a blessing and experience of God's grace, for the kingdom is at hand!

Mother Teresa in India, Mandela in South Africa and others in their mercy bore afflictions to help, heal and liberate persons in misery. On the cross, Christ received no mercy, yet in his mercy used his wounds to pour out love and blood for our salvation.

John Wesley, the Anglican evangelical preacher and founder of Methodism, encouraged his followers to conquer sin through spiritual self-discipline, godly living, purity of heart and holiness, '… without which no one will see the Lord' (Hebrews 12:14).

Christian peacemakers by their witness have inspired persons to work for world peace. Their love for peace and desire to exemplify the righteousness of Jesus Christ, the Prince of Peace, make them blessed and, therefore, 'they will be called children of God' (verse 9).

† O God of love, we pray that the beatific vision of persons hungering and thirsting after righteousness be a reality throughout the world.

For further thought

• In what way or ways does God give spiritual blessings to the merciful, pure in heart and peacemakers?

Tuesday 25 July
Kingdom people

Readings in Matthew (3) – Lesley G Anderson

Matthew 5:10–12

Blessed are those who are persecuted for righteousness' sake, for theirs is the kingdom of heaven. (verse 10)

The 'kingdom of heaven' (verse 10) belongs to followers of Christ who suffered persecution for causes higher than themselves. They lived lives directly opposed to that of the world. They experienced slanders, endured hardships and rejoiced in their tribulations. They were blessed for nobly and courageously sealing their faith with their blood for the sake of Christ and others.

Dietrich Bonhoeffer was a German Lutheran pastor, theologian, leading anti-Nazi dissident and opponent of Adolf Hitler. He died to save his country from evil personified.

Martin Luther King, Jr, an African-American Baptist minister and Civil Rights leader, died defending the civil liberties of the deprived in the USA, using non-violent civil disobedience.

Archbishop Janani Luwum, a leading Anglican voice in Uganda, was martyred for criticising and opposing the arbitrary killings and disappearances of persons by General Idi Amin's regime.

Archbishop Oscar Arnulfo Romero, a Salvadoran Roman Catholic, was martyred for responding to the cries, needs and prayers of his people concerning their poverty, oppression and social injustices. He opposed the tortures and assassinations of his nuns, priests and others.

Fatima Al-Mutairi of Saudi Arabia died for the faith at age 26 proclaiming to her family that 'the way of Christ is the most pure and most holy way of all'.

These Christians are the ones we know, but there are countless others who, although nameless, have kept the faith which authentically links them to Christ, who lived out the Beatitudes on Calvary's cross. He calls us, too, to take up our cross and walk the path of righteousness for ours 'is the kingdom of heaven'.

† Teach us, gracious God, how to bear persecution in your service without counting the cost, so that your will may be fulfilled in us.

For further thought

• There are Christians right now, being beaten, tortured, imprisoned and killed for their faith in and testimony of Christ. Remember to pray for them.

Wednesday 26 July
Visible and alive

Matthew 5:13–16

You are the salt of the earth … You are the light of the world … (part of verses 13 and 14)

My ministry began on the tiny island of Utila, Bay Islands, belonging to the Republic of Honduras. There my feet were my chief mode of travel. Everywhere I went I was visible.

Christians are called by Jesus to be both salt and light. We are challenged to season our lives with salt in order to make a difference in our society. We are to purify and impact lives; light exists to shine. Salt, although hardly visible, adds taste to our food, but light, however, is dominantly visible in the dark. They are both therefore immensely valuable. Salt at one time was the equivalent of money, for it was used to pay Roman soldiers their salaries (Latin, *salarium*). Christ tells us to season and preserve the best qualities of our lives to influence the lost, poor, needy, suffering, ostracised, neglected, perishing and others for the kingdom. Functioning as salt requires that we be lovable, merciful, peaceable and remain pure of heart. When we are no longer bearing our savour, our 'saltiness' (Mark 9:50), we will become dull, useless and tasteless. Jesus declares himself the Light of the World in John 8:12. He is both the energy and symbol of light. His presence and relevance are always revealed in the darkness of sin, political corruption, as well as the ills, fears and pains of daily living. Our light, as a reflection of the light of Christ, must shine throughout the world.

I pray that as one of many lights, I too led people living on the island of Utila to the true Light, Jesus Christ.

† Lord, season us with your salt and pour your holy light into our lives, that we may devote our lives, love, and mercy, in your service.

For further thought

• What must you do to become the salt of the earth and the light of the world?

Jesus fulfils God's holy law

Readings in Matthew (3) – Lesley G Anderson

Matthew 5:17–20

Do not think that I have come to abolish the law or the prophets; I have come not to abolish but to fulfill. (verse 17)

Christ is the key to how we Christians ought to relate to God's holy law (covenant, agreement, bond). The first law was necessary, but limited. As a result, we learn from Matthew 5:17 that Christ came therefore not to abolish the law, but to perfect or complete it. Interestingly, Jesus makes a paradigm shift by radicalising and making 'obsolete' the external value of the law (Hebrews 8:13). He introduces the internal value of the law by embracing 'the new covenant' of Jeremiah 31, the law written on our heart, the law within us, what Galatians 6:2 refers to as, 'the law of Christ'. Christ intends that in all our words and actions we be morally and socially guided by his Sermon on the Mount on a variety of subjects including murder, marriage, lust, divorce, adultery and others. He encourages us to keep God's holy law, written on our heart, the Christian's guide to holy living and change of life.

A change of life – being converted, being born again – is the work of the Holy Spirit.

When we are filled with the Holy Spirit, we are motivated to repent of our sins, turn to Jesus and accept him as our Lord. When we believe in him, the Son of the living God, who humbly and willingly died for us that we might have everlasting life, he becomes our great sacrifice and righteousness. May grace and mercy which are found in the Gospels enable us all to live and delight in the law of Christ!

† O God, we believe, hope, and love you, and by faith pray and thank you for Jesus Christ, who writes his laws on our heart.

For further thought

- Jesus writes his laws on our heart. What do you understand by this statement? Will you not sin or make mistakes?

Do not commit murder: to murder is a sin

Matthew 5:21–26

You have heard that it was said to those of ancient times, 'You shall not murder'; and 'whoever murders shall be liable to judgment.' (verse 21)

The church was filled with Sunday morning worshippers. They came to worship God and to celebrate Mothers' Day. Then the news came that a man had murdered his mother. What a shock! The circumstance which led to her death on such a day has left an indelible mark on my mind. The mother took the initiative to seek reconciliation with her son over a land dispute. He hardened his heart and committed the dastardly act. Now he must face the inevitable judgement, punishment for his crime: long life in prison or death.

Murder is forbidden by the sixth commandment: 'You shall not murder' (Exodus 20:13). To murder or kill someone is to commit a grievous sin which can never be trivialised. Recalling that Jesus went further than the law into the very heart of humanity, we must endeavour to uphold the law of Christ. The spiritual implication is enormous for it includes an act of judgement. The Christian is called to share the peace and love of Christ and to hunger and thirst after his righteousness. Our togetherness as humans must link us to God, who identified himself with us in human flesh and died for us on Calvary's cross.

Christ affirmed that greed, hatred, murder, violence, revenge all stem from within us. They are the result of our freedom of will. Certainly, we cannot blame others for what we say or do. We can, however, learn how to forgive those who will do us harm. Let us overcome evil with good and conquer our adversaries by a superior moral power: grace.

† O Lord, deliver us from every evil thought, and action, and give us the power to live what we profess.

For further thought

• In what way can you express or show love for those who seek to do you harm?

Challenges and tragedies

Matthew 5:27–32

You have heard that it was said, 'You shall not commit adultery.' … It was also said, 'Whoever divorces his wife, let him give her a certificate of divorce.' (verses 27 and 31)

Cecilio Patterson and his spouse were active laypersons at Wesley Methodist Church in Panama. He was a self-employed accountant. She was president of the Wesley Women's League. One Sunday after worship she suffered a stroke which disabled her. It was during that crisis Cecilio gave up his busy schedule to tenderly care for his wife until her death.

Marriage and the union it symbolises can be the most sublime of human experiences. Let your love for your spouse serve as a bond to keep you together in Christ. Mark writes: 'Therefore what God has joined together, let no one separate' (Mark 10:9).

Families who have experienced either adultery or divorce or both can speak of their painful, destructive and devastating effects upon the couple, their family and/or relations. In verses 27–28 we are informed by Jesus that lust is a form of passion, which if misused or misdirected will lead to sin. When a couple marries, there is a commitment to uphold trust and faithfulness. The couple are expected to be married until death. In 1 Corinthians 13:8 Paul tells us: 'Love never ends.' Lust on the other hand is temporary. It sees the other person only as an object – a body. It is a hidden sin, and our desire to flirt distances us from God and our spouse. Jesus as a result places adultery in the eye and heart (the centre of our emotions and affections) before the actual act is committed. Jesus claimed the intention to sin a sin. He advocates self-mastery of the mind and body (verses 29–30).

May our marriages, too, be the most sublime of human experiences – with the help of Jesus and our dedication.

† O Lord, our God, enable us to honour you by being faithful to each other until death do we part.

For further thought

- Read again Matthew 5:29–30 and consider some positive ways of living out the text.

Fresh from the Word 2018

It may seem early, but *Fresh From the Word* 2018 is now available to order.

Order now:
- from your local IBRA Rep*
- in all good Christian bookshops
- direct from IBRA

To order direct from IBRA
- website: shop.christianeducation.org.uk
- email: ibra.sales@christianeducation.org.uk
- call: 0121 458 3313
- post: using the order form at the back of this book

Price £9.99 plus postage and packaging.

E-pub and Kindle versions are available.

Become an IBRA rep
*Do you order multiple copies of *Fresh From the Word* for yourself and your friends or people in your congregation or Bible study group?

When you order 3 or more copies direct from IBRA you will receive a 10% discount on your order of *Fresh From the Word*. You will also receive a free promotional pack each year to help you share IBRA more easily with family, friends and others at your church.

Would you consider leaving a legacy to IBRA?

What's valuable about a gift in your will to the International Bible Reading Association's International Fund is that every penny goes directly towards enabling hundreds of thousands of people around the world to access the living word of God.

IBRA has a rich history going back over 130 years. It was the vision of Charles Waters to enable people in Britain and overseas to benefit from the word of God through the experiences and insights of biblical scholars and teachers across the world. The vision was to build up people's lives in their homes and situations wherever they were. His legacy lives on today in you, as a reader, and the IBRA team.

Our work at IBRA is financed by the sales of the books, but from its very start in 1882, 100 per cent of donations to IBRA go to benefit our local and international readers. To continue this important work would you consider leaving a legacy in your will?

Find out more

Leaving a gift in your will to a Christian charity is a way of ensuring that this work continues for years to come: to help future generations and reach out to them with hope and the life-changing word of God – people we may never meet but who are all our brothers and sisters in Christ.

Through such a gift you will help continue the strong and lasting legacy of IBRA for generations to come!

To find out more please contact our Finance Officer on 0121 458 3313, by email to ibra@christianeducation.org.uk or by writing to International Bible Reading Association, 5–6 Imperial Court, 12 Sovereign Road, Birmingham B30 3FH

- To read more about the history of IBRA go to page 29.
- To find out more about the work of the IBRA International Fund go to pages 369–371.

Readings in Matthew (3)
Love and prayer

Notes based on the New Revised Standard Version by **Bruce Jenneker**

The Very Reverend Bruce Jenneker is Rector of All Saints Anglican Church, Durbanville, in Cape Town, and Senior Priest of the Diocese of Saldanha Bay. He spent 26 years in the USA – at St Alban's Church and Washington National Cathedral in Washington DC, and as Associate Rector of Trinity Church, Copley Square, Boston. He has also served at St George's Cathedral, Cape Town. Bruce's interests are liturgy and worship. He chaired the Standing Commission on Liturgy and Music of The Episcopal Church, serves on the Liturgical Committee of the Anglican Church of Southern Africa and has taught liturgy at seminaries.

Sunday 30 July
Singleness of heart

Matthew 5:33–37

Let your word be 'Yes, Yes' or 'No, No'; anything more than this comes from the evil one. (verse 37)

The Jesus that Matthew presents in his Gospel stands in the tradition of the wise teacher, one who is attuned to the meaning of life and knows its lessons well enough to pass them on. His Jesus is also the fulfilment of all that the prophets foretold, the Messiah of their prophesies. More than just a wise life-coach, Jesus actually has the words of eternal life – his teachings and precepts in fact open the way to living life abundantly, here and now, in the fullness of all God's promises.

At the heart of Jesus' teaching is a call to a profound personal integrity that is a reflection of the image of God in which each human person is created. This integrity is fundamental, given and essential to human existence. It is not a legalistic adherence to laws or ordinances; in fact, this God-given integrity precedes all our choices. It is a reflection of the integrity – the honesty, truthfulness, trustworthiness, righteousness and holiness – of God. The divine integrity is lodged within us, hidden perhaps, but present nonetheless.

Jesus intends to lead his followers to the recognition, development and actualisation of that integrity – which is their nature, their vocation and their fulfilment.

† Pray for an understanding of the integrity of God and for the grace that will uncover that integrity in all you are and do.

Monday 31 July
Turning the world upside down

Matthew 5:38–42

But I say to you, Do not resist an evildoer. But if anyone strikes you on the right cheek, turn the other also. (verse 39)

In Matthew 5 the evangelist records five times that Jesus says: 'You have heard it said … but I say to you.' In each instance Jesus is overturning conventional wisdom: the prohibition on murder becomes a judgement on destroying relationships through anger and cruel words; the prohibition on adultery becomes a judgement of the lust that reduces another person to an object; the prohibition on swearing falsely becomes a judgement of claiming external, even heavenly support for one's actions and promises; the prohibition of the universal law of 'an eye for an eye and a tooth for a tooth' becomes an invitation to overturn hostility with generosity, to undermine violence with excessive, extravagant and costly bigheartedness. The last somersault in this series of revolutionary overturnings of common sense, fair play and good judgement is the most radical of them all: the time-honoured patterns of hatred and love must be reconfigured so that hatred is cast out and love conquers all.

Here again, Jesus is invoking the integrity of God as the essential identity of human persons. Not sordid murder, but divine connectedness defines the human person; not immoral and lustful diminishment of persons into sex objects, but divine recognition of the dignity and wholeness of every person; not the repugnant vehemence of calling the heavens to witness words and actions, but divine trustworthiness; not so-called blind justice and retribution, but divine generosity and kindness; not the narrow miserliness of refusing to share oneself, but the divine embrace of all others, those like us and those most different from us.

† Pray for a spirit willing to see your world of everyday actions and choices from God's perspective. How frequently and successfully are you turning your world upside down?

For further thought

• Why is challenging accepted wisdom and conventional choices so difficult? How have you turned your world upside down in the last few weeks?

Tuesday 1 August
The counsel of perfection

Matthew 5:43–48

Be perfect, therefore, as your heavenly Father is perfect. (verse 48)

In the original Greek, this statement of Jesus, often described as the counsel of perfection, is an imperative – an ideal and future hope expressed as a reality definitely to be achieved. A more fulsome translation of 5:48 would be: You must be perfect – all the time growing into more and more complete maturity of godliness in mind and character, reaching the divine height of virtue and integrity – as your heavenly Father is perfect. This verse serves as a conclusion to this section of Jesus' teaching; it sums up all that he has been trying to impart about the true nature of the human condition and experience: that it is ordered for and oriented to true godliness, nothing less.

It is a sad fact that in ordinary language the phrase, derived from this statement of Jesus – the counsel of perfection – is used to refer to something that of its nature cannot be achieved. It would be the counsel of perfection to ask someone to forgive some grievous hurt and woundedness. And yet that is precisely what should happen.

Abundant life, life lived fully, confidently reaching for the best of all possible worlds, is a life that recognises and celebrates the integrity of God, recognises and celebrates the human vocation to grow into that divine integrity, and with disciplined intentionality seeks to grow into it.

† Pray for freedom from pride so that you can recognise the perfection to which you are called, and the humility to ask for the grace to become what you are called to be.

For further thought

• What aspects of God's integrity are most missing from your life? What will help you reflect God's integrity more fully?

Wednesday 2 August
Purity of heart

Matthew 6:1–8

Your Father knows what you need before you ask him. (part of verse 8)

Having challenged his followers to grow into the perfection of God's integrity, Jesus turns now to the practice of religion. In the culture in which he lived, religion, religious practice and rituals were integral and unavoidable aspects of everyday life, both personal and social. It would have been hard to identify anything more important than religion and religious practice.

In these exhortations Jesus seeks to move his listeners away from the practice of religion to the spirituality of belief, from the doing of religious duties to an authentic engagement with God. It is one thing, Jesus is saying, to do what religious practice demands; it is quite another thing to live into the spirituality from which those actions and commitments derive and to which they are intended ultimately to lead us.

Here is the classic distinction between law and grace. The law prescribes the correct fulfilling of the defining precepts; grace is surrender into the embrace of God and life in that relationship – for which, at best, the law is a guarantee.

It is God who is the ground of our being; it is God who is at the heart of our reality. Jesus is inviting his followers to live into this truth, to claim it and to revel in it, rather than commit themselves to an unswerving focus on a burdensome set of laws that are impossible to fulfil. The God Jesus presents is not won over by works; rather, since God already knows what we need, it is our trusting surrender, confident faith and sincere gratitude that moves God's heart.

† Pray for an openness to experiencing God as the divine embrace that seeks and finds you, and finding you treasures you unconditionally, providing what you need.

For further thought

• How do you integrate meeting the demands of religious practice with commitment to loving God with all that you are?

Thursday 3 August
Forgiveness – our context and our vocation

Matthew 6:9–15

Do not bring us to the time of trial, but rescue us from the evil one. (verse 13)

In Matthew's version of the Lord's Prayer, it is debts that are to be forgiven, while in Luke's version it is sins that are to be forgiven. Perhaps, in their history of adherence to a legal code by Matthew's Jewish hearers, the legal imbalance of a debt most aptly described the reality of broken relationships. Luke, writing for Greeks, has the tragic flaw that undermines and the burden that crushes in mind when he chooses sin to describe what rends people asunder and fractures their relationship with God.

But while for both evangelists the point is forgiveness, this is all the more so for Matthew who adds further words about the need for forgiveness, the requirement to be forgiving and that God will withhold forgiveness from the unforgiving.

It can be said that forgiveness is at the heart of Christianity. God forgives the sin of the Fall in the loving gift of the Only-begotten. As he is dying, the Only-begotten prays that his betrayers and executioners should be forgiven, 'for they do not know what they are doing'. We affirm in the Creeds that we believe in 'the forgiveness of sin'. Forgiveness is the medium in which we live, the spiritual air we breathe.

In South Africa, imperialism, colonialism and apartheid have fractured and wounded, oppressed and exploited millions over centuries riddled with prejudice and racism. The Truth and Reconciliation Commission has forged a path of forgiveness and reconciliation. We are learning to walk that path. It is a path which all of us, everywhere, each on our own contexts, must learn to walk.

† Pray for a readiness to accept that life is a continually unfolding opportunity to be forgiving and be forgiven; to receive every day as unlimited opportunity to forgive and be forgiven.

For further thought

• What makes being truly forgiving difficult? Who and what have you found most difficult to forgive?

What's the bottom line?

Matthew 6:16–21
Where your treasure is, there your hearts will be also. (verse 21)

This passage will be familiar to many as the Gospel read on Ash Wednesday. When it is read on that occasion, the focus is appropriately on fasting and piety (and almsgiving, in the longer reading). But this teaching of Jesus is of a piece with all that has gone before in chapters 5 and 6. Jesus is calling his hearers to a thoughtful way of life in which they focus on the ultimate, understanding the particulars for what they are. Worship is adoration of God in the first, middle and last place. Fasting is an aspect of that adoration, as are all forms of piety, including almsgiving. They are the tasks and projects of religion and as such they are in service of a higher goal, that of surrender to and intimacy with God.

An often-repeated African proverb says: I pointed you to the stars and all you saw were my fingertips. Fasting, piety and almsgiving, like all other practices and duties of religion, are merely fingertips pointing to the amazing and life-giving wonder of intimacy with God. It is this incredible intimacy that we yearn for and seek; it is the impetus for all our religious practices. Of course when the intimacy is in place then what were religious practices become acts of love and devotion, offered freely, not because they are required.

Jesus ends this reflection by returning to his focus on purity of the heart. Singlemindedness, a clear and consistent focus on what truly matters, is expressed in his caution about storing up treasures.

† Pray for the gift of surrender to and intimacy with God: that God's embrace becomes the point of reading scripture, the benefit of study, the blessing of fasting, the joy of service.

For further thought
• Why is it easy to focus on fingertips and miss seeing the stars? What makes practices accessible and intimacy with God remote?

Readings in Matthew (3) – Bruce Jenneker

August

Saturday 5 August
Living with darkness – choosing the light

Matthew 6:22–24

The eye is the lamp of the body. So, if your eye is healthy, your whole body will be full of light; but if your eye is unhealthy, your whole body will be full of darkness. (verses 22–23)

We end our week of reflections on verses from Matthew 5–6 where we started. Jesus is calling those who follow him to a profound personal integrity that is a reflection of the integrity God. This divine integrity is fundamental; human existence is ordered and graced for it. The divine integrity is lodged within us, hidden perhaps, but present nonetheless.

There is an aspect of wholeness to integrity: it is not divided, compartmentalised, split into component parts. Like the unity of the Trinity in whose likeness we are created, we are differentiated and yet whole.

How we see things is crucial. The perspective we bring to bear on reality defines our relationship with it. Do we see the world, all that is in it and all that happens in it, as in the embrace of the Love-that-Holds-the-Universe-Together? Or do we see the world as numberless vortices of experience randomly spinning in and out of one another? Or do we see the world as elements for a magician's show with God as the magician?

It is often said that perception is half the truth. If the light of God's love and purposes radiates your perception, you will perceive reality in one way. On the other hand, if your perception is overcast with a pessimistic view of the destiny of humanity, then you will perceive reality as going to hell in a hand-basket. If you are focused, integrated and reaching for intimacy with God, you will engage reality from the perspective of wholeness and integrity. On that path lies salvation.

† Pray for the eyes of your spirit to be open and alert, able to see the light and ready to respond to it with all that you are and all that you have to offer.

For further thought

• What darkness encroaches on your sight? What can you do to allow the light to penetrate that darkness?

Readings in Matthew (3)
Building on rock

Notes based on the New Revised Standard Version by **Mandy Briggs**

 Revd Mandy Briggs is a Methodist minister who lives in Bristol. She is the Education and Outreach Officer at the New Room (John Wesley's Chapel), the oldest Methodist building in the world, on the Web at www.newroombristol.org.uk. Mandy and the New Room are on Twitter at @mandbristol and @NewRoomBristol.

Sunday 6 August
Don't worry, be happy!

Matthew 6:25–34

Therefore I tell you, do not worry about your life, what you will eat or what you will drink, or about your body, what you will wear. Is not life more than food, and the body more than clothing? (verse 25)

Over the next week we're going to continue looking at the Gospel of Matthew, focusing on passages from the Sermon on the Mount.

Today's reading encourages us not to worry about what we will eat, drink or wear. Very apt, considering that the readings we're going to be looking at from Matthew 6 and 7 are like a veritable feast of Jesus' teaching. We won't try to digest it all at once though – it's better in daily bite-size chunks!

It's very easy to live a life worrying about things; if we don't have enough to eat or drink, we want more; yet if we *do* have enough, we may still fret about what we don't have. Does that make sense?

There is a danger that we can lose perspective and fail to see the bigger picture – the fact that we are deeply loved and cared for by God, no matter what. Whatever our situation, worry doesn't work. There is a good analogy in the film *Van Wilder* relating worry to a rocking chair – rocking but going nowhere.

This week's readings are full of practical advice and sayings to puzzle over. Happy feasting!

† Jesus, as many people listened to you on the mountainside, may I also listen to your words this week.

Monday 7 August
Is there something in your eye?

Matthew 7:1–6

Why do you see the speck in your neighbour's eye, but do not notice the log in your own eye? (verse 3)

It was late afternoon and I was waiting for a bus. It had been a long day and I was tired. I wanted to get home as soon as possible but it was rush hour and the journey would be slow.

When it arrived, the bus was crowded. It was a double-decker and there were no seats on the bottom deck so I climbed the stairs to the top deck. There was a seat right at the front, so I took it gratefully, smiling at the young woman listening to her headphones who already took up the other half of the double seat.

I glanced across the aisle. A woman in her twenties, wearing fashionable makeup and clothes, had positioned herself across the other double seat so that she and her bag took up two spaces. 'That's terrible,' I thought. 'If someone gets on at the next stop and needs a seat, she'll just make sure her bag is in the way so they have to sit somewhere else.'

The next stop came. A mum with three children got on and they made their way up the stairs. Immediately, the woman shifted over to the window side of the double seat so one of the children could sit next to her.

I was immediately ashamed of myself. I had judged the woman to be selfish but in the end she shared the double seat with someone who needed it.

The log in my eye felt rather large at that moment.

† God who sees, help me to be aware of the ways in which I judge other people. Help me to see them with your eyes of love.

For further thought

• If you are going somewhere today, pray for those who are travelling alongside you, whoever they are.

Tuesday 8 August
Asking, seeking, knocking

Matthew 7:7–12

Ask, and it will be given you; search, and you will find; knock, and the door will be opened for you. (verse 7)

More than 40 years ago, an American singer named Janis Joplin sang a song that sounded like a consumer's prayer, asking the Lord to buy her a Mercedes-Benz to overtop her friends in their Porsches.

I must admit that when I have read this verse about asking, seeking and knocking before, I tended to place it in a personal context. What is it that I want, what is it that I seek, what is it that I want to knock on doors about?

It's all very well praying for a posh car, but it comes across as quite a selfish prayer. I would like to suggest that God promises to supply our *needs*, but not necessarily all our *wants*.

Have you ever considered this verse in a community context? What are the things that your community wants to ask for, what are they seeking, what issues do they want to knock on doors about?

In a global context, this particular verse challenges me to get involved. It challenges me to use the 'ask, search, knock' principle as a motivation to get involved, to call for change in government policy, to campaign against unjust practices which affect millions caught in poverty around the world.

Change will not come instantly. It takes persistence, courage, prayer. There may be frustration and impatience along the way. But this is about more than just a new motor.

† God, forgive me when I base my prayer life around myself. Help me to pray for the needs of my community and for the world.

For further thought
• Is faith in the God of Matthew 7:7 passive or active?

How low can you go?

Matthew 7:13–14

For the gate is narrow and the road is hard that leads to life, and there are few who find it. (verse 14)

It is an interesting experience trying to enter the Church of the Nativity in Bethlehem. This famous church, which is a World Heritage Site, is built over the place where it is traditionally considered that Jesus was born.

Tourists and pilgrims visit in their thousands every year, eager to pray and take photos of the grotto which is said to mark the exact spot where the infant was placed in the manger.

With the number of visitors dropping in, you would expect that there would be large, wide doors to make it easy for everyone to gain access. But you would be wrong.

The main entrance door to the Church of the Nativity is small and low and narrow, and you have to bend down to get through it into the main body of the church. There is something very profound about stooping low in order to gain access. Just as Jesus came into this world as a vulnerable child, so we have to lose our height and pride and bend low to come closer to the site of the manger. It's a very powerful thing to do.

Jesus said 'I am the Way.' Following this path of faith may mean taking a different route than the one our family and friends are taking. It may be difficult and there may be obstacles along the way. Yet Jesus promises that this way, the vulnerable way, will lead to life.

† Light the path before me, Lord Jesus, that I may follow your way even when the route is difficult to see.

For further thought

• Find out more about the Church of the Nativity at sacred-destinations.com/israel/bethlehem-church-of-the-nativity

Thursday 10 August
A good fruitcake?

Matthew 7:15–20

In the same way, every good tree bears good fruit, but the bad tree bears bad fruit. (verse 17)

I'm a big fan of the *Great British Bake Off*, which airs on the BBC in the UK and has been spread around the world. Amateur bakers compete against each other to produce mouth-watering delicacies including bread, pies and cakes. One baker gets sent home each week while another is crowned 'Star Baker'. Eventually the last three bakers compete in the final for the Bake Off title.

You might think that watching people baking on TV is utterly boring. You can't smell or taste the food, you can only see others creating it. But for me there is something fascinating about seeing how each baker chooses ingredients, plans their recipe and creates the final bake.

Most of the time the ingredients they choose go well together and they create something delicious. Sometimes, they go for slightly unconventional ingredients which do not always work (I think black squid ink featured in one recipe!). Sometimes things go very, very wrong – woe betide you if you get a 'soggy bottom' in your pie!

My point? It's important what goes in and it's also important what comes out. The passage from Matthew today emphasises this. How do you test a person's authenticity? By looking at the quality of their words and actions, their compassion and the way they treat others. In other words, what comes out!

† God, may the fruits of how I live out my faith and life bring nourishment to others.

For further thought

• How can you use your gifts and graces to bless someone else today?

Readings in Matthew (3) – Mandy Briggs

August

The moment of truth

Matthew 7:21–23

Not everyone who says to me, 'Lord, Lord,' will enter the kingdom of heaven, but only the one who does the will of my Father in heaven. (verse 21)

Presenters of singing and dancing reality contests have recently developed an annoying habit when announcing their results – there is often a HUGE pause before the winner is announced.

It may be there to string out the suspense, it may be there so that the cameras can capture tension and reactions … but it is always there, annoying the audience, who just want to find out who has won.

I wonder if, on the day of judgement, there will be a similar long drawn out pause. This is a difficult passage because the images it presents are harsh – here is Jesus suggesting that not everyone will get into the kingdom of heaven, only those who obey his Father. Even some of those who have been preaching and healing in his name may not be admitted.

We're back to the idea of false prophets and trees bearing good or bad fruit. Deeds and words look good on the surface, and even false prophets can do wonderful things; but what matters here is not the outward appearance, but a sound relationship with God.

These verses seem harsh; but for me they emphasise the fact that God knows us entirely and utterly. God knows the motives of our hearts. If we are not trying to follow God's paths, but are doing things to make ourselves look good or to build a personal powerbase, God sees. The challenge here is to examine our motives and walk humbly with our God.

† Search me, O God, and know my heart; test me and know my thoughts. See if there is any wicked way in me and lead me in the way everlasting (Psalm 139:23–24).

For further thought
• If we feel uncomfortable at the thought of being judged, consider how often we are the ones who actually do the judging.

Saturday 12 August
Firm foundations – for all

Matthew 7:24–29

Everyone then who hears these words of mine and acts on them will be like a wise man who built his house on rock. (verse 24)

I remember singing about this story as a young person in Sunday school and taking great pleasure in doing the actions to illustrate the rains coming down and the floods coming up, the house on the rock standing firm but the house on the sand falling FLAT (with an added handclap for dramatic effect).

The traditional approach to this passage is to emphasise the importance of firm foundations. Don't build your life upon the shifting sands of uncertainty, instead make strong foundations by making a commitment to follow the teachings of Jesus, which will underpin your life and strengthen you when storms come.

That's the traditional approach – but again, for me this story works itself out in a global way. Climate change, floods and storms mean that thousands of people who live in very basic housing are at risk from very real and dangerous weather situations. Their houses could very literally fall flat.

I think of organisations like Habitat for Humanity, who work at community level in over seventy countries around the world, enabling housing problems to be solved through collaborations between volunteers and local people. Or Shelter – the UK-based housing and homelessness charity which works and campaigns for safe and affordable housing for all.

The foundations which we seek to build are not just made of faith and prayer, they are also strengthened by practical action which make hope a reality for those who long for shelter and a place to really call home – whatever the weather.

† When we build, strengthen us. When we fear, comfort us. When we are in need, provide for us, O God of compassion and mercy.

For further thought
• What are the housing issues and needs in your community?

When I look at the heavens
Let there be light(s)

Notes based on the New Revised Standard Version by **Nathan Eddy**

Nathan Eddy is editor of *Fresh From the Word*, a freelance writer and editor, and an aspiring stargazer. He is proud of his roots in the United Church of Christ, USA, and he has served as minister in the United Reformed Church and as a university chaplain (he's now a student again, doing a PhD in the Psalms). He once spent a summer interviewing silver miners about their lives in Colorado, and lives in London with his wife Clare and their two daughters. You can find him in a library, or standing in the middle of the room having forgotten why he went in, or on Facebook through the Fresh From the Word Facebook group.

Sunday 13 August
Mindful of mortals

Psalm 8

When I look at your heavens, the work of your fingers, the moon and the stars which you have established ... (verse 3)

My four-year-old niece has a treasured possession: a snow globe with tiny snowman inside. She shakes it and holds it up to the camera when we are talking on the computer; all I see is the silent, swirling universe of tiny plastic flakes and her fingertips.

Something of the vastness inside that snow globe, and a child's hands, capture the vision the cosmos as seen by the Old Testament, including Psalm 8. Even the tiniest human creature is inseparable in the Bible from the vast heavens. 'What are human beings that you are mindful of them, mortals, that you care for them?' (verse 4).

There is no dispassionate stargazing in the Bible. To consider the stars is to do theology – to ask what it means to be human, to consider the grandeur of God. Why we are here? What is God up to?

Take the chance this week to reflect both on the majesty of the cosmos and on the deepest questions of human life. We, too, do theology when we stargaze. God has entrusted us with a breath-taking responsibility in a fragile world; a world as alluring, and as vulnerable, as a globe held in a child's hands.

† God of the starry sky, humble us with your majesty, charge our world with your grandeur, and lift our gaze.

Monday 14 August
Light of light

Genesis 1:14–19

And God said, 'Let there be lights in the dome of the sky to separate the day from the night; and let them be for signs and for seasons and for days and years, and let them … give light upon the earth.' And it was so. (verses 14–15)

The high point of the annual carol service in Union Chapel, London, is the passing of the light through the dark wooden sanctuary. Candle by candle, a thousand worshippers pass the flame throughout the curved space until the darkness is pricked with flickering points of light.

The creation of light is the first act of God's creation (Genesis 1:3), and God's separating of light from darkness marks the start of day and night. Yet not until today's reading, Day 4, does God create the heavenly bodies. In between, dry land has emerged and bushes and trees have sprung up and borne fruit. Light, apparently, comes from God himself. Like the play of light on a shimmering surface, this light of God dances across the Bible; the shining of God's face is a blessing in Numbers 6:25, and, like a bookend to Genesis 1, light is central to the concluding vision of the whole Bible in Revelation 22.

Only God, who clothes himself in light as with a garment (Psalm 104:2), is the author of light. Yet God sees it as 'good' that the sun, moon and stars all have power of their own and rule over day and night (verse 16). The heavenly bodies are not objects of worship, but they have an essential role to play all on their own: lighting the earth, sending messages, and marking the seasons (verse 14).

I am struck that God sees fit to give these crucial roles to the sun, moon and stars. We, too, even if we just hold up a candle, can bring that everlasting light of God into the world.

† Creative God, open our eyes, that in your light we might see true light (Psalm 36:9).

For further thought

• What do you think the primordial, uncreated divine light would look like, and feel like?

When I look at the heavens – Nathan Eddy

August

Tuesday 15 August
Of stars and families

> **Genesis 26:1–5**
>
> *I will make your offspring as numerous as the stars of heaven, and will give to your offspring all these lands. (verse 4)*

Most astrophysics textbooks don't delve into the ups and downs of family life, but the Bible is different. The star-throwing God of Genesis 1 and Psalm 8 has no qualms about not only shaping the first humans with his hands (Genesis 2) but also calling an individual, and staying faithful to his family over generations. Stars might seem distant and even impersonal to us, yet in Genesis 26 they are a sign of a very personal promise. God tells Isaac that his descendants will be as numerous as stars (verse 4). God's faith extends to the human family as surely as it does to the heavens.

A display window in Selfridges on London's Oxford Street gave me pause in December the year before last. The theme was the zodiac and the universe; one window was brim-full with cut stones representing the 300 billion stars in our galaxy, the Milky Way. Star upon star, upon star.

Sometimes I just want stars to be stars; I don't want the majesty of the night sky to be reduced to human concerns. Yet this family of Isaac is special; it is God's concern that it flourish, for the sake of all the nations (verse 4). A star guided the wise men to the holy family, and here, too, stars are a sign of great things to come for Isaac's family. What are all mortals, God, that you are mindful of them?

† God of Isaac and Rebekah, to whom ordinary families are as important as the starry host, help us to value our families as much as you do.

For further thought

• The Milky Way is tiny compared to so-called elliptical galaxies, which can be twenty times its size.

Wednesday 16 August
Against idol worship

Deuteronomy 4:15–20

When you look up to the heavens and see the sun, the moon and the stars, all the host of heaven, do not be led astray and bow down to them and serve them. (part of verse 19)

Near the southern tip of the island of Manhattan, around the corner from Wall Street, stands the National Museum of the American Indian. One summer we stumbled into it, and were transfixed by the displays of contemporary art and design. My daughters in particular were struck by the video footage of a recent rain dance playing on a massive screen.

Like many cultures in ancient times and today, ancient Israelites believed their behaviour, their faith, was connected to the coming of the rain. Deuteronomy is particularly insistent on the connection between faithful observance of the heart and God's gift of rain: 'If you will only heed his every commandment that I am commanding you today – loving the Lord your God, and serving him with all your heart and with all your soul – then he will give the rain for your land its season' (11:13). Confuse the stars for gods and God would make plain his displeasure by turning the sky to bronze and the earth to iron (28:23). If no rain fell, then the Israelites needed to take a hard look at themselves.

We might be reluctant to see God behind all weather, but in the age of global warming, I wonder if we, like ancient Israel, understand that our practices profoundly impact the environment. Our worship at the false idols of constant consumption and limitless development will have consequences. We, too, need to choose the God we worship in our fragile world, and turn from idols to the true and living God of Israel, the God of Jesus Christ. God desires true worship of the heart and the flourishing of all life here on earth, and the stakes are very high indeed.

† God of creation, inspire in us a holy zeal to renew the earth and live on it in peace.

For further thought

• What idols need knocking down in your walk of faith? Ask for God's help to identify them.

Starry army

Joshua 10:12–15

And the sun stood still, and the moon stopped, until the nation took vengeance on their enemies. (verse 13)

It is not exactly clear how the stopping of the sun helped Israel. It may be that the lengthening of the day enabled the hailstorm that God sent to inflict maximum damage on the Amorites (see verse 11), or that the sun and moon were imagined to block the exits of the valley. Regardless, it is significant that for the writer of the passage, the miracle in view is not the 'laws of nature' being circumvented, but God obeying a human being. In verse 14, we read that 'there has been no day like it before or since, when the Lord heeded a human voice; for the Lord fought for Israel'. The stopping of the sun indicates as much God's compassion and desire to save as it does his raw power. Given the slaughter in view in the passage, it might sound morally suspect to see God's compassion there, but this seems to be the perspective of the ancient passage itself.

Whatever else happened in the battle that day, the very cosmos itself showed itself to be God's loyal servants. Sun and moon were agents of salvation and deliverance. Christianity in particular occupies a different place in society today than the fledgling, upstart nation depicted in Joshua. We are wary today of stories of a violent God, and we should be. But we can find hope that all the starry host are aligned with God's purposes of peace and justice in the Bible. This, perhaps, is the true miracle – that the cosmos listens to God, and God that day listened to Joshua.

† God of peace, all creation yearns for your just rule. Like the sun and moon, help us be your agents, that peace might reign on earth.

For further thought

• If someone asked you, what stories from the Bible would you say highlight God's concern for peace?

Friday 18 August
Solomon's house

2 Chronicles 2:1–12

I am now about to build a house for the name of the Lord my God and dedicate it to him ... for burnt offerings morning and evening, on the sabbaths and the new moons and the appointed festivals of the Lord our God. (part of verse 4)

One of the pleasures of my day is a cup of coffee and a stretch or two listening to early morning radio before the school rush. I grew up in dairy-farming country in New England, USA, and living now in London I take a special delight in *Farming Today*, a news programme about farming and agriculture in the UK. The animal sounds and down-to-earth tone are slender threads that connect me to the food I buy and to the cycle of the seasons.

They didn't need a radio show to be reminded of the agricultural year in ancient Israel. Life depended on crops and the weather. After a hot, dry summer, life-giving rains came (and come today) in the autumn to Palestine, and a wet winter provided the water necessary for growth. The main harvest festival, Sukkot, or Booths, took place at the autumn harvest, before the rains returned and the cycle started again.

As Solomon suggests in his prayer, the cycle of the moon, sun and stars was intimately related to the liturgical season. Life depended on God's faithfulness to crop and field. In the UK today, as I know from *Farming Today*, farmers use remote controls to manoeuvre their tractors and apps on their phones to record the movement of livestock. But their livelihood, their survival, and ours, depends just as much on the cycle of moon, sun and stars sustained by God. As Solomon says, 'Who is able to build him a house, since heaven, even highest heaven, cannot contain him?' (verse 6).

† Living God, in this moment of study and reflection I offer this small sacrifice of my life itself.

For further thought

• Temples were seen in the ancient world as dwellings for God and as a connection between earth and heaven. How are worship spaces conceived in your tradition?

Not one forgotten

Isaiah 40:12–26

Lift up your eyes on high and see: Who created these? (verse 26)

I confess to a certain snobbery when I stumble across a horoscope in the newspaper. Star signs seem like random or wishful thinking at best, and a suspect practice at worst.

Horoscopes are a far cry from Genesis 1, but this week we have seen that stars and star signs were taken with seriousness in the ancient world. Partly this is because nature was not wholly separated from divine forces for these ancient writers. As we have seen this week, sun, moon and stars ruled day and night, marked the cycle of the seasons and even acted co-operatively as God's army. Light in particular was hardly just what helped you find your way at night; it could also be viewed as an aspect of God's garment – God's self.

I am not about to start reading my horoscope, but I am fascinated by the intimate way God is attentive to the cosmos, and the cosmos to God. Not one star is missing because of God's attentive care (verse 26). Each one is named and known by God, even those unknown to us – stars so far away from earth that their light hasn't reached us yet. God's ways are ultimately as mysterious as the universe is immeasurable (who except God, indeed, has marked off the heavens with a span, as verse 12 says?). But the sun and the night sky can indeed offer witness to a personal God who creates, who empowers, who elects a people and who saves. That is something special indeed.

† God of the world's salvation, I praise you for your care for little and great.

For further thought

• What do stars symbolise today? Notice them in books and magazines around you.

When I look at the heavens
The heavens proclaim

Notes based on the New Revised Standard Version by **Ian Fosten**

Ian Fosten is a director of a community theatre, a poet and leader of the ministry team for Norwich Area United Reformed Churches in the UK. He lives on the Suffolk coast with his wife and youngest children. He helped set up the St Cuthbert's Centre mission project on Holy Island (Lindisfarne). He has a particular interest in connections between theology and landscape. His poetry and writing is found at www.fosten.com.

Sunday 20 August
The heavens proclaim

Psalm 19

The heavens are telling the glory of God; and the firmament proclaims his handiwork. ... The law of the Lord is perfect, reviving the soul; ... the precepts of the Lord are right, rejoicing the heart. (verses 1, 7a and 8a)

Generally speaking, the thrust of Western education has been to train students in focused investigation. All life is seen as raw material to be examined, analysed, dissected, explained and understood. You need only to consider the achievements of science, technology and a range of disciplines to see what benefits flow from this approach. There are, however, limits to its usefulness, not least the implied belief that to understand something is to be its master. It only takes a spell of extreme weather, a stock exchange wobble or even finding ourselves without an Internet connection to undermine the shakiness of this perceived mastery.

Our readings this week encourage us to consider the world in a different way. Instead of hunched, close focus we are invited to straighten up and lift our eyes to the vastness and wonder of all that God has made. We are given permission to explore those things which are sometimes better appreciated by the heart rather than solely by the intellect. Today's reading replaces investigation with wonder and so draws us into the psalmist's delight in the order and splendour of creation, and also into the wholesome purpose of living well in God's way.

† Quietly take notice of your surroundings without attempting to classify or explain. Receive as a gift the people, the sights that are there before you.

Monday 21 August
Song of the stars

Job 38:1–7

Then the Lord answered Job out of the whirlwind: 'Where were you when I laid the foundation of the earth? … On what were its bases sunk, or who laid its cornerstone … when the morning stars sang together and all the heavenly beings shouted for joy?' (verses 1, 4, 6 and 7)

Cornwall, the county in the farthest south-west of England, is a place associated with spiritual sensitivity. Throughout the landscape, notably in sight of the two highest moorland peaks, large stones were levered into position thousands of years ago. Their purpose is not known for sure but veneration of 'the numinous' seems the most likely explanation. In August 1999, a group of youngsters travelled down to Cornwall in order to witness a total eclipse of the sun. The group was boisterous and full of fun and conversation as they sat on a cliff top and waited. As the eclipse began, the morning darkened, the birds ceased their singing and the youngsters all fell quiet, awed by the intense 'otherness' of the moment. Many of those bright young people could easily have explained the mechanics of this astronomical event, yet they realised intuitively that they had participated in something more than simply the alignment of earth, sun and moon. When the sun reappeared and the day took up where it had left off and conversation returned with the birdsong, each person carried with them an experience which words, somehow, could not enclose.

In God's response to Job's questioning, we are shown a point at which human explanation becomes redundant and the mystery of God's purpose flows in its place. To find ourselves in this place is not to experience intellectual failure but to pass through a doorway from knowledge into faith, and to travel lightly in the company of him who 'laid the foundation of the earth' and taught the stars to sing.

† Loving God, when I am overwhelmed by circumstances that I can neither control nor understand, may fear and anger be replaced by trust in your mysterious yet all-enfolding love.

For further thought

• Today, parts of Western Europe and North and South America will experience a solar eclipse. If you are able to, make an effort to safely observe it.

Tuesday 22 August
Namer of the stars

Psalm 147:1–11

How good it is to sing praises to our God; ... He heals the brokenhearted, and binds up their wounds. He determines the number of the stars; he gives to all of them their names. ... [He] takes pleasure in those who fear him, in those who hope in his steadfast love. (verses 1b, 3, 4 and 11)

I have always rather admired architects, not for their sometimes impressive earning potential, nor because, of all professions, they are allowed (or so it seems) to wear flamboyant bowties, but because of their ability to hold in mind both the overall plan and layout of a large built structure while, simultaneously, attending to the most minute detail of the finished project. Anyone who can deal with foundations, drainage, steelwork, bathroom taps and cupboard door handles with equal fastidiousness is, in my view, worthy of respect.

And the psalmist agrees with me! The God who sets the stars and names them, yet also cares intimately for individuals who are wounded and broken is indeed worthy of notice and respect. To contemplate with awe God who is vastly beyond our ability to comprehend and yet to know God in the tiniest joys and needs of everyday life, requires that we suspend our usual way of trying to grasp difficult ideas – overwhelming yet intimate? ... how can that be? – and instead relax into that intuitive way of knowing which is present in our deepest relationships. When we no longer need to explain or account for our affection, admiration or love we are then free to simply delight in the Beloved. How good it is to sing praises to our God!

† Rest comfortably and breathe in the vast incomprehensibility of God. After a few minutes, with each breath now draw in people and places about whom you are concerned. End with silent praise.

For further thought
- Are we so readily controlled by the need to be purposeful that we find it hard simply to praise God?

A star and the Messiah

When I look at the heavens – Ian Fosten

August

Matthew 2:1–12

In the time of King Herod, after Jesus was born in Bethlehem of Judea, wise men from the East came to Jerusalem, asking, 'Where is the child who has been born king of the Jews? For we observed his star at its rising, and have come to pay him homage.' (verses 1 and 2)

Taken at its face value, the story of travellers from the East seeking out the baby Jesus carries with it a burden of implausibility. Put bluntly, how could anyone follow a star in the night sky in order to discover a precise geographical location on the earth?

Of course today that is exactly what we do when we use some bundles of complex electronics hanging out in space to guide us with pinpoint accuracy to a precise grid reference. But, pre-GPS positioning, how could these travellers possibly have done it?

The answer is partly that the ancients were pretty smart in the field of celestial observation and mathematics and, as we see in today's reading, combined this knowledge with some shrewd on-the-ground research. However, my guess (encouraged by T S Eliot's splendid poem 'The journey of the Magi') is that following the star to Bethlehem was less a matter of arithmetic, still less the product of sophisticated technology, and much more about intuitive prompting of the heart.

My own journey to find and know the child and subsequently the man and saviour born in a stable at Bethlehem was helped by diligent Sunday school teaching and adult study, but it really began in such heart-moving childhood moments as when a choir with soloists sang carols in a candlelit church and 'knowing' came as a gift without the prior need to understand.

† The question, 'Where is God to be found?', might be asked out of anger, despair or simply being intrigued to know. In your prayers ask it honestly out of your circumstances today.

For further thought

• Is the 'truth' of Bible stories best understood through historical or scientific enquiry, or by 'hanging loose' and letting the story speak?

Thursday 24 August
Signs in the heavens

Mark 13:24–37

But in those days, after that suffering, the sun will be darkened, and the moon will not give its light, and the stars will be falling from heaven … Then they will see 'the Son of Man coming in clouds' with great power and glory. (verses 24, 25 and 26)

There is a common conceit among people of every age in that their time represents the culmination of human history – either triumphantly, or in terms of the end of civilisation as it has been known. Often the supporting evidence is strong such as when the 'Black Death' plague killed 200 million people in fourteenth-century Europe, and elsewhere at times of volcanic eruption, large scale war, prolonged drought or other ecological catastrophe. Today's reading may well draw upon such a worldview and may be inspired by the first-century destruction of Jerusalem and the scattering of the Jewish people.

I wonder whether such a linear view of history is mistaken and that human history actually suggests we take a more circular view. Usually, what is happening today has happened before and will probably happen again. Maybe the world darkens and the stars tumble often – but, if that is so, God's brightness also occurs with matching regularity and dependability. If we take this circular view of history we will see that God in Jesus, far from waiting in the wings before starring in the post-Armageddon or super-heated climate finale, is in fact present with us continually.

The psalmist looked to the hills or to the heavens in times of need or despair and asks, 'From whence cometh my help?' Always, without fail, writes the mystic Julian of Norwich who wrote at the time of the Black Death, from the God who 'is maker and lover and keeper' of all that is made (Robert Llewelyn, ed. *Enfolded in Love*: DLT 1993, p. 3).

† Dear God, when in the intensity of our present need we cry out, 'When will it all end?' help us to know that your light, love and peace are always readily to hand.

For further thought

- How might choosing to take a 'circular view' help provide some helpful perspective for situations which cause you stress?

When I look at the heavens – Ian Fosten

August

God our light

Revelation 22:1–7

And there will be no more night; they need no light of lamp or sun, for the Lord God will be their light, and they will reign forever and ever. And he said to me, 'These words are trustworthy and true.' (verses 5 and 6)

For many Christians the book of Revelation seems a little too obscure and lurid to be useful. If that is your view, I invite you to read these words from Revelation less as a future hope and more as a statement of present possibility. When I read Revelation in that way this is the understanding I come to:

Even on the brightest of days
dark thoughts, regrets and memories
might obscure the light
and render life's landscape
fearful, featureless and dull.
The close intimacy engendered
by carefully positioned lighting
might not sufficiently subdue
the glare of a broken relationship
or fractured trust.
Yet, somewhere deep within there burns
eternally an inextinguishable brightness,
powered independently of
mood or circumstance:
The light of God shines on
and ever will.

† Help me to see, dear God, when those around me stumble in the darkness of confusion or sadness that I might be the bearer of your light and the giver of your hope.

For further thought

• Why is it that a single candle flame in a darkened room inspires, moves and reassures us more than any elaborate electric lighting scheme ever could?

Saturday 26 August
Praises of the heavens

Psalm 148

Praise the Lord! Praise the Lord from the heavens; praise him in the heights! … Praise him, sun and moon; praise him, all you shining stars! … Let them praise the name of the Lord, for his name alone is exalted; his glory is above earth and heaven. (verses 1, 3 and 13)

In the year 1224 when St Francis was recovering from illness, he wrote his famous *Canticle of the Sun* – sometimes called *Canticle of the Creatures* – in which he invokes the sun and moon, the wind and the rain, all creatures that populate the earth and even death itself to collaborate in a hymn of praise to God, the source of all life. I suspect that he found much of his inspiration in today's reading, Psalm 148. In a way which prefigures a twenty-first century understanding of the interdependence of all that is created, both Francis and the psalmist express their exuberant delight as they orchestrate the cosmos, the landscape and all its creatures into a symphony of praise to the Creator. In both pieces the handbrake is off, the mooring ropes are untied, all reserve and restraint is jettisoned and these writers just go for it!

As a child, and alongside all that I learned in church, I too received a deep sense of the presence and purpose of God in both the awesome wonder and the intimate intricacy of creation. To this day, though I am often moved by worship and even more so by shared silence in church, it is the buffeting wind on a Cornish cliff top that, almost literally, lifts me off my feet in praise and connectedness to our creator God.

In an age that is sometimes excessively cerebral and dismissive of sensations as a route to understanding I hope you will allow yourself to take a 'wild ride' with today's psalm.

† Today, tonight, for ever, may I be caught up in the song that all creation sings; a song of praise to our God.

For further thought

• How best might you incorporate this invitation to 'lift your eyes to the heavens' into the prayer and worship of your everyday life?

Politics of food
Food in the Old Testament

Notes based on the New Revised Standard Version by **Vron Smith**

See Vron's biography on p. 198.

Sunday 27 August
An apple a day took wholeness away

Genesis 3:1–7

So when the woman saw that the tree was good for food, and that it was a delight to the eyes, and that the tree was to be desired to make one wise, she took of its fruit and ate. (verse 6)

I remember, when working on a maternity ward, watching a newborn trying to suckle, desperate for his mother's milk. His efforts to feed were as powerful as his need to breathe so that sometimes he tried to do both with disastrous results!

From birth, we seek nourishment and food. Hunger drives an instinctive desire for survival and a need to be fed. Our world, our creation provides us with food and as Christians we recognise this is a gift from the goodness of God who desires us to live. However, like Adam and Eve, we are people of desire, and sometimes desire distorts the ways in which we see and use what is given. Eve saw the apple as good food, attractive and giving wisdom. In reality, a few bites of an apple brought instead fragmentation and separation. We need to become wise in our use of the gift of food, ironically the one thing that Eve desired but failed to be in that moment of eating. Yes, food is good and appealing but more so, as we'll see in the next days, it is an invitation to co-operate with the Giver so that all may be fed.

† God of goodness, thank you for the gift of food, the gift of life. Give me wisdom to use them well for all people.

What are you hungry for?

Genesis 25:19–34

Esau said to Jacob, 'Let me eat some of that red stuff, for I am famished!'
Jacob said, 'First sell me your birthright.' Esau said, 'I am about to die; of
what use is a birthright to me?' (verses 30–32)

My friend and I had been out walking in the hills all day. We were cold and tired and near to our destination when, as we passed by a cottage, the smell of frying bacon hit our nostrils. We said almost simultaneously, 'I'd give anything right now for a bacon sandwich!'

Jacob and Esau are twin brothers. Jacob is a domestic herder who has ambition to be the number one but isn't; Esau is a hunter who is the firstborn but does not value all that being the firstborn brings. Imagine Esau coming home, famished after hard physical work and saying, 'That smells really good! I'm dying of hunger. I'd give anything for some hot food!' Here, though, Jacob takes advantage of Esau's hunger to meet his own ends. Esau ends up selling Jacob his birthright, giving up power and status for a bowl of red lentil stew and some bread.

Back to hunger and a bacon sandwich. Would we have given anything? I hope not! But what actually might eating a bacon sandwich or any other food really cost me? How often do I think about where it came from, the farmers and their livelihood? My hunger to eat what I choose, when I choose, could mean that without much thought I am selling my birthright as a disciple of Christ called to justice and integrity. 'I am about to die. Of what use is a birthright to me?' As a Christian, that birthright is everything.

† Lord, let my hunger be for your justice and your peace for all people.

For further thought
- Choose one of your favourite recipes and make an effort to cook it using only ethical ingredients.

Politics of food – Vron Smith

August

God likes a good feast

Politics of food – Vron Smith

Exodus 23:10–19a

For six years you shall sow your land and gather in its yield; but the seventh year you shall let it rest and lie fallow, so that the poor of your people may eat; and what they leave the wild animals may eat. (verses 10–11)

Our garden at home had fruit and vegetables and as a child I would help my dad plant various seeds, watch for green shoots, then flowers and, eventually, pick the fruit and dig up the vegetables. Apples, raspberries, carrots from the garden always tasted so much better! Nature and the weather often meant a mixed harvest, but we were not dependent on it.

Not so for the people of Israel. Their lives were intimately linked with the land and its produce, where the goodness of creation reflected the goodness of God towards the whole people. Imagine the delight at harvest times when the labouring on the land produced enough to keep them from famine for another year. That joy and thankfulness overflowed into celebrating Passover, Harvest and Ingathering. In their feasting, the people of God offered back to God with grateful hearts the best of their harvest. They also had concern too for the poor, those without land who therefore could not have the same experience of God's bounty.

It is easy to lose the connection between the food that we buy, the land and people that produced it and God who gifts us in creation. Today there is an invitation to us to solidarity with God, creation and the poor. I wonder how often do we even think to thank God before we eat? A simple prayer before or after eating may not seem like much but to God, all offerings, however meagre, are acceptable.

† Lord, all life is your gift of love to me. Teach me to cherish creation which you sustain for our good.

For further thought

• Make a conscious effort to say a simple prayer of thanks at meal times for the rest of the week.

Wednesday 30 August
Come dine with me

> ### 1 Kings 13:7–22
>
> *'I also am a prophet as you are, and an angel spoke to me by the word of the Lord: Bring him back with you into your house so that he may eat food and drink water.' But he was deceiving him. (verse 18)*

One of St Ignatius Loyola's gifts to the church was that of discernment and learning how to make decisions that co-operate with God's desire for us and the kingdom. Sometimes those choices can be clear, and we can see what is more of God and what is not, but sometimes it's difficult. Something that appears good is not necessarily always where God is inviting.

Take our young prophet who has just healed the king. He has no problem in making a choice to refuse the king's invitation to dine. He recognises easily the temptation offered as a gift and holds to what God has asked of him. He will not be compromised by eating with the king. However, he then encounters the old prophet. Here is someone seen to be a man of God, someone who shares the same calling, who being older should be wiser. So when the old prophet says that God has changed his plan and that the young prophet is to eat with him, he does not question the message, does not stop to reflect if this indeed is God's doing, does not see a far subtler deception under the guise of good. As a result, the young prophet eats and drinks where he should not and reaps the consequences. Discernment is something we learn and we do get it wrong. The important part is to look at the fruits of our choice and see whether they seem of God. As the saying goes, 'The proof of the pudding is in the eating.'

Politics of food – Vron Smith

August

† Give me, Lord, the gift to see you at work so that I may choose what is the greater good that you desire.

For further thought

• Think back to a good decision you made and notice how you proceeded to make it and its consequences.

Thursday 31 August
For need or for greed?

Proverbs 13:23–25

The field of the poor may yield much food, but it is swept away through injustice. (verse 23)

Today's reading from Proverbs has truth in it that applies today just as much as in the culture of the sixth or fifth centuries BC. Proverbs are a collection of wisdom accumulated over the centuries that give a glimpse of life, of its meaning and mystery, of understanding God within it. They are usually pragmatic and about the everyday and come from experience handed down from family to family.

Imagine if the writer were to find himself in this world today. Would he make changes to what he wrote? Or would he still pen similar words – that the lot of the poor is such that their fields are still yielding more food but even now it is swept away from them by a whole political and global system of food production that encourages injustice.

He may then turn to find that indeed the belly of the wicked is still never satisfied. Mohandas Gandhi once said, 'There's enough on the planet for everyone's needs, but not for everyone's greed.' Food is big business and big money because it's one thing we can't do without. Small co-operatives have to struggle against large corporate monopolies which are always hungry for more. More food production, more money, more power, more control, more food production. And so the cycle goes.

As Christians we need to understand what is happening and be ready to speak out. The writer of Proverbs also said that those who love, discipline. A more modern version might be, 'Love does not grant unbridled freedom.' We need to become prophets who can speak out those words.

† Guard my appetite, Lord, so that you are the One who satisfies me, the One who frees me to love.

For further thought

• Look up some of the facts about world hunger on the World Food Programme website.

Friday 1 September
Fasting from, fasting for

Isaiah 58:1–14

Is not this the fast that I choose: to loose the bonds of injustice, to undo the thongs of the yoke, to let the oppressed go free, and to break every yoke? (verse 6)

One of the disciplines of monastic life is fasting where at certain meals the food would be limited and simple. Whenever it was a fasting breakfast, I came to notice that even though I woke up happy, having to fast left me grumpy for the remainder of the morning until lunch. Eventually I realised that the focus of fasting was all about me! It was not about God, nor about the people who were starving who would be given help through the money that we donated. God was inviting me to look at my underlying desires that needed some attention!

Isaiah doesn't pull his punches as he tells God's people in no uncertain terms that their fasting is lacking the change of heart that God desires. Fasting has become all about them and their interests; it is a means to try and bargain with God. You can almost hear them saying, 'Rather than stop quarrelling, I'm going to fast instead for you God. Rather than treating my workers fairly, I'm going to miss a meal.'

Fasting has a purpose and a fruit. To choose to fast when in fact God is inviting me to develop the self-control to stop gossiping or judging others unfairly is unlikely to bear fruit or delight God. So, does your fasting remove hunger or homelessness, bring freedom to the oppressed? Does it show what God's care is about? If so, you will find God will satisfy your needs in parched places.

† Let my fasting be for your purpose, God of integrity. Let its fruit delight you.

For further thought

• For one day, choose to fast from a behaviour which lacks love.

Politics of food – Vron Smith

September

Saturday 2 September
A diet of love

Daniel 1:1–16

Daniel resolved that he would not defile himself with the royal rations of food and wine; so he asked the palace master to allow him not to defile himself. Now God allowed Daniel to receive favour and compassion from the palace master. (verses 8–9)

Walking through the university halls of residence, you could often smell the exotic aromas of a stir-fry here or a spicy peanut stew there, all accompanied by the chatter of people. Sharing food was a way of foreign students remaining connected with the place and people where they felt they belonged. This was even more apparent for those who had dietary laws that they followed. For them food was about shared beliefs and living faithfully together before God.

Daniel was having a struggle about food. A captive of war, he was being offered an education in the king's court with the guarantee of a good job, accommodation and food all provided. Daniel is under real pressure to conform, to eat what's given to him. But he refuses to eat royal rations because he wants to hold to what is pleasing to God. He risks it all because his relationship with God is more important to him than anything else.

To us, religious dietary laws may not appear helpful. But we can ask ourselves, 'Are there ways in which the things I eat can prevent me living faithfully with God?' Do I boycott the food companies who treat their workers unfairly? Do I buy food grown locally? Our shared belief is that Christ is to be found in all our brothers and sisters and he calls us to respond. Perhaps we need to choose more wisely what passes our lips. Not for dietary laws, but the law of love.

† Show me, Christ of my brother and sisters, how to live more faithfully in my choices of food that I may build up the body of Christ.

For further thought

• Consider helping in some way at a local food bank or food co-operative.

Politics of food
Food in the New Testament

Notes based on the New International Version (UK) by **Pete Wheeler**

Pete Wheeler spent 20 years working as a musician, composing, producing and licensing music for film and TV before becoming an associate pastor, and subsequently being ordained in 2016. He trained at St Mellitus College and is currently curate for the Deanery and St Mary's Church in Aylesbury, UK. He's married to Ali, a graphic designer. As well as being kept busy by two teenage children and music, Pete's creative life also involves making sausages and wine; garden design; not enough golf; a bit of footie; the odd geeky board game; Lapsang Souchong tea; and keeping chickens.

Sunday 3 September
Getting your hands dirty

Mark 7:1–13

'These people honour me with their lips, but their hearts are far from me. They worship me in vain; their teachings are merely human rules.' You have let go of the commands of God and are holding on to human traditions. (verses 6–8)

Tom, a friend of mine, is a gardener on a country estate. We are chatting about the significance of how we grow food and eat it, and, as we do so, he makes no effort to clean his grubby hands before eating his sandwiches. Clearly his immune system is well used to a little mud!

Imagine a similar scene as Jesus' disciples gather to eat. Their hands are dusty and dirty, and, while not a scriptural necessity, the Jewish custom was to eat with ceremoniously washed hands. Immediately, the Pharisees seize their opportunity to criticise this lack of religious observance.

Yet Jesus points out that it is the Pharisees who are unclean! Their sustenance is found in their continual exploitation of the law so as to leverage importance and position. By contrast, the disciples are 'getting their hands dirty' – getting stuck in to the everyday mission of Jesus!

This week we explore the hugely political resonances of our consuming, becoming, being, sharing and providing Christ's body – the food that brings in the kingdom of God.

Like the disciples did, is it time to get your hands dirty? Perhaps in a situation that needs addressing, or with a friend who needs some practical help?

† Lord Jesus, as I pursue holiness, and cleanliness of heart, show me times and places that you long for me to get my hands dirty.

Monday 4 September
Master chef

Matthew 14:13–21

Jesus replied, 'They do not need to go away. You give them something to eat.' (verse 16)

I have used my fair share of church PA systems in my time, of varying quality! But I am perplexed as to how Jesus speaks to a crowd approaching 10000 (including women and children) without any sort of PA or amplification available. Has that question ever crossed your mind? It certainly has mine!

I suspect that Jesus knows the very best way in which to engage this huge crowd is to physically demonstrate who he is, and what he's about (echoing the actions of Elisha in 2 Kings 4:42–44 as he does so). In an oral tradition and culture, the impact of this miracle of provision would have spread like wildfire through the hills. This is a meal that says 'I am the only provider you need' – a message full of political resonance!

I also wonder who performed the miracle here. Was it Jesus, or was it the disciples? When did the bread and fish actually multiply? While this story appears in each of the four Gospels, none of them make the answer clear.

Yet Jesus intended for his disciples to distribute genuine sustenance to the people, saying 'You give them something to eat.' Likewise, we are charged with taking the small fragments of what we bring to be offered up, multiplied and enabled by the Holy Spirit to nourish the world around us. Why spend your life on what doesn't satisfy (compare with Isaiah 55:2)? Jesus is the ultimate provision: the real thing; the bread of life!

With thanks given to the Father, his body is broken and shared out. And there are leftovers too!

† Jesus, you are the great sustainer. Teach me to rely on your provision alone, so that you might multiply the fragments of my offering back to you.

For further thought

- Not a great cook? Nor me! Instead, I keep chickens so I can give the eggs away! How can you become a provider of good things for people around you?

Tuesday 5 September
The Last Supper (it's not about you)

Mark 14:12–26

While they were eating, Jesus took bread, and when he had given thanks, he broke it and gave it to his disciples, saying, 'Take it; this is my body.' (verse 22)

At my church we have taken to gathering right around the table to celebrate communion. Standing in rough circle, we gently jostle so that everyone can see, and inevitably our eyes alight on each other as we gather face to face around the table. It is at this moment when, as Rowan Williams once said, 'we see each other as we really are'. Jesus chooses to eat with his friends, and eat with sinners. Presenting himself as the Passover lamb, he even chooses to share food with the man who will betray and offer him up to become the sacrificial lamb. Looking around the table, Jesus really sees each of them, as they really are.

But it's not about them, it's about him. This is a meal that remembers mercy and restoration; a meal that commemorates the miraculous rescue and redemption of ancestral kinfolk. Yet suddenly Jesus, taking the table elements in his hands, says, 'do this in remembrance of me'. I would have loved to have seen the expressions on the disciples' faces as Jesus, breaking the bread before them, makes yet another politically charged statement revealing who he is, and who they are to be. Taking a tradition they are all used to, he completely reorders it, presenting himself as the fulfilment of its meaning – even before the events which it will come to celebrate have even happened! With Jesus, a meal is never just a meal.

This is not about me, it's about Jesus. After all, as my former tutor, theologian Lincoln Harvey, points out, it's called the Eucharist – not the You-charist.

† Jesus, I want to put you at the centre of my worship. As I do, help me to see others as they really are – unreservedly, completely and utterly loved by you.

For further thought

• Read Andy Matheson's book *We Not Me* for a perspective on how the Christian life is never about individualism, but a Jesus-centred community.

Wednesday 6 September
Politically providing

Acts 6:1–7

'We will turn this responsibility over to them and will give our attention to prayer and the ministry of the word.' This proposal pleased the whole group. They chose Stephen, a man full of faith and of the Holy Spirit.'
(from verses 3–5)

Have you ever wondered why Stephen becomes the first martyr for Christ? It is not one of the twelve apostles, who rightly wanted to focus on their ministry of the word, who is seized, charged and put to death first for their 'blasphemous words'. Instead it is one of the seven men chosen to distribute food who is persecuted!

As we saw earlier in the week, to usurp the state in its role as provider was to make a serious political statement; one that clearly identified Stephen as being subject to a 'Lord' other than the state. Providing food to widows and orphans was a direct challenge to these authorities, whose only plan was for such burdens on society to quietly die away.

So it is that Stephen, a man full of faith and of the Holy Spirit, is stoned to death.

As an occasional town chaplain in the centre of Aylesbury, I have experienced first-hand criticism for feeding the homeless, for siding with refugees, for helping drunk party-goers get home safely and for befriending those of other cultures and faiths. It would seem to some that I am making a political statement. And they may be right, but it's probably not the one they imagine! Indeed, while I find national party politics hard to navigate, I hope to actively usurp the politics of apathy, indifference and injustice.

To feed, to love and to provide for others is to actively bring in the coming kingdom which Jesus heralds and teaches us to pray for. Won't you join me, Stephen, and others, in playing your exciting part in the reordering of the cosmos?

† Lord Jesus, give us courage to become activists who, through the provision ourselves, nourish and feed your people, and usher in your kingdom.

For further thought

• In what areas might showing that 'Jesus is Lord' of your life be seen as a challenge to others?

Thursday 7 September
Divine tablecloth

Acts 10:9–16

He saw heaven opened and something like a large sheet being let down to earth by its four corners. It contained all kinds of four-footed animals, as well as reptiles and birds. (verses 11–12)

Have you ever heard someone say something, or read something, but not realised its significance until later? In this passage we see Peter struggling to understand his tablecloth vision, and yet looking back to Sunday's reading (Mark 7:1–13), we might remember that Jesus had openly challenged the Jewish customs and food laws received by the Israelites in the wilderness.

Once again, for Peter, it's a recurring moment of forehead-slapping realisation as he begins to understand exactly what Jesus was going on about! It seems that all this time Peter had continued to only eat kosher food (verse 14). Yet the Holy Spirit was at work, challenging and growing Peter to see what (and who) is clean and unclean very differently.

Sometimes we are slow to change our behaviour to reflect our beliefs. For example, we may understand that consuming responsibly is to the advantage of God's creation, but our old habits are hard to break. But the politics of what we consume, and how we treat our bodies, really matters – for now we are Christ's body.

Throughout my life it has been the times of looking back and reflection that has allowed me to see where the Holy Spirit is leading me. Looking back over the past few days to Sunday again, let me ask you now – have you seen areas where the Holy Spirit is challenging you to 'get your hands dirty'? Or, to go a step further, can you identify the people who you might have thought were beyond your ability to love, to reach or to witness to?

† Father, I thank you that you have sent your Holy Spirit to grow me. Challenge the ways in which I have become accustomed to see, do and consume. Clean my heart, and dirty my hands.

For further thought

• Looking back to the stories of Rahab and Achan (Joshua 6 and 7), can you see further resonance here of whom God deems clean and unclean?

Politics of food – Pete Wheeler

September

Friday 8 September
Feed your enemy

Romans 12:9–21

On the contrary: 'If your enemy is hungry, feed him; if he is thirsty, give him something to drink. In doing this, you will heap burning coals on his head.' Do not be overcome by evil, but overcome evil with good. (verses 20–21)

We once had an unexpected visit from the angry parents of my son's friend, wanting to know why we had handled a situation in a certain way. Instead of engaging them at the doorstep my wife and I invited them in, and before they knew it we were sitting around the table with wine and breadsticks. I believe that conversation would have gone very differently on the doorstep!

Did you even realise your enemy was hungry? Paul tells the Romans to 'practice hospitality' (verse 13). When we start to look behind anger we often find hunger – a hunger for meaning, for security, for relationship and for food!

So when you start loving and feeding your enemy instead of fighting against them it turns the world upside down, upsetting the status quo. As we have already seen, it has such serious implications that Stephen is martyred for what amounts to civil disobedience. The world just doesn't know how to handle the revolutionary nature of the kingdom of God, and thus we might expect to face opposition. It's no coincidence therefore that this passage follows Paul's teaching on Christ-like sacrificial love and service, and directly before his teaching on 'governing authorities'. So, what exactly will you feed your enemy?

The fruit that we bear in the Holy Spirit (Galatians 5:22–24) can spiritually feed those around us. When you are patient, loving, gentle and kind in the face of your opposition you are feeding your enemy with a nutritious meal! When you invite your angry neighbour in to share some bread and wine you grow and nourish health and well-being.

† Bread of life, who truly satisfies, grant me the grace to forgive, the eyes to see and the courage to face my opposition with a humble heart.

For further thought

• So, is it time to invite that neighbour round for something to eat? Or maybe that person you know who rubs you up the wrong way?

Saturday 9 September
Faith and works together

James 2:14–18

Suppose a brother or a sister is without clothes and daily food. If one of you says to them, 'Go in peace; keep warm and well fed,' but does nothing about their physical needs, what good is it? In the same way, faith by itself, if it is not accompanied by action, is dead. (verses 15–16)

I love chocolate. However, I recently made a commitment to buy only fairly traded chocolate after listening to a presentation on how men, women and children are commonly trafficked to work on African cocoa farms.

This is where the politics of food really hits home. This tiny action I choose to make has eternal consequence – 'eternal' being a very present concept, not just a future one. Living under his kingdom rule, and under his grace, we are called, as William Cavanaugh says about the Eucharist in his article in *The Blackwell Companion To Christian Ethics*: 'to be now what we will perfectly be later – the body of Christ' (p. 217). Therefore, I know that even my small action is part of a common kingdom purpose. It is in knowing that we are inheritors of what we do not deserve that we are compelled to live out faith through our actions.

In the UK, I have noticed a recent change in sentiment towards the poor. Whereas it was common to envy the rich for what they have, now it is common to envy the poor for what they seemingly get, particularly when they are deemed as 'undeserving'. Jesus challenges this idea of 'who is deserving' in his parable of the vineyard workers (Matthew 20:1–16). Who do you see as deserving or undeserving – of your support, your encouragement, of a place at the table, or your time?

When we acknowledge that we have nothing of our own to give, we affirm God's sovereignty over all we have. To participate in the subversive and revolutionary politics of food is to bring in this very present kingdom of God.

† Lord and sovereign God, we know that all things come from you, and of your own do we give you. In the light of this, your grace, use me to feed your people.

For further thought
• No step or action you take is ever too small to make a difference in God's economy. Commit to making small changes that will have kingdom consequences. Start today.

Politics of food – Pete Wheeler

September

Acts 13–28
A new phase begins

Notes based on the New Revised Standard Version by **Alesana Fosi Pala'amo**

 Alesana Fosi Pala'amo is a lecturer in practical theology at Malua Theological College in Samoa. Ordained as a minister of the Congregational Christian Church, Samoa, his teaching and research interests include Christian ministry, youth and social ministries, pastoral theology, worship and pastoral counselling. Alesana is completing his PhD research in pastoral counselling through Massey University, New Zealand. As a counsellor Alesana works with church members as well as Pacific Islanders living in Auckland. Alesana is married to Lemau, and their sons Norman, Alex and Jayden attend primary school.

Sunday 10 September
Sent on a mission

Acts 13:1–15

So, being sent out by the Holy Spirit, they went down to Seleucia; and from there they sailed to Cyprus. (verse 4)

Any mission has three key areas: first, the purpose of the mission; second, knowing who the sender is; and finally, the ability and character of the one being sent to undertake the mission. A successful outcome largely depends upon a clear understanding between all three.

From today's reading one could identify the sender for Paul and Barnabas' mission as the church at Antioch. But with a divine purpose of taking the message of Christ to the Greco-Roman cities during the first century AD, the sender must be of divine origin. It is suggested that the sender here is the Holy Spirit.

In our lives, sometimes we get caught up in our own agendas and lose sight of the purpose of our missions. The one being sent takes on the mindset of sender, and thus the purpose of the mission becomes lost. This was not the case for Paul and his travellers. Since the Holy Spirit was behind the mission that Paul and Barnabas were sent, it is fair to say that the message of God reached the masses back in the first century CE and has continued to spread throughout the world even today. For this, mission accomplished!

† Lord, remind us to function for your purpose so we do not become self-centred and lose sight of you as our Sender and Creator. (In Samoan) *Amene*

Monday 11 September
Storytelling

Acts 13:16–31

So Paul stood up and with a gesture began to speak: 'You Israelites, and others who fear God, listen.' (verse 16)

Samoans love to tell stories. This is a way that many traditions and practices are passed down through the generations: through the practice of storytelling. The elders in the family often talk about events 'back in their day' to illustrate life-experiences and the worldviews of their times. Such stories and reflections are then used to teach and instruct the younger and developing members of the family. Stories of myths and legends of Samoa are told; explanations of proverbial sayings significant and meaningful for Samoans are given; and biblical stories are recited and memorised by children at *Aoga Faifeau* or pastor school as well as at Sunday school. Several lessons are taught and learnt through storytelling. Samoans love to tell stories and more importantly, enjoy listening to stories being told.

At the beginning stages of the apostle Paul's missionary journeys, he had won over many listeners of the stories of Jesus that he spoke. It was not a case of telling an unknown story of God to residents of the Greco-Roman cities that Paul visited; many had already heard about God and the miracles and teachings of Jesus. The story that Paul shared about the history of Israel to the death and resurrection of Jesus gave an understanding of God that made his listeners take note. The truly amazing part of the story told is that although we are sinners and inadequate, we are saved through our faith in Christ, our Risen Lord. What good news the story of God tells to those who listen and understand the blessings of God's love!

† Lord, thank you for the story of your love that guides us. Give us ears to listen to stories of others, the heart to understand and insight to know when to share our stories. *Amene*

For further thought

• In this digital age have we forsaken our storytelling with electronic devices that occupy us? Tell a story this week, or even listen to one being told!

Tuesday 12 September
The excitement of inclusion

Acts 13:42–52

For so the Lord has commanded us, saying, 'I have set you to be a light for the Gentiles, so that you may bring salvation to the ends of the earth.' (verse 47)

Being included is something that many strive to achieve. Inclusion can mean to be 'liked' by friends on different mediums of social media or friends in person. Inclusion can also mean being involved in decisions that have an impact upon your life. To have someone else decide and know what is best for you is something that many young people in the church have expressed as a major 'dislike' in their lives. *Amana'ia* is a Samoan word that can be translated as 'to be acknowledged'. When a visitor arrives to a new place, home or village, traditionally the first exchanges of welcome include acknowledging the origins of the visitor. This may include any chiefly titles one may hold, village, family and any other significant designations. Likewise, the visitor must acknowledge the same for the host. Acknowledgement for whatever reason is important because it shows that the person's worth has been recognised. The opposite *lē amana'ia,* translated as 'not being acknowledged', again is something that many Samoans dislike. To be included brings excitement because it means that your voice, opinion and presence are valued by someone else.

The message that Paul took to the Gentile cities informed them that they too were included in the promise of salvation through Christ. They were reminded of an impartial God; whether Israelite or Gentile, both are included in God's salvation. Faith in Christ is the key, so who wouldn't be excited at being included in such a blessing? We, too, share the excitement of inclusion into God's salvation and ultimately, God's everlasting kingdom.

† Lord, thank you for including us in your salvation for the world. Remind us to include and acknowledge those around us, just as you have taught us about the importance and value of inclusion. *Amene*

For further thought

• Do you exclude those who should be included? Acknowledge everyone around you then inclusion will come naturally.

Wednesday 13 September
Not because of us but unto you, Lord!

Acts 14:8–23

Friends, why are you doing this? We are mortals just like you, and we bring you good news, that you should turn from these worthless things to the living God, who made the heaven and the earth and the sea and all that is in them. (verse 15)

Do we sometimes worship the message-giver and lose sight of the message itself? As preachers it is easy to get caught up in the hype of everything; where we are placed on pedestals and forget who we serve. *Faifeau* is the Samoan word translated as 'minister'. A literal translation is 'doer of chores' or 'someone that serves'. Both transliterations are great because these titles highlight the role of the minister in the villages. Doing chores of God: healing chores, cleaning-up chores, cooking chores, maintaining chores – these symbolise the role of the *faifeau*. *Faletua* is the Samoan word for 'minister's wife'. A literal translation is 'house at the back'. In traditional Samoa, the house at the back serves the front house, *fale tele* or large house. When the title-holder or *matai* of the family makes a request to the 'house at the back', then food, gifts, fine mats or whatever are sent from the house at the back to serve the guests. How significant these two titles are as God's servants for Samoans; a doer of chores and a house at the back, because both titles show humility as being servants for others and for God.

This is precisely where Christians should be especially those called as preachers and missionaries of God's work. Just as Paul and Barnabas discovered, it was not their right to take credit for the work they were doing. Such praises belong to God whom they serve. Praise and honour is for God, as it is not our doing, but through God we are able to do all things that we do.

† Gracious God, help us to remember that we are only able to do what we do through you our Lord. Praise and honour are yours always. *Amene*

For further thought

• What words from your culture would you use to describe servant leadership? Share them on our Facebook group today.

Acts 13–28 – Alesana Fosi Pala'amo

September

Thursday 14 September
God's astounding grace

> ### Acts 15:1–11, 28–29
> *On the contrary, we believe that we will be saved through the grace of the Lord Jesus, just as they will. (verse 11)*

Upon reflecting on the text for today, it really struck me the division between 'us' and 'them', between one group of people and another. There existed a division between the Israelites and Gentiles at the time these words were written. The division was about being recipients of God's saving grace, or not. The Israelites claimed inclusion to salvation through Christ. In order for the Gentiles to also be included in this salvation, they were required to uphold certain Israelite traditions that included circumcision. The message that Paul and his assistants preached on their missionary journeys for the Gentiles was that God's salvation through Christ was not exclusive for any given group of people. Israelite or Gentile, all had access to salvation through the grace of our resurrected Lord.

At times we may focus so much on our own cultures and traditions that we lose sight of the gospel message that Jesus taught. We may focus too much on the actions and practices, while forsaking the underlying message of Christ and what he has done for us. We are not saved by any actions of our own, or any culture or tradition that we uphold; we are saved by God's action, grounded in his everlasting love: the grace of God that saw Jesus sacrificed for our sins, and risen from death. An action that happened only once, and yet one that will lift up all faithful believers in Christ to God's eternal kingdom.

† Lord God, thank you for our salvation through Jesus Christ. Help us to remember that we are not saved by our actions, but by your grace. *Amene*

For further thought

- What is a contemporary dividing wall in your church, and in our world, that needs to come down?

Friday 15 September
Different carriers; same message

Acts 15:30–41

Judas and Silas, who were themselves prophets, said much to encourage and strengthen the believers. (verse 32)

A Foundations of Teaching course run by Massey University has taught me that effective, deep learning depends largely upon the willingness of the learner to engage with the subject matter. Regardless of how lively, charismatic and well-informed the teacher is, the learner is the key for getting the message across. The challenge for learners or anyone listening to a message being preached is that sometimes we may get caught up and misled by the carrier of the message. If we don't like the preacher for whatever reason, either personally or professionally, we may switch off from listening to a great message. Or if we like the preacher too much, we may get carried away and focus too much on the preacher at how great he or she is, and miss the gospel message entirely.

Reading today's passage has reminded me that all Christians have the opportunity to carry the gospel message. This is the beauty of God's message. It is not only ministers, pastors or missionaries who can spread God's word, but anyone who has received Christ into their hearts. What people see as displayed in us will help to spread the message of Christ. The gospel and the good news is that God loved us so much, that he gave his only Son to die for our sins. He rose from death so that we as believers can have eternal life. What a great message, and a message that needs to be shared by all believers.

† Lord God, help us to carry the good news of your love to everyone around us. *Amene*

For further thought

- What can you do today to make real the gospel of encouragement?

Moved to act

Acts 16:1–10

When he had seen the vision, we immediately tried to cross over to Macedonia, being convinced that God had called us to proclaim the good news to them. (verse 10)

When I attended a recent Pacific *fono* (meeting) for practitioners in New Zealand helping youth with mental health problems, I was struck by the courage of some youth who shared their stories and testimonies. In my heart I felt like approaching the young teenager who had just shared her story and giving her a comforting hug. However, I considered the inappropriateness of my intention due to the trauma she had experienced from men in her life. To my surprise, a female attendee got up from her seat and did exactly what I felt like doing in my heart, but which my mind had doubted. Upon reflection, the feelings that both my fellow attendee and myself experienced I can identify as examples of being moved by God's Spirit.

Paul's second missionary journey to spread the gospel message was riddled with challenges from its very beginning. A dispute with his trusted companion Barnabas was enough for the pair to part ways. But others like Silas and Timothy filled in the gap and joined the travelling preacher to take the gospel message to the Gentiles. They, too, were moved just like Paul and Barnabas to stand up and preach the word of God across the Greco-Roman cities that they visited.

Christ has paid the price for our sins through his life and death, and rose victoriously to eternal life. Let us open our hearts and be moved by the Spirit of God, and make a difference for someone's life beginning with our own.

† Lord God, may your spirit move us always to do good for the benefit of others and for ourselves, and move us to honour and worship you our Lord. *Amene*

For further thought

• Where can you see God's Spirit in someone's actions today?

Acts 13–28
Paul on tour

Notes based on the New Revised Standard Version by **Liz Clutterbuck**

Liz Clutterbuck is a curate in the Church of England, working part time in a North London parish, and freelancing as a researcher and writer. Ordained in 2015, she trained at St Mellitus College, completing a MA in which she explored the role of hospitality and mission in the Eucharist. This was inspired by her involvement with Matryoshka Haus, a missional community based in both London and Dallas, and its weekly communal meals. She is passionate about social media, mission, baking and travel – and loves it when she manages to combine as many of her passions as possible!

Sunday 17 September
Missionary encounters

Acts 16:11–34

When she and her household were baptised, she urged us, saying, 'If you have judged me to be faithful to the Lord, come and stay at my home.' And she prevailed upon us. (verse 15)

From Acts onwards, the New Testament chronicles the missionary journeys Paul and the apostles took to spread the gospel. It tells the stories of the founding of churches; the building of relationships; conversions; and the persecution that some Christians continue to suffer today.

Two thousand years later, Christians are still on a missionary journey. We may not cross borders and we may not think of ourselves as 'missionaries', but our daily lives regularly bring us into contact with those that do not know Christ. Paul's experiences have much to teach us about how to engage society with the gospel message.

This passage also provides a blueprint for how Christians should interact with one another. Lydia opens her home to the apostles, and this is a pattern followed by other Christians they meet along the way. Homes were of huge importance to the followers of this new faith – it was where they met together, where they ate the meal in which Christ was remembered, and where teaching took place.

Does this take place in our homes today? Do we welcome in the stranger? Provide food for the body and for the soul? Perhaps this is something to consider as we begin this week's readings.

† Lord, touch our hearts as you touched Lydia's. Strengthen our faith so that we might give ourselves and our possessions away for the sake of the Gospel.

Turning the world upside down

Acts 17:1–15

These people who have been turning the world upside down have come here also, and Jason has entertained them as guests. They are all acting contrary to the decrees of the emperor, saying that there is another king named Jesus. (verses 6b–7)

When was the last time you turned the world upside down because of your faith? These early Christians were shaking up society, and the authorities did not like it!

By associating himself with Paul and Silas, hosting them in his home, Jason was representative of all that the authorities feared in this new religious movement. And Jason paid the price for it.

Throughout history, Christians have turned the world upside down because of their faith. Sometimes this has been an action that has affected a whole society – for example, Luther's actions that triggered the Reformation in Europe. On other occasions, Christians have responded to the way in which the world around them has been turned upside down by forces outside Christianity – such as the response of the Confessing Church in Germany to the Nazi government. At other times, individual Christians have allowed their lives to be turned upside down in order to do the work of the kingdom and to follow the call that God has placed upon their lives.

As a priest, I have had to allow my life to be turned upside down, at least a little bit! Beginning training involved moving house, leaving a job and accepting that this was the beginning of a lifetime of sacrifices made in order that I might follow God's call. It's not always easy – but it is a walk in the park compared to the sacrifice Jesus made on the cross, and the martyring of countless Christians throughout history.

We need to allow our lives to be disturbed by the great gospel message we carry!

† Lord, come in and disturb my life today! Show me the way that your gospel might turn the society in which I live upside down and give me strength to share it.

For further thought

- Read a document written by a Christian who turned the world upside down (e.g. Luther's theses, the Barmen declaration or a Kairos Document) and reflect on how it might inspire you.

Tuesday 19 September
False idols

Acts 17:16–34

Then Paul stood in front of the Areopagus and said, 'Athenians, I see how extremely religious you are in every way. For as I went through the city and looked carefully at the objects of your worship, I found among them an altar with the inscription, "To an unknown god."' (part of verses 22 and 23)

The church at which I work is less than half a mile from Arsenal football club's stadium. On match days, the streets are full of fans wearing red shirts – and if it's a Sunday, the church is full of Arsenal fans too! The atmosphere at a football stadium has been likened to that of worship – only the worship is not offered to God, it's to the cult of football.

Something about the sport draws millions of fans into its stadiums every week across the globe. If Paul was to visit earth today, he might regard football as akin to the gods the Athenians worshipped – an idol that bears little resemblance to the Lord of heaven and earth.

A love of sport is not incompatible with a love of God, but it is an example of something in modern society that can distract us from our faith. Our lives today are full of 'idols' – the latest technological gadget, fashion item or a compulsion to keep up with our neighbours – but the challenge is how we can hold on to these things lightly, prioritising our walk with God.

Just as Paul told the Athenians that God does not live in 'shrines made by human hands', so we must remember that 'In him we live and move and have our being' (verse 28). We bring God into those places in which the idols of modern society are worshipped, and it is our role to show what God has to offer.

† God of heaven and earth, make your presence known in the face of today's idols so that all may know the way of truth.

For further thought

- Take some time to examine your lifestyle and ponder whether there are any false idols within it. What are they, and how might you change this?

September   Acts 13–28 – Liz Clutterbuck

Wednesday 20 September
Where are the Lord's people?

Acts 18:1–11

One night the Lord said to Paul in a vision, 'Do not be afraid, but speak and do not be silent; for I am with you, and no one will lay a hand on you to harm you, for there are many in this city who are my people.' (verses 9–10)

Do you know how many Christians live in your city, town or province? In London, according to the 2011 census, 48.4 per cent of the population would call itself Christian – although far fewer actually attend church regularly.

Compared to some parts of the world, this is quite a high number, but it can often feel like Christians are very much in the minority within society, and that can make you feel quite isolated.

Paul has a similar experience in Corinth. He is disheartened by the way in which the worshippers at the synagogue treat him, and the lack of impact his message appears to be having (despite the conversion of Crispus). Thus, the Lord speaks the words we find in verses 9 and 10 and tells Paul that despite appearances to the contrary, 'there are many in this city who are my people.'

This is a message many Christians may need to hear today. When it appears that secularism has taken hold, or when living in a nation where a faith other than Christianity is dominant, it may feel as though we are alone in our walk with God. This passage ought to raise confidence that not only is God alongside us in this journey, there are people unseen and unknown who share our beliefs.

† Dear God, thank you for your assurance that we are not alone. Would you reveal those who believe in you and deepen existing relationships?

For further thought

• If you feel isolated in your faith, how might you find fellow Christians? How might you reach out to those who could feel like the only Christian in their community?

Acts 13–28 – Liz Clutterbuck

September

266

Thursday 21 September
Disagreeing well

Acts 19:1–20

He entered the synagogue and for three months spoke out boldly, and argued persuasively about the kingdom of God. When some stubbornly refused to believe and spoke evil of the Way before the congregation, he left them, taking the disciples with him, and argued daily in the lecture hall of Tyrannus. (verse 9)

I love the social network Twitter, but I have a few rules about how I use it. One of my biggest rules is not to get embroiled in arguments, particularly theological ones, on the platform. Because tweets can only be 140 characters each, it is very difficult to get a clear point across without misunderstandings or simplification. The speed at which a tweet can be replied to also makes things difficult – hurtful comments can be made in the blink of an eye and cause much damage.

Twitter is really not a place to discuss the deep theology of Christianity, especially not with the many atheists who use the social platform with the aim of baiting those who do have a faith. I would much rather have those sorts of discussions in person, perhaps in a pub or over dinner so that there is space for explanation and listening.

That's the approach that Paul took in Ephesus. First in the synagogue, where for three months he 'spoke out boldly' until people spoke evil of him; and then in a lecture hall for two years, arguing daily with anyone who cared to disagree with him. Imagine putting yourself in such a position! Most people do not like intentionally getting into arguments with people, but Paul did it day after day for years – because of how strongly he believed in the message he was carrying with him. Not only did he do this intentionally, he was equipped by God to argue well and share the gospel.

† Lord, bless us with the Holy Spirit as you did the Christians in Ephesus. Equip us with all we need to be great defenders of the faith.

For further thought

- Spend some time equipping yourself to defend the Christian faith – pray, do some reading, talk with others – and then find a suitable place in which to discuss it with someone.

September   Acts 13–28 – Liz Clutterbuck

Friday 22 September
Accepting difference

Acts 21:15–26

Then Paul took the men, and the next day, having purified himself, he entered the temple with them, making public the completion of the days of purification when the sacrifice would be made for each of them. (verse 26)

Differences of opinion can be difficult to overcome. In fact, it could be argued that disagreements between churches, denominations and individual Christians are the biggest barriers to Christian unity. We let our differences get in the way of enabling us to be the body of Christ to its fullest potential.

In Jerusalem, Paul was drawn into conflict between two Christian factions – Jewish Christians and Gentiles. James had aligned himself with those who believed that a Christian needed to follow all the laws of Israel, in addition to being baptised, in order to that they might enter God's kingdom. Paul strongly believed that Christ's death and resurrection was for all, not just the Jews like himself, and that righteousness was achieved through faith in Christ, not the keeping of laws.

Chapter 15 of Acts has already covered the issue, and Paul's letter to the Galatians goes into more detail as to Paul's issues with the Jewish Christians in Jerusalem, but this passage is an excellent illustration of compromise – of agreeing to disagree.

Instead of reopening the argument, Paul agrees to join the men going through the rite of purification. In doing so, he avoids a disagreement that would have furthered division within the still very young church. Whether or not it works we will leave for tomorrow's reading …

† Christ, show your church the path to unity, so that we might be your body to its full. Let division cease and your peace reign.

For further thought

- Spend some time reading about the differences between different churches around the world and pray for those who seek unity in the face of division.

Saturday 23 September
Following the crowd

Acts 21:27–36

Then all the city was aroused, and the people rushed together. They seized Paul and dragged him out of the temple, and immediately the doors were shut. (verse 30)

Paul's act in yesterday's reading did not manage to appease the Christians in Jerusalem. In fact, a piece of gossip resulted in the Jews turning against him, too. They believed that he had brought a Christian Gentile from Ephesus into the Temple, thus defiling the Temple. However, Paul had not done this and the result is an illustration of what can happen when a crowd believes an untruth.

A crowd is easily roused. Gossip spreads like wildfire and violence can be sparked quickly. The result in this instance was the beating of Paul, who had to be carried away to comparative safety by soldiers – not how he may have imagined his journey to Jerusalem ending.

Continuing yesterday's theme of church unity, this passage poses a challenge to all those who allow themselves to be swayed by hearsay or a crowd who believes in it. It is easy to believe in stereotypes, misunderstandings or gossip – which can result in big divisions in a faith that so many share.

One of the best weapons against such division is education – understanding more of theology and how it has been shaped in different traditions; finding out about what the church looks like in different countries; and sharing that knowledge with others. The other is prayer. Pray for a healing of divisions, so that the church might truly work together in God's mission on earth.

† Lord of all, break down barriers that divides your church and give a greater depth of understanding to all Christians.

For further thought

• Intentionally get to know a church that is different to your own.

Acts 13–28
And so we came to Rome

Notes based on the New International Version (UK) by **Tim Yau**

Tim Yau spent over a decade in Christian youth ministry before being ordained as an Anglican Pioneer Minister. He trained as a curate in Peterborough, growing a church plant in a new housing development, while also serving rural churches. He is now the Emerging Church Pioneer Minister for the Eastern Synod of the United Reformed Church, establishing missional projects in Ipswich, and ministering across East Anglia as an advocate for Fresh Expressions of church. To his wife's dismay, he is a *Star Wars* geek and still dreams of becoming a superhero.

Sunday 24 September
Missionary model

Acts 26:19–32

Paul replied, 'Short time or long – I pray to God that not only you but all who are listening to me today may become what I am, except for these chains.' (verse 29)

One of the maxims of modern Western culture is: 'be yourself'. This saying has encouraged a generation to do what feels right for them, whether it be in relationship matters, personal conduct or identity issues. As a teenager I was a vandal: breaking bottles, smashing windows and tagging mindless graffiti. It felt liberating, but it was destructive. Thankfully Christ transformed my negative behaviours into constructive ones. Consequently, as much as I applaud the prevalent sentiment of personal liberty, if unchecked I think it can become rampant individualism, where people put themselves at the centre of *their* universe, often at the expense of others. This stance couldn't be further from Paul's prayer to 'become what I am'.

Paul was an apostle, theologian and writer, but primarily a missionary to the Gentiles, the non-Jewish nations. In his letter to the Philippians Paul offers an account of his ministry, his impeccable Jewish pedigree, his religious rigour, his defence of the faith and his faultless morality. Could you top that? Thankfully, he dismisses all that as rubbish; the only thing that really qualifies him is Christ. This is the antithesis of modern individualism and what sends him to Rome, the heart of the empire, in chains.

† Lord God, help us to be like Paul, forsaking the cult of self, and instead following Jesus.

Maritime malcontent

Acts 27:1–20

So Paul warned them, 'Men, I can see that our voyage is going to be disastrous and bring great loss to ship and cargo, and to our own lives also.' (verses 9b–10)

Speeding across the narrow lanes of rural Norfolk is never a good idea, but in the midst of winter, on a moonless night and with a fully laden car, it's asking for trouble. With a guitar clamped between my knees, staging equipment by my side and a lighting rig over my shoulder, my colleague's small vehicle couldn't have been any fuller. We were on our way to a remote church to lead a Christmas presentation and our driver was eager to get there. Being thrown around in the back seat, with various pieces of kit falling on me I declared, 'If you don't slow down we'll crash in a minute!' My co-worker loved his car, and enjoyed the thrill of a cross-country drive, and decided to ignore my warning. Seemingly seconds later there was an almighty jolt, props and paperwork were thrown forward and we came to an abrupt stop. The car was in a ditch, the wheels were bent under and the performance was definitely off.

Paul was an experienced sea traveller. He'd already been shipwrecked three times and had spent awhile drifting in the open sea (2 Corinthians 11:25); he didn't need divine revelation to see that carrying on with the voyage would end in disaster. However, Paul was not the pilot, he was the prisoner, and he was in no position to dictate the course of action. Paul was a powerless passenger being swept along by the foolishness of those who should have known better, yet even as a lowly captive he still spoke up. Are we willing to do the same?

† Lord God, we recognise that in the plans of the powerful, your church is often seen as a small and insignificant. Give us courage to speak out when we perceive impending disaster.

For further thought

• What are the approaching difficulties on the horizon for your community? How will you speak out about them, and who will you tell?

Acts 13–28 – Tim Yau

September

Messenger and the message

Acts 27:21–32

Last night an angel of the God to whom I belong and whom I serve stood beside me and said, 'Do not be afraid, Paul. You must stand trial before Caesar; and God has graciously given you the lives of all who sail with you.' (verses 23–24)

At Christmas 1979 the Swedish pop group Abba was number two in the UK charts with 'I Have a Dream' – a catchy melodic tune with a children's choir and sentimental lyrics about belief in angels. The song embraced a wistful fantasy, a coping mechanism to help them through reality. Not so much a heavenly messenger, but more the good in everything around them.

Fast forward to 2014 and I'm at a Mind, Body, Spirit Festival, a place where alternative health therapies, paranormal practices and new age spiritualities coalesce. I'm standing by a stall bursting with angelic knick-knacks and books about how to contact and commune with angels. I get chatting to the stallholder who is obviously enthusiastic about the reality of angelic spirit beings in her life. She tells me about the close encounters she's had with them and the feelings of peace and serenity they'd given her.

Now back to Paul out on the stormy sea, faced by experienced sailors unsure of if they're going to make it through the tempest alive. In the midst of that turmoil Paul declares that an angel came to him and told him not to be afraid. For him the angel was simply a messenger from God. He doesn't dismiss it as a fanciful humanist notion of goodness in all people, nor does he enthuse ecstatically about the nature and qualities of the spirit being. For Paul, the message and who it was from was fundamental and not the messenger. We may never meet an angel in this life, but we can learn to trust the message and its author.

† Lord God, help us to hear your voice in the day-to-day, so that when the storms of life hit we're prepared to listen to your message, no matter how hard it is to hear.

For further thought

- Hebrews 13:2 equates strangers with angels. How would you recognise an angelic messenger? In what ways are you fostering an attitude of listening to God?

Wednesday 27 September
Meal in the maelstrom

Acts 27:33–44

'Now I urge you to take some food. You need it to survive …' After he said this, he took some bread and gave thanks to God in front of them all. Then he broke it and began to eat. They were all encouraged and ate some food themselves. (verses 34a, 35–36)

I was at the end of a messy relationship and I was an emotional wreck. The last thing I wanted to do was go to church, especially not the one where my former partner had until recently been employed as the community worker. The neighbourhood, the building and the congregation all reminded me of what I'd lost, but I couldn't escape the feeling that I should be there. Arriving on her old territory I was bombarded by reminders of her: the kids asked me her whereabouts, the church contained her work and the noticeboard still displayed her photo. Nevertheless, I was there, even though my rational mind was telling me it was a mistake.

It was a communion service and before we took the bread and wine we went and passed peace to one another, usually by a smile and a handshake. I was not expecting this. I'd quietly made it to the back row, but now I'd be faced by all the people; maybe I could make a swift exit! Too late, they spotted me, but what I found in those embraces was that here were heartbroken people too, it wasn't just me who was grieving; everyone felt the loss. Then to the holy meal, something I'd eaten many times before, but this time something different, feelings of peace, love and hope filled me, I was not alone, Jesus was with me in my brokenness and so were his people.

Paul's simple meal with the sailors may not have been 'communion', but like communion all were fed and encouraged in the midst of chaos.

† Jesus, in the great commission you said, 'I am with you always, even to the very end of the age.' When we are emotionally lost and spiritually drained feed us by your holy presence.

For further thought

- Where do you go when you are feeling broken? Who feeds you when you're spiritually empty? What's stopping you from being fed by God?

Thursday 28 September
Maltese mystery

Acts 13–28 – Tim Yau

September

Acts 28:1–10

The people expected him to swell up or suddenly fall dead; but after waiting a long time and seeing nothing unusual happen to him, they changed their minds and said he was a god. (verse 6)

Growing up I had little contact with wildlife; the closest I got was a stray dog. Although we do have snakes in England, to me they were something distant, foreign and exotic. However, my dad grew up in rural Hong Kong and he was well aware of the dangers of snakes. To him snakes meant pain, incapacity or even death, they were to be avoided at all costs. Consequently, my father never took us for wholesome family walks in the countryside because a snake might be hiding, waiting to bite.

The fear and suspicion of snakes is found in many cultures and has obvious allusions to Genesis 3:15 and the tempting serpent. However, in the minds of the Maltese hosts of Paul and his guards, the highly poisonous viper was simply an agent of their goddess Justice. Their simplistic and somewhat superstitious belief was that if a bad thing happened to you, you'd obviously done something to deserve divine punishment. So even though the shipwrecked party had survived their stormy ordeal, the snake was sent to finish off Paul.

Today many people's lives still come to untimely ends, and this could easily have been the termination of Paul's journey, but God had other plans. The islanders' suspicion and judgement turned to wonder and acclaim when he cheated death, so they declared Paul a god. No longer suspected as a criminal, he was welcomed as a divine healer and honoured with hospitality and gifts. Paul was seemingly unfazed by the snake and the attention; his focus was on God and the destination, and not the passing brouhaha.

† Lord God, give us courage and determination to stay focused on your destination for us in this life and help us not to be swayed by the miseries, mysteries and vanities of our journey.

For further thought

• In what ways is your faith in God swayed by circumstance? How can you develop a trust in God beyond difficulties, triumphs and self-reliance?

Friday 29 September
The Messiah mandate

Acts 28:11–22
For this reason I have asked to see you and talk with you. It is because of the hope of Israel that I am bound with this chain. (verse 20)

What is it that people hope for? In the traditional Chinese culture of my father's generation, their hopes are often explicitly exhibited in the statues of Fu, Lu and Shou, gods personifying the ideals of prosperity, status and longevity. Often in modern Western culture people hope for personal happiness, even if it causes the unhappiness of others. Whatever our culture's prevailing hopes are, they seldom comprise elements of hardship, suffering and imprisonment. Yet, this is what Paul embraced 'because of the hope of Israel'.

To establish a relationship with the Jewish leaders of Rome, Paul calls a meeting; however, they've never heard of him before. Paul appears to look like a chained criminal, so he endeavours to explain his judicial predicament. Also, not missing the opportunity to share the good news of the kingdom of God, he evangelises them. To the sceptics among them, he defended himself by suggesting that he was simply a faithful Jew. He had had first-hand experience of the fulfilment of prophecy, by encountering the resurrected Jesus, the long awaited Messiah, God's anointed one. His subsequent incarceration was not due to disloyalty to his people, but because of his faithfulness to the hope that they all shared. However, that hope was not about the prosperity, status and longevity of the Jews, but the poverty, humility and sacrifice embodied in Jesus.

Hope is more than just wishful thinking, blind optimism or desperate desire. Hope is a solid fact, a physical person, a resurrected reality. Jesus is the hope of Israel, the hope of the world, and the hope of you and me.

† Lord Jesus, when we are hopeless, help us to lift our eyes to you. When we are hopeful, allow it spread beyond ourselves, and when we are hoping, let it be in you alone.

For further thought

- What do you personally hope for? Are there things you have compromised on to see it realised? Have your own hopes eclipsed hope in Jesus?

Saturday 30 September
Mission matters

Acts 28:23–31

For two whole years Paul stayed there in his own rented house and welcomed all who came to see him. He proclaimed the kingdom of God and taught about the Lord Jesus Christ – with all boldness and without hindrance! (verses 30–31)

This is the end to the cinematic sweep of the writer Luke's description of the spread of the gospel, specifically to the non-Jewish Gentiles, through the lens of the apostle Paul. However, taken at face value it finishes neither majestically with the salvation of Rome, nor tragically with the execution of Paul, but rather perplexingly abruptly, which is highly frustrating. It leaves so many questions unanswered and might as well say, 'and they all lived happily ever after!' It almost reads like Luke suddenly ran out of papyrus to write on, consequently cramming in a hurried conclusion so as not to end mid-sentence. Maybe this is the point of Luke's final enigmatic brevity: we are invited by the absence of narrative to fill out the story for ourselves, joining the dots and making the connections with what has already been implied. At the start of Acts (1:8) Luke has Jesus declaring: 'You will be my witnesses in Jerusalem, and in all Judea and Samaria, and to the ends of the earth.' Luke concludes Paul's epic journey with his arrival in Rome, accomplishing all that Jesus had anticipated. After the mundane, miracles and mayhem, Paul finds a place of God's favour to minister from, but that's not the end!

† Father God, call us into your mission; Jesus, send us to the ends of the earth; Holy Spirit, empower us to deal with all adversity. May we faithfully fulfil what you ask of us.

For further thought

• How can you and your church community be living out the end of the story of Acts?

Friendship in the digital age
Friends with God

Notes based on the *The Message* and the New International Version (UK) by
Joshua 'Spanky' Moore

 Joshua 'Spanky' Moore is an Anglican minister and university chaplain based in New Zealand. He received his somewhat unconventional nickname from his teenage years playing in a punk band, and it has stuck ever since. Spanky has been involved in planting a now-expired Fresh Expression called The Kitchen, and he specialises in working with that exotic and elusive creature The Young Adult. He currently lives with his wife and daughter in Christchurch while struggling to grow asparagus.

Sunday 1 October
Fostering friendship

Proverbs 17:9–17

Overlook an offense and bond a friendship; fasten on to a slight and – good-bye, friend! (verse 9, The Message)

One of the strangest and yet most profound things a close friend has ever told me was 'You know what, Spanky? I like you so much, that even if you snapped and committed mass murder, I think I'd still come and visit you in prison.' As crazy as that sounded, I realised that in this person I had a truly loyal and deep friend.

Three years on, that unlikely conversation opened up an ongoing question around what God's 'Key Performance Indicators' of deep friendship might be. And I've come to the conclusion, as our passage from Proverbs points out, loyalty and forgiveness seem pretty high up on God's list.

And yet these are the very things our age of virtual friendship seems to struggle with most. Instead of sticking with each other through thick and thin, it's so easy for us to constantly assess our friendships against how useful they are to us, and how socially embarrassing someone is.

But what if one of the big ways Christians could bear witness to the good news in the world was through the way we went about our friendships? What 'Key Performance Indicators' would you put on God's friendship list?

† Father, thank you for the gift of friendship, and the close friends that you have given me. I'm especially grateful for having _____ in my life.

Monday 2 October
Friends with God

Friendship in the digital age – Joshua 'Spanky' Moore

Exodus 33:7–11

And God spoke with Moses face-to-face, as neighbors speak to one another. (verse 11, The Message)

For a number of years, I worked as a breakfast host on our local university radio station. One of the highlights was interviewing famous people – where for a glorious ten minutes I got to talk with normally untouchable people as if we were best friends. One morning as I walked into the studio, my producer informed me we had a late unscheduled interview with some 'theatre' actor. 'I'm not sure who he is. Sir … Ian … someone.' he said dismissively. I groaned inside. Just another boring interview to keep our advertisers happy.

The interview went fine. He had a very theatrical sounding voice. Almost like a wizard, even. But it wasn't until I got home, and my wife screamed with excitement as I walked through the door, 'YOU SPOKE TO GANDALF???'. It suddenly clicked. I'd just interviewed Sir Ian McKellen, one of the biggest stars from *The Lord of the Rings* films. It was the biggest interview of my career, and at the time I didn't even realise it.

I suspect the Exodus people of Israel must have had that same sense of utter disbelief about Moses's relationship with Yahweh. Spending time face to face – not just as a king with his servant, or a creator with his creature – but as friends. That was simply unthinkable.

We still struggle to get our heads around this mind-blowing God who doesn't just want to rule over us, or just intimately love us, but also wants to know us face to face as friends. Now, if that doesn't cause us to realise friendship is a gift that should be treated as something sacred, then surely what will?

† My God and friend, thank you for not just loving me, but liking me as well. Help me to seek your face and friendship every day.

For further thought

• Would 'FaceTime' on a smartphone have sufficed for the conversations between God and Moses?

Tuesday 3 October
Choosing your friends

Proverbs 22:22–25

Don't hang out with angry people; don't keep company with hotheads. Bad temper is contagious – don't get infected. (verses 24–25, The Message)

One of the most influential mentors in my life is a chap named Phil. He sought me out when my faith was on a knife edge and would serve me coffee. He's a man of exceptional faith and character. But I still remember the first time I got into a car with Phil behind the wheel. Suddenly an impulsive and impatient man had materialised in his place. Hand gesturing! Erratic braking! Horn tooting! Dangerous overtaking! Where had that calm, composed guru full of sagely wisdom gone?

You see, the encouragement from Proverbs to avoid hanging out with hotheads isn't as straightforward as it first appears. Because in my case having an (occasionally) hotheaded friend was one of the best things that ever happened to me! So where does this proverbial advice leave us when it comes to working out how to choose our friends?

I think it's pretty clear from Jesus' teachings that Christians aren't called to just hang out with nice, well behaved, easy people. But this passage reminds us to use wisdom and have a realistic view of our own weaknesses as well. So, if you struggle with gossip, think twice before befriending a big mouth. If you struggle with self-worth, don't befriend someone who's full of their own importance. If you struggle to care for 'the least of these', perhaps befriending a wealth-obsessed property tycoon isn't a great idea.

So, next time you're faced with a possible new friendship, ask yourself this: Will this relationship ultimately help my character move towards God's kingdom, or pull me away from it?

† God of wisdom, help me to discern the people you are calling me to befriend in my life – both sinners and saints.

For further thought

- Which of your friends help move you towards God's kingdom? Are the friends that come to mind Christian, or religious, or neither?

Friendship in the digital age – Joshua 'Spanky' Moore

October

Jonathan and David

---

1 Samuel 18:1–5

By the time David had finished reporting to Saul, Jonathan was deeply impressed with David – an immediate bond was forged between them. He became totally committed to David. From that point on he would be David's number-one advocate and friend. (verse 1, The Message)

I'm not ashamed to admit it. I have 1498 friends on Facebook. I probably know two-thirds of them personally, would say hi to about half if I walked past them in the street and would happily hide in a skip to avoid interacting with about a twentieth of them.

And all of this constant connection with so many people seems to have helped create a phenomenon among younger people: Mass Loneliness. Case in point: I had a friend over for dinner who told me about their flatmate who studies at my university. 'He's about to finish his degree, and he still doesn't have a single friend from his four years on campus.'

Sherry Turkle wrote the book *Alone Together: Why We Expect More from Technology and Less from Each Other*. In it she notes that social media 'offers just the right amount of access, just the right amount of control ... it puts people not too close, not too far, but at just the right distance. The world is now full of people who take comfort in being in touch with a lot of people whom they also keep at bay' (p. 15).

But in Jonathan and David's friendship we see something so different from this. Most of us can only maintain close friendships with a handful of people, and yet many of us have ploughed all of our energy into maintaining a huge catalogue of acquaintances.

So who in your life might God be inviting you to go deeper with? Are you brave enough to invest less of your time into the big crowds and to make yourself vulnerable to a few?

† Father, all that I am, have been and shall be is known to you. Help me to be myself around the friends I love the most.

For further thought

- Is Facebook a good medium for intimate friendships? What are its advantages and disadvantages?

Friendship in the digital age – Joshua 'Spanky' Moore

October

Wounds of a friend

Proverbs 27:5–19

Better is open rebuke than hidden love. Wounds from a friend can be trusted, but an enemy multiplies kisses. (verses 5–6, NIV)

I've always struggled with conflict. My family's motto was essentially 'Why can't we all just smile and get along?' and so I've spent a lot of my life trying not to rock the boat. When I confessed this to my psychologist friend recently, she told me the prescription she gives people with my conflict-averse streak is to order a burger from Burger King (this bit I liked the sound of), but then to complain about it and request a replacement burger. The mere suggestion made my palms go clammy! Lurking deep down in me is the assumption that 'correction is rejection'. I don't want anyone to feel rejected, and I certainly don't want to experience rejection myself – and so I often shy away from truth-telling.

But our passage in Proverbs challenges this and offers us a pointer towards forming deeper friendships. Yes – the best friendships involve loving acceptance, but we also need our friends to challenge us, correct us and even wound us. The irony is, people often challenge us from a distance via social media, while the ones we're closest to often choose to keep the peace rather than say hard truths. Many a Christian friendship has come to a tumultuous end because they've been built on superficial foundations that can't withstand truth-telling, correction or even a healthy difference of opinion!

So how might we begin to live into the idea that 'wounds from a friend can be trusted'? How can we become brave enough to speak the truth in love and allow ourselves to hear the truth when we're on the receiving end?

† Loving God, help me to be brave enough to speak and humble enough to receive your truth in love from my friends.

For further thought

• In your own words, what does God think of friendship? What is friendship for?

Friendship in the digital age – Joshua 'Spanky' Moore

Friday 6 October
Who can you trust?

Micah 7:1–7

Right-living humans are extinct. They're all out for one another's blood, animals preying on each other … Don't trust your neighbor, don't confide in your friend … But me, I'm not giving up. I'm sticking around to see what God will do. I'm waiting for God to make things right. (from verses 2–7, The Message)

From 2006 to 2009 I headed up a Fresh Expression of church called 'The Kitchen'. Over those three years the big thing God led our community towards was the rediscovery of Christian hospitality. On first impressions that sounds like a pretty cushy calling, right? And yes – plenty of pizza, pasta and red wine was consumed in the name of God over those years. But the much tougher part was exploring the 'Christian' dimension of 'Christian hospitality': what does it really mean to welcome the least to eat around our table?

One of the conversations that's stayed with me from this time was with a nice, upstanding, theologically educated couple, who shared with our group a vividly told story about some friends of theirs who'd once welcomed a hard-up person to dinner, only to have them take advantage of their hospitality – stealing jewellery and cash while pretending to go the bathroom. For them, the moral of the story was obvious. 'Sure, hospitality is fine and dandy, but don't push the Christian bit too far or you'll just end up with hurt feelings and poorer off.'

But our reading from Micah gives us a wake-up call in the face of these terrifying hospitality war stories. Anyone can expect the worst of people. But Christians! Now, we're called to constantly flirt with potentially dodgy company, to not give up and to stick around to see what God's doing in the world. Even if that means getting ripped off every now and then. So, who was the last person you had over for dinner?

† God of bread and wine, as you have welcomed me around your kingdom table, help me to welcome the least, the last and the lost around my table.

For further thought

• Invite someone new over for dinner this week.

Saturday 7 October
'Unliked'

Psalm 55

This isn't the neighborhood bully mocking me – I could take that. This isn't a foreign devil spitting invective – I could tune that out. It's you! We grew up together! You! My best friend! (verses 12–13, The Message)

Most of us understand that when a loved one dies, the healthy response is to grieve. We encourage people not to bottle up their emotions stoically – but instead to feel the pain of loss.

So why is it that when we experience the death of a friendship we don't usually allow ourselves to grieve in the same way? Is there anything more painful than experiencing the breakdown of a close friendship? When a mortal wound is inflicted? When harsh words are uttered, bridges are burned and the sweetness of friendship turns sour? And how much more painful is all this when Christians fall out with each other and still can't navigate the stormy waters of forgiveness. Jesus himself experienced the ultimate betrayal by one of his friends and then total abandonment by the others. And Psalm 55 perfectly expresses the fact that so often the death of a friendship can feel just as painful as the death of a loved one.

No doubt you can call to mind the grief of friendship lost in your own life. So how are followers of Jesus to respond to the reality of being 'unliked', when reconciliation is beyond grasp?

Of course, there are no pithy solutions – but what if we could allow our friendships to die gracefully, and to do our best to love those from a distance whom we no longer can like up close?

† God of grace, help me to grieve the friendships I've had that have died, while still holding on to your spirit of peace, hope and forgiveness.

For further thought
• Where have you seen Psalm 55 lived out in your church or friendship group?

Friendship in the digital age – Joshua 'Spanky' Moore

October

Friendship in the digital age
Face to face

Notes based on the New Revised Standard Version by **Helen Van Koevering**

Living in Mozambique for 28 years has challenged Helen Van Koevering, raised in England, to look for God's goodness in a post-colonial, post-conflict, rapidly changing context. Helen is a parish priest in the largely Muslim town of Lichinga, and Director of Ministry with the Anglican Diocese of Niassa, a diocese which has experienced a church-planting people movement that has doubled members and congregations since 2004.

Sunday 8 October
Friends and family

Proverbs 18:24 – 19:7

Some friends play at friendship, but a true friend sticks closer than one's nearest kin ... wealth brings many friends, but the poor are left friendless. (verses 18:24 and 19:4)

This week we look at the nitty-gritty of face-to-face friendships, starting with a reading from the book of Proverbs. Everyone loves a good proverbial cliché to live by, to read on a fridge magnet, to throw out when it seems a wise word is called for. It leaves out much that falls between, much like the two quotes here, written as they are at the beginning and end of our reading today.

And what 'falls between' is context and time, history and space. There is the role of walking in integrity, foolish speech, desiring relationship without giving time to knowing someone, the speed at which we live our lives, anger and actions that kill relationships.

How can we learn what a 'true friend' is? How can we be a 'true friend'? Possibly through recognising the brokenness in all of us, including and mostly in me. Possibly by trying to listen to rather than speak over. Possibly by taking time out of a schedule to sit down and visit someone. Possibly by remembering that the only person you can really change in this world is yourself.

† Jesus, the true friend who sticks closer than my nearest kin, may I know you more nearly today.

Jesus' friendship

Luke 7:31–35

Look, a glutton and a drunkard, a friend of tax collectors and sinners!
(verse 34)

Before Jesus enters into the Pharisee's house as the invited yet unwelcomed guest, and yet the place where a woman was to anoint his feet with her oil, tears and kisses and receive forgiveness for her sins, we learn something of Jesus' friendship.

Both John and Jesus are God's messengers. John's ascetic lifestyle was rigorous: people said he had a demon. Jesus, who doesn't use food and drink as a means of marking what and who is holy, but rather as a means of uniting himself with all, is criticised. To point a finger at either is to keep our minds closed and ignore Wisdom, who wants to befriend all men and women. Wisdom, who sees the heart and need of someone and not just the exterior judged clean or unclean by society, doesn't just reach out to help someone be better, presentable and acceptable, but meets everyone where they are.

What can we learn from Jesus' friendship? 'Wisdom is vindicated by all her children' (verse 35): all those who hear and follow the way of God are Wisdom's children. Jesus' friendship was marked by hospitality, whether as the guest or the host. He was the guest of all who invited him, but also became the host in his welcome of all. May we be encouraged to follow Jesus in this pattern of friendship, regardless of whom we meet or have contact with today, and hear Jesus' call to friendship as radical hospitality.

† Lord, may we follow you on this path of hospitality, and have our eyes opened to see opportunities for friendship God's way, with all the different people we mix with today.

For further thought

• Whether as a guest or host, take note of each person you meet today. Pray for what is hidden from sight, for any burden they may be carrying and not showing. Intentionally try practising hospitality!

Friendship in the digital age – Helen van Koevering

October

Don't invite your friends

> ### Luke 14:12–14
> *When you give a banquet, invite the poor, the crippled, the lame and the blind. (verse 13)*

When it comes time for the invitation to 'come and receive' during communion, the congregation I serve come forward, kneel and wait together with open hands for the priest to offer the bread and the wine. It is a beautiful moment, seeing the women and men: the Director of Education in our town and the old widowed Ana; Tomás in his wheelchair and young choir master Osvaldo; all kneel side by side in equal need and responding to the same invitation to the banquet's life.

We hear more on the theme of radical hospitality in our reading today. In the invitation to the banquet, we have an image of the heavenly feast to which we are all invited, and of which we can catch a glimpse in our churches, whether it be called Holy Communion or Eucharist. We also have an image of those who will be there at the banquet – all those marginalised, hurt and humbled by the world. This will be the company into which we are called to be a part, now and in the future.

It is as we open ourselves to be radically hospitable friends that we might learn to see ourselves also in need of receiving radical hospitality in ways that go beyond friendship with others like ourselves – or in whose circle we would like to be seen. Those are the ones we have most easily and willingly called 'friend', and we are the ones who need to hear God's welcome to the banquet for all. There, we all will be in the company of the forgiven and the just.

† Jesus Christ, Son of God, in your invitation we see the potential of your loving mercy and reconciliation for all people. Thank you.

For further thought

• Next time you are present at Communion or the Eucharist, pray for those around as those who are sharing this meal with you. Thank God for the world's diversity and the beauty of the vision of the banquet.

Wednesday 11 October
Sharing bread

Psalm 41

Even my bosom friend in whom I trusted, who ate of my bread, has lifted the heel against me. (verse 9)

The hurts of those closest to us go deep. Broken trust and betrayal by those whom we have held closer than others affect our very being. Those who have known this describe themselves as 'scarred for life', and it can take time for them to recover, if they ever do.

But here in this psalm we are given permission and guidance to lament our hurt, and in lamenting recognise God's presence again with trust and thanksgiving. Look at the pattern seen in Psalm 41. In this personal prayer are all the elements of a psalm of lament: calling on God's name, describing the present need, a call and a reason for God's intervention, and praise to God. Between the beginning and the end petitions to God, nothing is spared from telling it as it is, honestly laying it out in prayer. The situation has been evaluated and found to be what it is: threatening and insecure. With integrity and recognition of any of his own sin in the situation, the psalmist asks for healing from God. Then, in the often abrupt way of a psalm of lament, the psalmist, holding on to his knowledge of God, returns to a confidence in his ever-present God. The lament for hurt has turned towards remembrance and praise. The psalmist has responded with 'Yes' to the ongoing blessing of God, not just for him but for all.

That's the truth! Working through our pain and hurt, experiencing the depths and discovering the way through, we learn what others around us may need to hear some day, too: that God is with us.

† Lord, you hold us in your presence for ever. May I grow in that knowledge even in the hardest times.

For further thought
• Try writing a psalm of lament.

Friendship in the digital age – Helen van Koevering

October

Thursday 12 October
Vulnerable, self-offering friendship

John 13:12–30

So after receiving the bread, he immediately went out. And it was night.
(verse 30)

The Last Supper provides us with an image of friends around a table. Friendship, and friendship's betrayal, are right at the heart of the gospel. But darkness can happen and can rock the community of the church, and make you wonder what we're all doing.

A visiting priest preached on this theme. She asked the question of why people stay with the faith community, why do they hold on when hurt happens in this community of Jesus' friends? It takes a choice to remain, to find meaning, love and God in this way. It takes a choice to continue to learn and give through difficulties and struggles with friendship and betrayal in the Christian community. Jesus, through vulnerable and self-offering love, revealed that God wouldn't allow anything to separate God from those he loved. This self-giving and accompanying love is the heart of God. To identify in that way with Jesus brings the choice of aligning yourself with people who are trying to make God's presence a palpable reality in the world. Together, we are choosing to learn to love through the pain, hurt and difficulty.

One of Jesus' friends, Judas, left and the night came in. Evil is present and possible even in such a community. Jesus, by his death and resurrection, came to show us that darkness doesn't have the last word. The last word belongs to love's work in the friendship he calls us to.

† Loving and holy God, teach us the meaning of friendship in the work of love which you lived in your community of disciples.

For further thought

- Consider any recent reactions you may have had to hurt in your Christian community. How did you react? How might thinking of friendship as a work of love change anything for you now?

Friday 13 October
'O Verbo'

Luke 21:5–19

You will be betrayed even by parents and brothers, by relatives and friends; and they will put some of you to death. You will be hated by all because of my name. But not a hair of your head will perish. By your endurance you will gain your souls. (verses 16–19)

These are wise words in our reading today, words to keep in our hearts for those harder days that will come. Listen well: don't prepare defensively, nor harden your heart and be fearful of reaching out and testifying to the love of God. That love is wisdom, the word and the keeper of your soul.

In Mozambique, the national language inherited from the Portuguese colonial centuries is Portuguese. Not that everyone speaks nor writes this, because more than 21 other languages exist in Mozambique, none of which are spoken in our diocese. Here, in this language, Jesus as the Word of God is heard as 'o Verbo', the Verb of God. The active, living, known and knowing love of God is Jesus, God's Son, who speaks in this passage today. Through Jesus' Spirit we live and more than endure life's ups and downs: we are transformed, made new and whole. And that potential is also there for our families, communities and neighbourhoods as it is for the church. There is nothing that can separate God's love from the Beloved, a love that cares about even the words and the details, 'the hair of your head'. Not only has Jesus taken the initiative to warn us of troubles ahead but he has paved the way through his death and resurrection. He lives by his Spirit. In us and this world.

Mozambicans know this, as they now live in peace after a war where 'brother killed brother' and all of life was destabilised by others. That love remains is their testimony.

† God, we know your presence with us, living and breathing love for our souls. May we remain always aware of that love, the love that remains for all time and place, guiding us always.

For further thought

- Investigate the presence of the church in post-conflict places of the world like Mozambique and hear the testimony to the remaining life and love of the Spirit. Be encouraged.

Friendship in the digital age – Helen van Koevering

October

Saturday 14 October
A new commandment

John 15:12–17

You are my friends if you do what I command you. I do not call you servants any longer, because the servant does not know what the master is doing; but I have called you friends, because I have made known to you everything that I have heard from my Father. (verses 14–15)

Friendship lived in our face-to-face realities has been the theme of this week. Today we see the example that Jesus left for us.

Here, in what is known as the Farewell discourses in John's Gospel, Jesus speaks definitively of his pattern and purpose of friendship. The love of friends is seen in the laying down your life for your friends: this is underlining the sacrifice, commitment and sometimes pain (and the imminent death on the cross of Jesus) involved in relationships that follow his pattern and purpose of friendship. It is a self-giving that Jesus modelled towards all and is most beautifully captured in the song of humility of Philippians 2:5–11. The self-emptying of Jesus is to be in our own minds when we seek true friendship.

Yet today's verse also points towards the purpose of such friendship. It is to mirror the mutuality seen in the relationship of friendship that Jesus shares with his Father. It is similar to that of an adult child with the parent that nurtured, protected, guided during his years of growth towards maturity, and the now peer relationship that is a sign of equal regard, mutuality and mature friendship. It is the purpose beyond the sacrificial parental investment of loving care and provision for a child: mutuality of loving friendships both with the parent and new friends and partners, spouses and the child's own children.

Sacrifice and mutuality: two sides of the same coin called friendship.

† Teach me, Lord, to be a friend in the pattern you revealed: friends with my spouse, my children, my neighbours, my community. In this way, may I be transformed to be part of your transforming presence in this world.

For further thought

• How can this model of friendship be made real in online friendships?

Stories from Judges
Triumph and victory

Notes based on the Revised Standard Version by **Anthony Loke**

Dr Anthony Loke finished his PhD in Old Testament from the University of Wales in 2011. He teaches Old Testament in the local seminaries and in churches. He has written ten books and numerous articles mostly in the area of the biblical books and Bible characters. His wife teaches English in a Christian private school. Their daughter, who graduated from Brown University in the United States, is also an English and art teacher in a local government school while their son is studying cognitive psychology at the University of Nottingham branch in Semenyih, Malaysia. The family members are cat lovers and they share the house with their feline friends.

Sunday 15 October
Caleb's daughter makes a claim

Judges 1:9–15

She said to him, 'Give me a present; since you have set me in the land of the Negeb, give me also springs of water.' And Caleb gave her the upper springs and the lower springs. (verse 15)

In many cultures, daughters are not given the same prominence as sons. For a long time, China implemented the 'one child' policy to curb rising birth rates. Parents who had a daughter often continued to try a second time, hoping for a son. China just recently relaxed their ruling and now allowed couples to have two children. We can see the same preference for sons rather than daughters in ancient Israel, as in Numbers 27, for example. In the patriarchal society, daughters had no share of the inheritance.

In today's story, Caleb's daughter, Achsah, was given to Othniel as the 'prize' for taking the city of Kirath-sepher or Debir. While her new husband got a city, a bride and a good marriage, she in comparison received a pittance from her father as a wedding dowry – the dry land of the Negeb. She came and asked him to give her a more suitable dowry – springs of water – in order that the land of Negeb be fruitful. Her action can be seen as subversive as she didn't dutifully accept what was given to her. By asking her father in public, he had to respond positively to save face. Thus, Othniel got more than he bargained for – a smart wife and a wedding dowry!

† Lord, you also taught us to ask in order to receive. Help us to ask well in order to receive what you desire to give to us.

Ehud's tribute

Judges 3:12–30

But when the people of Israel cried to the Lord, the Lord raised up for them a deliverer, Ehud, the son of Gera, the Benjaminite, a left-handed man ... (verse 15a)

The stories in the book of Judges follow a template: sin of apostasy, oppression, cry for deliverance, sending of a judge as saviour and rest in the land. The people entered into this vicious cycle when they sinned against God but, even though God delivered them from oppression by their enemies and gave them rest, they never came out of the downward spiral. The first saviour (called a judge) was Othniel and he did exactly what was expected of him. However, the subsequent judges were less idealised and each had weakness and imperfections.

The second judge, Ehud, had to use deception to garner victory. Firstly, we are told by the storyteller that Ehud was left-handed. This can mean that he was ambidextrous and was trained to also use his left hand. This is the key to his story. If he was left-handed, he would conceal his sword on his right thigh. The soldiers would normally think that a right-handed person would conceal a weapon on his left thigh and missed the concealed weapon on the right thigh! Secondly, Ehud pretended to have a secret message from God only for the king's ears, thus paving the way for him to carry out his assassination in private and getting away undetected. By using deception, Ehud was able to get near to King Eglon to deliver the fatal blow with the sword.

Is victory achieved only through deception? Is victory by any means truly acceptable to God?

† Lord, do I need to resort to deception in order to get my way? Can I not trust you more in my life? Show me your way in all I do.

For further thought
• Does the end justify the means or does the means justify the end?

Prophetess Deborah

Judges 4:4–22

… Nevertheless, the road on which you are going will not lead to your glory, for the Lord will sell Sisera into the hand of a woman. (part of verse 9)

In the time of the fourth round of oppression, God allowed Jabin, king of Canaan, and his general, Sisera, to oppress the people of Israel. The Canaanites had military supremacy in the presence of nine hundred horse chariots. When God raised the fourth judge to deliver his people, it was not a man but a woman and prophetess called Deborah. What happened to the men? Were there no men qualified to be the next judge? Instead, Deborah took the initiative and summoned Barak to be the commander of the forces of Israel to fight against Sisera near the river Kishon. Like a good soldier, Barak sensed something wrong in the choice of the battleground. One doesn't engage an army of chariots with infantry on flat ground as it would be suicidal! Barak also realised the difficulty in mustering the tribes to go to war without a divine representative, the 'male' judge.

Deborah's response to Barak's reluctance was to predict that the victory will not be won by a man but by another woman. What a blow to the man's ego! And indeed it was Jael, the wife of Heber, who achieved victory with a tent peg and hammer, not a sword or chariot. She allowed the fleeing Sisera into her tent, gave him warm milk, and then sent him to eternal sleep. This is definitely not the way for a general to die, at the hands of an ordinary woman. The fourth victory came through the avenue of two resourceful women who took up the initiative when the men failed to do so.

† Lord, help us to remember that help can come from any quarter and, in such times, we must do our part to rise up and answer the call.

For further thought

• Judges, we will see, is a violent book. What do you make of God's relationship to the violence we have encountered so far?

Stories from Judges – Anthony Loke

October

Call of Gideon

Judges 6:11–16, 34–40

... Pray, Lord, how can I deliver Israel? Behold, my clan is the weakest in Manasseh, and I am the least in my family. (part of verse 15)

The fifth judge was Gideon, and a rather reluctant one. When God first appeared to him, he refused to believe that he was the chosen one to deliver Israel (verse 15). His excuse, like Moses, was based on the belief that he was weak and that he came from the least of the clans and tribes. God's assurance to Gideon was that he was with him and therefore he cannot fail the mission. Gideon's request for a sign was fulfilled. The angel of the Lord touched the food and fire came out from the rock and consumed it. We would expect Gideon to faithfully obey God's call and begin his mission. In verses 34–35, we read that Gideon raised an army ready to fight but in the following verses, Gideon continued to test God. He asked not for one more sign but two, the second being a reversal of the first. We are familiar with the sign of the fleece on the threshing floor – the fleece to be wet while the floor was to be dry. Even though God performed the sign, Gideon was not fully satisfied and requested for the sign to be repeated in reverse.

Did Gideon falter in his resolve like Jephthah (chapter 11)? Did he want more assurance from God, a form of insurance of victory? Only when he had received, by now, the third sign, did Gideon lead his people to victory. How many times does it take for us to believe in God and his promises?

† Lord, I believe but help my unbelief!

For further thought

• Discerning God's will is not always straightforward. How have you discerned it in your life?

Sifting of the soldiers

Judges 7:1–8

With the three hundred men that lapped I will deliver you and give the Midianites into your hand … (part of verse 7)

Everything is ready for the battle to begin. Gideon has mustered his men, all 32 000, from the Abiezrites and four other tribes. But God intervened at this point and decided that because of the large number, the people may judge the coming victory as entirely due to their human effort. The first sifting reduced the army to 10 000 men. God decided again that the number was still large. This time God set the parameters to weed out a suitable number to fight. The soldiers were asked to drink water and those who knelt down to drink were separated from those who lapped the water like a dog. No explanation is given by the storyteller. Perhaps those who lapped the water showed that they were more alert to the surroundings and therefore more ready to act in times of danger. That left Gideon with only 300 men. At this point, the reader can identify himself with Gideon. The hesitant hero who decided to bring a large army to fight has his army drastically reduced to the size of an expeditionary force. Yet victory in battle was achieved through the reduced number (verses 22–23).

Was this the way God had to teach his hesitant hero? No matter how many proofs he was given, Gideon needed to be convinced each time. The reduction of his army demonstrated that God can overcome any obstacles in delivering his people from their enemies. Victory is solely due to God.

† Lord, with you on our side, we can put a thousand to flight!

For further thought

• Do we put our trust in numbers or in God?

Stories from Judges – Anthony Loke

Gideon defeats the Midianites

Judges 7:9–22

When Gideon heard the telling of the dream and its interpretation, he worshiped; and he returned to the camp of Israel, and said. 'Arise; for the Lord has given the host of Midian into your hand.' (verse 15)

The reluctant hero has his army reduced to a mere 300 men. But God gave him the promise that even with the 300, the Midianites will be given into Gideon's hand (verse 7). However, our reluctant hero is still unconvinced of victory. He needed another sign just before the battle. God told him to go incognito into the enemy's camp to hear for himself what the Midianites were talking about. God knew he was scared to go alone and suggested that Gideon take his servant Purah with him. Together they entered the camp and overheard one soldier telling another of his dream. Through the enemy's dream and the interpretation of the dream by the comrade, God used the non-Israelites as the voice of assurance that everything was in God's control. It seemed that the enemy had more faith in God's power than the Israelite counterparts.

With that final assurance, Gideon returned to camp, rallied his men and routed the enemy's camp. The surprise attack caused confusion within the enemy camp. Using lighted torches, the smashing of the earthen pots and the blowing of trumpets, the enemy was thrown into utter confusion, and the hysteria allowed Gideon and his small band to cut the enemy down to size. It is strange fact that God continued to use this reluctant hero despite his insistence on many signs. Perhaps at times we are not very different from Gideon.

† Lord, help me not to always make excuses for not following you or believing in you.

For further thought

• Moses was also like Gideon in making excuses for not believing in God. What other biblical characters come to mind?

Abimelech usurps authority

Judges 9:1–21

Now therefore, if you acted in good faith and honour when you made Abimelech king, and if you have dealt well with Jerubaal and his house …
(part of verse 16)

Gideon, known also by his nickname Jerubaal, had a large family of seventy sons. He also had a son, Abimelech, through his concubine from Shechem. Abimelech means 'my father is king'. Was that the way of Gideon saying that his favourite son was expected to take over his leadership after his death? But Israel's judges were not hereditary. When the judge died, God would raise another judge to counter the enemy. The people of God proved to be unfaithful, and they went into the vicious cycle forgetting the previous deliverance by God. In Judges 8:35, the storyteller gives another hint of their unfaithfulness – they would also forget the kindness of Gideon in delivering them, and instead did a great injustice to Gideon's family.

Abimelech had less chance of becoming the next leader since there were seventy brothers ahead of him. Instead of relying on God, he sweet-talked his way, convincing the people of Shechem, his mother's relatives, that one ruler was better than seventy. He got the people of Shechem to side with him and brutally killed his seventy older brothers, except one who got away. Abimelech was proclaimed king at Shechem. The youngest son, Jotham, escaped and told an allegorical parable to demand justice for his murdered brothers. In essence, the parable foretold Abimelech's eventual downfall and demise.

Brother killing brother to get position and power? That is not uncommon, and people often resort to such devious ways to get power and stay on in power. Where is justice, one may ask?

† Lord, the ground is often soaked with innocent blood which cries out for justice. Hear their cry!

For further thought

- The traditional Christian and Jewish answer when justice does not come on earth is that justice definitely be served in the hereafter. What do you make of this?

Stories from Judges – Anthony Loke

October

Stories from Judges
Death and disaster

Notes based on the writer's translation from the New Revised Standard Version by
Alexandra Wright

Alexandra Wright is senior rabbi of The Liberal Jewish Synagogue, St John's Wood, London. She studied at Leo Baeck College, London, where she also taught classical Hebrew after ordination in 1986. She was volunteer chaplain at the North London Hospice and is drawn particularly to accompanying those who are journeying towards their final days – which really includes all of us.

Sunday 22 October
Death of Abimelech

Judges 9:22–29, 50–56

But a certain woman threw an upper millstone on Abimelech's head and crushed his skull. Immediately he called to the young man who carried his armour and said to him, 'Draw your sword and kill me, so people will not say about me, "A woman killed him."' So the young man thrust him through, and he died. (verses 53–54)

There are two kinds of leaders in the book of Judges: charismatic military heroes who rescue the Israelites from oppression and self-proclaimed, often violent, brutal and reckless individuals, driven by mercenary motives, vengeance and a thirst for victory.

Abimelech, who has killed seventy of his brothers, belongs to the ignominious group. His name means 'my father is king', an ironic label, given that his father, Gideon, has refused the crown and that Abimelech, who does accept kingship, appears to have no personal relationship with his Father in heaven. In fact, God's place is supplanted by Abimelech himself – it is not God who raises him up as king, but the man himself who 'lords it over' Israel for three years. Four ruthless battles bring down the people together with Abimelech.

His comeuppance, killed by a millstone that cracks his skull, is God's measure for measure, a punishment for the murder of his brothers, whom he has killed 'with one stone' (9:5). Even worse for Abimelech, he is maimed by a woman, and calling for his arms-bearer to finish him off, he seeks to avoid the dishonour and shame of having his male supremacy emasculated!

† Eternal God, school us in your teachings and make us loyal to your commandments. May we never consent to evil, or surrender to temptation or self-contempt.

Monday 23 October
The call of Jephthah

Judges 11:1–11

Now Jephthah the Gileadite, the son of a prostitute, was a mighty warrior. Gilead was the father of Jephthah. Gilead's wife also bore him sons; and when his wife's sons grew up, they drove Jephthah away, saying to him, 'You shall not inherit anything in our father's house; for you are the son of another woman.' (verses 1–2)

Jephthah's unfortunate birth makes him an outsider to his own brothers. Disinherited and forced to flee from home, 'men of low character' gather around him. They are the joyriders of the Hebrew Bible, raiding whatever comes within view.

But Jephthah is also a *gibbor chayyil* – a man of strength and military prowess – and when Israel finds itself at the mercy of the Ammonites, the elders of Gilead – the very men who had rejected him – beg him to return to be their commander and chief. If God delivers them into my hand, says Jephthah, then I'll be your commander.

Here is a man marked by his birth and background, rejected by family and tribe, attracted to worthless types – the Bible calls them *reikim* – 'empty'. Why doesn't he stand up to his brothers to ask for a share of his father's inheritance? We are reminded of the daughters of Zelophehad in the book of Numbers, who are not afraid to demand a share of their father's property, even though they are excluded from the inheritance because they are women.

What does it feel like to be an outsider? To be excluded and always harbour a sense that one doesn't belong anywhere? For centuries, the Jewish people were foreigners, outsiders in the lands in which they lived, unwanted, expelled and oppressed.

But with our books and rituals, with our profound sense of history and the values that sustain us, we have found a way to contribute the fruits of our heritage to the well-being of the world of which we are a part.

† Give us the courage, O God, to keep alive in dark ages a vision of humaneness and harmony.

For further thought

• How do we create a sense of belonging somewhere and the confidence that we each have something to contribute to the well-being of society?

Stories from Judges – Alexandra Wright

October

Tuesday 24 October
Jephthah's rash vow

This is how the outsider addresses his daughter, as one who has brought 'trouble' upon him. She, nameless, an only child without brother or sister – and where is her mother? – emerges from her home, clasping a timbrel and dancing. In her own eyes, she is like Miriam, the sister of Moses, who takes a timbrel in her hand and goes out with all the women following her dancing and singing. Had news of her father's routing of the Ammonites preceded his arrival? She came out to see the conquering hero, innocent of the terrible vow that whatever comes out of the door of his house to meet him on his safe return would belong to God and be offered as a burnt offering.

Yet, he sees not the loveliness of her youthful purity, but only calamity and trouble. The vow must be honoured and she knows, as her father also knows, that it cannot be retracted. Unlike the companions of her father's youth, those 'empty fellows' who fall in with him when he is rejected by his family, her friends, who accompany her into the hills to weep and 'bewail her maidenhood', hold her in their memory and mark her life with songs of lament for four days each year.

Like David's lament for Jonathan, grieving for his 'brother', whose love was 'wonderful, more than the love of women', this young girl's companions teach us about the enduring love and loyalty of friendship and the comfort and strength it brings at times of grief and sadness.

† Do not entreat me to leave you, or turn back from following you. For where you go, I will go … your people shall be my people, and your God, my God.

For further thought
- When we have lost our way, our lives bleak and lonely, let us ask, how can we honour and be faithful to our friends?

Birth of Samson

Judges 13:1–14, 24

'Now be careful not to drink wine or strong drink, or to eat anything unclean, for you shall conceive and bear a son. No razor is to come on his head, for the boy shall be a nazirite to God from birth.' (parts of verses 4–5)

Manoah's wife is barren and has borne no children – according to the angel who makes no bones about her condition. The midrash – ancient rabbinic commentaries on the Bible – tells us that it might have been her husband who was sterile – their lack of children the result of marital discord.

When she does become pregnant, Manoah's wife is careful to observe the rules of her pregnancy – no wine or spirit, no unclean food. And when the child is born, she allows his hair to grow, in accordance with the laws of the Nazirite in Numbers 6, for the boy is to be consecrated to God, with priest-like responsibilities.

His mother names him Shimshon (Samson), a name connected with the Hebrew word *shemesh* ('sun'), no doubt a mythological allusion, but also as her wish-fulfilment that this child will aspire to be full of light, goodness and strength. God does indeed bless him and he is filled with the divine spirit.

But like most teenagers and young adults, his hormones get the better of him and his parents are bewildered by his dangerous liaisons with foreign women. It is, of course, all part of God's hidden plan; Samson will marry a Philistine woman and eventually be seduced by Delilah, who discovers the secret of his strength and delivers him into the hands of the Philistine enemy. It is only a matter of time until his hair grows back, his strength is regained and he takes his revenge on those by whom he has been betrayed.

† Purify our spirits, O God, that we may serve you in truth.

For further thought

• Do we have the courage to allow our children to be what they are destined to be without imposing our own expectations on them?

Stories from Judges – Alexandra Wright

October

Samson and Delilah

Judges 16:4–22

So he ... said to her, 'A razor has never come upon my head; for I have been a nazirite to God from my mother's womb. If my head were shaved, then my strength would leave me; I would become weak, and be like anyone else.' (verse 17)

The Italian artist Caravaggio's painting of Samson and Delilah shows the sleeping, shorn Samson lying with his head in Delilah's lap. The light falls on his forehead and shaven head, his face and neck in shadow. Her buxom form is leaning over him, one finger held up to her lips indicating to the two Philistines, shackling his wrists, that they are to keep quiet. In the other hand, she holds a razor. Her almost innocent round face is bathed in light, her mouth slightly apart, only the folds of her red gown and breasts betraying her sensuality.

This is the man who has torn asunder a full-grown lion, killed thirty citizens of Ashkelon; he has caught 300 foxes, tied their tails together, set alight torches between each pair of tails to set fire to the Philistines' grain, vineyards and olive trees. With the jawbone of an ass, he has killed 1000 men and torn down the doors and gateposts of the town gate and carried them to the top of a hill near Hebron.

Now, exhausted by Delilah's nagging, 'Tell me, what makes you so strong?' he sleeps. He has strung her along with stories, but wearied to death by her constant pressing – the rabbis interpret this to mean her intimacy with him – he gives way and tells the truth. Unaware of his own helplessness, he imagines he will break loose and shake himself free as he has done before.

Samson lives somewhere between the physicality of his strength and the illusion of love with the women he encounters.

† Source of mercy, when my body and mind fail, be my rock and my strength, for in you do I put my trust.

For further thought

• How can we know when the pleasure we pursue is fleeting and illusory? And how do we recognise the enduring power of love and happiness?

Death of Samson

Judges 16:23–31

Then his brothers and all his family came down and took him and brought him up and buried him … in the tomb of his father Manoah. He had judged Israel for twenty years. (part of verse 31)

Jewish funeral rituals are simple: the deceased is buried as quickly as possible, so that mourners are not left in limbo for too long. The dead are dressed in white shrouds and buried in a plain wooden coffin, rich and poor alike, for neither silver nor gold will be carried into the grave. Mourners recite a prayer of praise to God, affirming their acknowledgement of God's sovereignty even in times of sadness and grief. The mourners sit for seven days (*shivah*), reciting prayers, visited by family, friends and community who bring food, companionship and memories of the dead.

Here Samson, who has brought the temple crashing down on to the Philistine people, is carried by his brothers and father's household to the tomb of his father Manoah. The promise of a child who would be consecrated to God seems far away. The light of his mother's life is extinguished. We are left with the image of a man paradoxically weakened by the strength that allowed him to overcome his enemies. He is hungry for intimacy with women, yet harassed by their nagging for answers; he seeks vengeance against the Philistines, but is blind to the enticements of Delilah.

At the end of his life, eyeless in Gaza, a small boy appears, leads him by the hand and places him, according to his instruction, between the pillars of the temple. And one cannot help but imagine that the story has come full circle – that the boy is the child promised to his mother, now to be gathered to his fathers in the family tomb.

† What are we, Eternal One, that you take note of us? What is our worth, that you consider us? We are like a breath, our days are as a passing shadow.

For further thought

• How do we cherish and hold on to the memories of those we love and who are no longer with us? And how can we express our gratitude for all the blessings they brought to us?

Stories from Judges – Alexandra Wright

October

Saturday 28 October
Death of a concubine

Judges 19:1, 16–30

As morning appeared, the woman came and fell down at the door of the man's house where her master was, until it was light. (verse 26)

In December 2012, in India, a young physiotherapy student was gang-raped on a bus, beaten and assaulted and left with horrific injuries. Jyoti Singh subsequently died. The rape and murder prompted outbreaks of protests in India and a demand that the law be made more stringent for sexual assault against women in a country that has not always seen women as victims.

How many centuries mark the time between this horrific event of our own century and the story of the nameless concubine in the book of Judges, who is pushed out of the house where she is staying by her husband, raped and abused by strangers all night long until morning? In the growing light of dawn, she makes it back, but collapses at the entrance of the man's house. Unresponsive to her husband's demand to get up, he puts her on the donkey and sets out for home.

Why, when he returns to his home, does he take hold of the concubine and cut her up limb by limb into twelve parts, posting them throughout the territory of Israel?

In an age of awareness of human rights and the preciousness of human life, does it not seem shocking and frightening that there are still places that tolerate and even encourage contempt of women, and worse, violence and abuse against them?

What is the name of the concubine in the story? Where is her voice among the voices of her husband, father-in-law, host and depraved attackers? Anonymous and silent, she symbolises all women who remain oppressed and abused in the world.

† Out of the depths I call to you, O Eternal God. O God, listen to my cry.

For further thought

- How can we be more attentive to the plight of those whose human rights are diminished or violated by abuse?

Here I stand
(Martin Luther 500th anniversary)
I can do no other

Notes based on the New Revised Standard Version by **Raj Patta**

 Raj Patta is ordained in the Andhra Evangelical Lutheran Church, a South Indian church of approximately 1.5 million members and the largest Lutheran denomination in India. Until 2014 he was the National General Secretary of the Student Christian Movement in India and previously worked for National Council of Churches in India in their advocacy work for Dalit Christian rights. He is from Andhra Pradesh, India, and is married to Shiny. They have two sons. Raj blogs at www.thepattas.blogspot.com and is passionate about reading the Bible from the margins of society.

Sunday 29 October
Hidden and revealed

Isaiah 45:15
Truly you are a God who hides himself, O God of Israel, the Saviour. (verse 15)

This year marks the 500th anniversary of the day that a Catholic monk nailed 95 theses to a door in Wittenberg and began the Protestant Reformation. In the next three weeks we shall look first at others in the Bible who have, like Luther, stood firm for what they believed God was asking him to do. Luther felt impelled to act as he did: Here I stand, I can do no other. Whatever the consequences, we must obey God rather than human beings.

The prophet who wrote Deutero-Isaiah was one such figure who stood firm, even when God was absent. The oracle of Isaiah says that on one hand God hides God's self and, on the other, God is revealed as Saviour. Luther explained this by saying that God is hidden in the context of captivity and oppression, and God reveals God's self in the saving and liberating acts of our times. In other words, when humans create contexts of oppression and violence, God's self is concealed, and when such situations are addressed and overcome, God's self is revealed, for only then salvation and liberation are realised!

† God, challenge us to be your channels by participating in your struggles of creation, justice and liberation.

Here I stand – Raj Patta

October

305

Standing firm

Isaiah 7:9b

If you do not stand firm in faith, you shall not stand at all. (verse 9b)

What does it mean to stand firm in faith? For Martin Luther, 'faith alone' was a way to understand justification, for in his day the church was dominated by the rule of Rome alone.

I am a Christian from a Dalit background, historically called the 'untouchables'. As I consider Luther's position, and I as reflect on being a Dalit Christian, I remember many times of being looked down on for being Dalit. The mindset of some in the community was that they were upper caste and knowledge was theirs. Our teachers taught us that knowledge was their domain. Church was liberating because it gave us a different education. When we started getting educated and improving ourselves, the mindset of the upper caste did not change. They continued to look down on us. But Christian faith gave us a sense of dignity, it empowered us and it gave us self-respect. We had internalised a certain way of thinking. My Dalit consciousness arose at seminary; and now I am able to question and speak back. Faith helped us to stand firm in a profound way.

Today, many societies today define themselves as secular, for there has been a decline of the public role of faith. However, being firm in our faith is as important as ever. For it is our faith in Jesus Christ that inspires us to seek the transformation of our society. Such a faith, like Luther's, compels us to translate faith into action and roots us firmly in life and life-giving mission.

† O God, the origin and the beginning of faith, transform our faith into action so that we can become channels of life in situations of lifelessness and death. In Jesus' name we pray.

For further thought

• Find out more about Lutherans in India, including on the National Council of Churches in India (NCCI) website, www. nccindia.in

Here I stand – Raj Patta

October

Tuesday 31 October
Always reforming

Acts 5:17–29

But Peter and the apostles answered, 'We must obey God rather than any human authority.' (verse 29)

Today as we mark the 500th anniversary of the Reformation, we remember that for Luther, the Reformation was an act of God. He was courageous in being obedient to God alone and not to any human authority, which in his times was the papal authority. Faith and grace were liberated from the captivity of the then-human authority.

For me, it is caste which has been the dominating authority, causing injustice and oppression to several million Dalits across the globe. The call of the Reformation today is to reject and defeat the authoritarian, unjust practice of caste and allege total obedience to our liberating God, so that our public spaces no longer tolerate discrimination. For Jesus, it was 'Roman Empire or kingdom of God', and he chose the latter over against the former. For Luther it was 'Rome or Christ', and he chose Christ over against any other ecclesial authority. Today it is 'caste or Christ', and our ultimate choice is Christ over against caste. Such a thing is now required in the re-formation of our churches. We all share in this call to re-formation today. As Martin Luther King said, 'Injustice anywhere is a threat to justice everywhere'!

† God of justice, enable us to invoke Luther's spirit in reforming our churches today. Teach us to speak truth to all powers and authorities and strive for your liberation here on earth.

For further thought

• What needs re-formation in your community and country?

Here I stand – Raj Patta

October

Wednesday 1 November (All Saints Day)
Remembering the forgotten

> **Revelation 7:9–17**
>
> *After this I looked, and there was a great multitude that no one could count, from every nation, from all tribes and peoples and languages, standing before the throne and before the Lamb, robed in white, with palm branches in their hands. (verse 9)*

Today, which certain traditions observe as 'All Saints Day', we take time to remember those who have entered eternal glory before us. We thank God for their lives and contributions, taking inspiration from their witness, and we pledge to live out their legacy that they have left with us.

John in his vision in Revelation chapter 7 sees that 'a great multitude' gathers before the throne. Who are these standing before the throne? It was 'a great multitude'; a crowd, a no-people, a throng, rather than a 'recognised people'. This communicates that it would be the 'no-people' who are uncountable, from all nations, from all ethnicities, from all peoples and from all languages that would stand before the throne. These are the no-people 'who have come out of great ordeal' (verse 14) worshipping God.

Today, there are 'no-people' of our times, who have been crossing borders and the seas with great risks, fleeing wars and poverty as refugees. It would be these 'saints' that would stand at the throne as 'a great multitude', for they died with no documents, passports or any recognition. On this day, let us accept the challenge to consider these refugees and such other people as 'people' and welcome them into our midst. For it is in the ministry of hospitality that All Saints Day will have its meaning and purpose.

† Gracious God, today we remember all our dear ones who are laid to eternal rest. Enable us to recognise the 'no-people' among us, and help us welcome them into our midst. In Jesus' name we pray.

For further thought
• Re-member the dis-membered communities this All Saints Day!

Thursday 2 November
Alternative vision

> **Acts 7:51–60**
>
> *Then he knelt down and cried out in a loud voice, 'Lord, do not hold this sin against them.' When he said this, he died. (verse 60)*

Stephen spoke of his faith conviction in Jesus Christ in a public space to a council of religious leaders, who arrested him for expressing his loyalty and allegiance to Jesus' movement and for reinterpreting and retelling their own history from an underside. If Stephen was merely 'lobbying' for this movement, I guess he would have been spared death, but instead he was seeking to create a space that enraged the religious hierarchies, and he was eventually stoned to death. For 'speaking truth to the powers' Stephen was martyred by those powers.

Like Luther, Stephen represents a threatening voice. Dalits and all oppressed peoples, too, have been constructing such visions of transformation and have been courageously speaking truth to the powers and principalities of their own contexts. And they, too, have been attacked, silenced and even murdered. There are scores of whistle blowers, social justice activists and prophets for justice, who have been martyred for standing for their convictions. Today, as churches we are called to recognise these voices, join along with them in creating stories of liberation and spaces where such stories are nurtured and celebrated. Let our churches be such alternative spaces that strive to create alternative societies!

† Gracious God, grant us your courage to speak truth to power, and embolden us to witness for your liberation here on earth. In Jesus' name we pray.

For further thought

- How can churches move from 'lobbying' to being and becoming truly alternative public spaces?

Here I stand – Raj Patta

November

Friday 3 November
Struggle for freedom

Ephesians 6:10–17

For our struggle is not against enemies of blood and flesh, but against the rulers, against the authorities, against the cosmic powers of this present darkness, against the spiritual forces of evil in the heavenly places. (verse 12)

Paul exhorts the Ephesian church to be strong in God, for as disciples of Christ, we are called to struggle against the evil present in our context. One of the important features of Jesus' ministry, too, was this kind of struggle, for he fought against the rulers, authorities, cosmic powers and evil forces to establish justice and liberation.

When I read these verses of Paul and consider Luther's struggle, I think of the struggle of Dalits around the world for justice. For me, the struggle is against the caste system in Andhra Pradesh, all across India and indeed around the world. The struggle is against the whole system which causes injustice and inequality and perpetrates violence. Individuals are caught up in this system. The principalities and powers of our time, in my view, are represented by this system which divides human beings by colour, occupation and descent.

Reformers like Martin Luther engaged in this mission of Jesus in addressing the unjust practices in his church. We, too, are called to fight against the systemic and structural sins of our times; casteism, racism, fundamentalism and extremism have all left scores of people in the claws of discrimination, exclusion and lifelessness. Let us therefore make a pledge today to contest these forces of evil, and strive for solidarity, justice and peace, wherever we live!

† Gracious God, help us to fight systemic and structural evil in our times. We seek the guidance of your Holy Spirit in this mission.

For further thought

- How can you translate and participate in the mission of contestation in your own context?

Here I stand) – Raj Patta

November

Radical healing

> **John 9:13–17, 24–38**
> *Jesus said, 'I have come into this world for judgment so that those who do not see may see, and those who do see may become blind'. (verse 39)*

Jesus gives sight to the blind in this story, but he does more – he also blinds the short-sighted, selfish, nominally religious people, for they try to obstruct Jesus' healing. When Jesus said he has come to give 'good news to the poor', have we ever translated it as 'bad news to the rich?' It is a tough saying, but I believe that this is the strength of the good news! As a Dalit Christian, I have hope when I hear, 'You will be paid for what you have done', 'You will reap the consequences right here in this world for what you have sown'. It gives me strength to know that injustice will be rectified in our world, not only in a world to come.

I wonder if a focus on being rewarded or judged after death has sidetracked the relevance of Christ's mission. This statement, instead, calls our churches to seek repentance and reconciliation after injustice, as well as the removal of caste forever. Mission according to Christ's way is to give sight to the blind and to call for reconciliation, repentance and reparation from those who have oppressed others, for justice shall be exercised accordingly. Luther, too, sought to bring about change in his world. Can we make Jesus' vision a reality in our own?

† God of justice, may we as churches be channels of justice for all peoples. In Jesus' name we pray.

For further thought

• How do some seek to inhibit the healing of the poor in your community?

Here I stand – Raj Patta

November

Here I stand
(Martin Luther 500ᵗʰ anniversary)
Grace

Notes based on the New International Version (UK) and the New Revised Standard Version by **Malcolm Carroll**

Malcolm Carroll works for Greenpeace, organising volunteer activities. He's a Baptist minister and has served in churches in Sheffield and Nottingham. He also worked for the Church of England for 10 years. He spends some of his time living on a boat near London, the rest of it in a cottage in mid-Wales with his wife Becky, where they rear children and other poultry. He enjoys outdoor activities, classical music and is an Arsenal supporter.

Sunday 5 November
This grace in which we stand

Romans 5:1–11

Therefore, since we have been justified through faith, we have peace with God through our Lord Jesus Christ, through whom we have gained access by faith into this grace in which we now stand. (verse 1, NIV)

Her name was Grace. I found her attractive in her own way. She was squat, ugly, with bits hanging over the sides. 'Grace' suggests poise, the elegant movement of a dancer. Grace was a barge, and she was crammed full of all sorts of interesting things. Just as barges should be on the UK's inland waterways. I was reflecting on Romans 5 as I cruised past, and yes, 'grace' in Romans is a barge and not a ballerina. Paul has crammed many keywords and concepts of the Christian faith, including the three persons of God, into the first six verses of this chapter. But one word carries them all: grace. Grace is the amazing and unchangeable fact that God has declared his enemies to be his children. And God has made it so.

I was once gently rebuked by a fellow minister. I'd described a core part of the minister's work as calling people to believe in God. Softly he asked, 'Isn't it our job to tell people that God believes in them?' – grace.

† Lord, help me never to get over the shock that you have made me your child. And the shock that so many around me don't yet know that they too are children of the King.

Monday 6 November
That grace might reign

Romans 5:12–21

… so that, just as sin reigned in death, so also grace might reign through righteousness to bring eternal life through Jesus Christ our Lord. (verse 21, NIV)

I read about the permanent grounding of an aircraft, described in the article as 'graceful' – the Royal Air Force's Vulcan bomber. It came into service in the 1950s, and one of its roles was to carry the UK's nuclear deterrent ('weapons of mass destruction' when possessed by others). Grace and awful power. The word 'grace', too, has to carry strong ideas. It may suggest elegance rather than brute strength, but still, in Romans, it's more bomber than ballerina. Grace is how the whole being of God and the whole power of God are committed to us to bring us to eternal life.

The starting point of the Christian journey is that God gives himself for those who were enemies. It is the end point too and the defining character of our relationship with God. Each day for the Christian begins in precisely the same way the journey first began. This way of grace is how things forever are.

In Martin Luther's day, the church obstructed access to God. It placed itself between the Christian and God, dictating punishment for sins (and how, with payment, punishment could be reduced). Luther's great contribution was to bring Christendom back to basics: God declares us his children; God gives us faith. Faith is the trusting willingness to receive the gift. God, for us, gives; God, in us, receives. The church is vital but secondary, derivative, subordinate to the reign of grace.

† Lord, grant me the courage – the absolutely huge courage – to see where my church is outdated and, worse, makes access to God's grace harder, not easier.

For further thought
• Maybe there are churches today that could do with a little more humility.

Here I stand – Malcolm Carroll

November

313

When superheroes dream

Romans 6:1–14

Offer yourselves to God, as those who have been brought from death to life. (part of verse 13, NIV)

We have dreams – I used to dream of playing for Arsenal. But what happens when superheroes dream? There's Iron Man, an ingenious engineer who creates for himself a powered suit of armour. His special powers are external. Then there's Dr Manhattan, a nuclear physicist who reconstitutes himself after a very hi-tech accident. His special powers are internal. There are other superheroes with other types of superpowers. But – do superheroes ever dream of being anything better?

How about joining, not with mere superheroes, but with God himself in striving for truth, justice and the Christ-like way? How about fighting for victory over everything that is wrong and unjust? Superheroes can only dream of such things. For us, it's our day job. The new life which we receive as a gift is an out-reaching of the life of Christ.

Brought from death to life, to the life of Christ, we are now gifted to participate in Christ's activity in the world: we share in the mission of Christ. Grace has brought us to a newness of life where our significance, purpose, worth, belonging, are all redefined by God himself. The possibility of our righteousness, just like our faith, is generated entirely by God's faith in us. Righteousness, which is the purposeful new life of Christ, is a gift, just like faith. Are we up to living a righteous life? It's a gift, guaranteed us by the fact of Jesus Christ.

† Think on a story from the Gospels where Jesus encountered ordinary folk: what will people encounter when they meet me today?

For further thought
• What is this new person like? Take a long look at Jesus.

Wednesday 8 November
The new world order

Romans 6:15–23

What then? Shall we sin because we are not under law but under grace?
By no means! (verse 15, NIV)

I saw the phrase 'new world order' in a memorial document at Hiroshima, 2005. The document argued that, had President Franklin D Roosevelt lived, there would have been no atomic bombing of Hiroshima, that Roosevelt had been looking towards an era of co-operation, especially with Russia. Roosevelt died in April 1945 and was succeeded by President Harry S Truman. The document suggested that Truman dropped the bomb in August 1945 to stop Soviet Russia, that, having seen how much of the West Russia had acquired, the bomb would end the war, scare Russia and prevent Russia mopping up the East. The Russians didn't cower from the bomb but copied, so began the Cold War and a new world order characterised by the bomb.

Who knows how the world would now be if co-operation rather than Cold War doctrine had followed from 1945. But on such decisions, the world turns. In yesterday's reading we saw a glimpse of the new person. This passage today describes the new world order: we live under grace. Our new world order is supported only by grace. No bomb to back us up, simply that God wills it this way.

In this new world order, there are enemies still. Part of our job is to reach out to them in the same way God has reached us. An American president was once criticised for being too courteous to his enemies. Abraham Lincoln replied: Do I not destroy my enemies when I make them my friends?

† Lord, by your grace, what enemy can I destroy today?

For further thought

• Grace and peace are often coupled together. How does one help explain the other?

Here I stand – Malcolm Carroll

Thursday 9 November
The way of the Spirit

Romans 7:1–12

We serve in the new way of the Spirit, and not in the old way of the written code. (part of verse 6, NIV)

Yesterday's passage introduced us to the new order, the new way of doing things. The new order is not just another place, here we discover it is a person, the Spirit of God. The full being of God – Father, Son and Spirit – is at work for our salvation.

In this part of Romans, Paul grapples with heavy themes such as the law and death (two key themes to keep in mind to help understand Romans 7). At first glance you might see the obvious answers, that instead of the law we are brought to freedom, instead of death we are brought to life. But it is more. Instead of law, it's the new way of the Spirit, instead of death, the new life of the Spirit. This new way of the Spirit is not some supernatural code to replace a written code, it is God himself. The God who gave for us is the God who dwells in us; the saving work of God is not external to us, but within.

The law can tell you what you should do and is particularly keen on telling you what you can't. Do something wrong and guilt comes galloping in. Life in the Spirit is about who we are. Get it wrong and, well, that's quite likely as we seek to make sense of our new life in a mingled world. Right or wrong, we remain who we now are, those forever gifted with and gifted into the life of God.

† God, help me to be happy making mistakes seeking to achieve your purpose rather than never make mistakes because I serve no purpose at all.

For further thought

• What written laws have I created for myself and now condemn myself every time I break them?

Friday 10 November
Being dead can have its advantages

Romans 7:13–25

Who will rescue me from this body of death? Thanks be to God through Jesus Christ our Lord! (part of verses 24 and 25, NRSV)

There are five species of frog that survive being frozen to death. Seventy per cent of the fluid in the animal freezes, the heart stops pumping. Come spring, the frog thaws, the heart restarts and, after a period of repair, off it hops.

Paul uses death to try to explain how we come to live. And how, being saved, we yet sin. How can you legitimately leave a marriage? Death – the dead cannot be unfaithful. Law is so powerful – unless you are dead, because the dead can do no wrong. The dead can receive no punishment. Death itself has no power and can do nothing to those already dead. By what mechanism can we say we are saved from law, sin, death? How is that by God's grace we are justified? It is because we died. We died in Christ, therefore these things no longer have dominion over us. We are justified in him to live a risen life; Christ's righteousness.

In this world, the dominion of the old order is broken, but we're still a part of it. Righteousness isn't perfection. We will sin, even our best falls short, we will fail and we will die. But the power of these things is broken. Death is an explanation of how this can be.

Remember the frog that can freeze? But when it lives again, it is still a frog, still in the same natural order. We are raised as new people in a new world order living the life of Christ.

And Happy Birthday to you, Martin Luther (10 November 1483).

† Loving God, Salvation is a gift from you, and even the faith to accept that gift is itself a gift; here I stand with open hands.

For further thought

• Hands open to receive are hands open to help, to heal, to hold another's.

Here I stand – Malcolm Carroll

November

Heirs of God

Romans 8:1–17

Now if we are children, then we are heirs – heirs of God and co-heirs with Christ, if indeed we share in his sufferings in order that we may also share in his glory. (verse 17, NIV)

A friend was in the Territorial Army, the UK's part-time force. I spoke of him to a full-time soldier and he had nothing but scorn for the part-timers. The only two polite terms he used were SAS – 'Saturdays and Sundays', and STABS – 'Stupid T.A. Bs ... well, just one polite term. Two thousand years ago 'Christians' was a derogatory term too: 'little Christs'. In a world of big religions where some had an arsenal of laws and others a stockpile of esoteric wisdom, along comes this little band worshipping a carpenter.

Grace: the amazing and unchangeable fact that God has declared us to be his children. More: he has declared us his heirs, co-heirs with Christ. Grace isn't just God's action, but God's being; the gifting God who gives his Son who sends his Spirit. His pleasure is to include us in himself.

It is of course amazing good news, that we share fully in all that has been accomplished in Christ. All the work of salvation is now accomplished in him. A full share of full forgiveness, a full share of the Spirit life. Our full share, though, is not merely the results of God's activity but is in the being of God himself.

Those making the derogatory comments could never have guessed. We do not imitate and live as little Christs; by God's amazing grace we are gifted participation in God and live as full Christs. Which is why to share his sufferings comes to us as privilege and joy.

† Lord, help me to see how participation in your life means necessarily means a participation in the challenges facing this world.

For further thought
• Each day refresh me with the amazing fact that I live simply by your grace.

Here I stand
(Martin Luther 500ᵗʰ anniversary)
Faith

Notes based on the New Revised Standard Version by **Kristina Andréasson**

Kristina Andréasson was ordained as priest in Church of Sweden on 7 June 2007. With over six million members, the Church of Sweden is the world's largest Lutheran denomination and is established in twenty-four different countries around the world. Kristina worked in parishes in south Sweden before she moved to London in January 2013 to work for the Swedish Church in the UK. She travels around the UK and values her city life in London. To her it is often there that God becomes the most present, in a crowd of people.

Sunday 12 November
Saved, again and again every new day

Romans 10:4–13

If you confess with your lips that Jesus is Lord and believe in your heart that God raised him from the dead, you will be saved. (verse 9)

In London in November it is autumn and leaves are falling. It gets darker and colder. Perhaps a grey sky can capture what's dark in our life and in our world; the rain can allow tears to fall. Is waiting for light in life sometimes like waiting for that spring far away? Is 'to be saved' something but far, far ahead?

In *The Large Catechism*, Martin Luther claims that having a God is like having something in which the heart entirely trusts. Faith is having something for the heart to rely upon every day, not only one day in the future. When hope dies like leaves falling to the ground, when tears fall like autumn rain, faith in God who rose from death and conquered darkness tells us that the good, and love, will have the last word.

The autumn leaves' colour is now becoming a more intense red; red like love persisting no matter what, like Easter day's red morning sun. In the little red leaf, my faith is reflected and perhaps something of Martin Luther's. In the coldest autumn day, I still feel saved; my heart entirely trusts a love that can go into the darkest moments, and still come through.

† God of life, let me in some way, if even only a little, sense your love that has the power to endure even coldest autumn wind.

Monday 13 November
Faith through the words of other people

Romans 10:14–17

'How beautiful are the feet of those who bring good news!' … So faith comes from what is heard, and what is heard comes through the word of Christ. (verses 15 and 17)

Can I see them, the beautiful feet of those who bring good news? Can I see them in the crowd, while walking down Oxford Street? Can I spot them among the hundreds of people in the tube station? Can I discover them while walking in my neighbourhood? Can I hear the word of Christ?

Yes, I think so. The middle-aged lady on a busy street, taking the time to explain directions to tourists. The ticket officer smiling and saying good morning to everyone who passes him on the tube station. The old man at the mirror shop in my neighbourhood, asking me how I'm doing, hoping my weekend was good, telling me to take care.

In Lutheran tradition the word is central; the word of God is there to create faith.

I don't know about the lives of the helpful lady, the smiling ticket man or my kind neighbour; I don't know a thing about their faith. But it strengthens my faith, their lovely words.

In their words, I sense God. Because if you listen to their words, it won't leave you unaffected. It warms your heart and leaves something beautiful around the person that brought you the words.

How beautiful are the feet that bring good news. If we listen, we might hear their words today. And that might be just what you need to make your next step be an easier one to take. I believe that's a part of what God is about, being there in some way on your steps through life.

† God of life, thank you for that your word of hope and joy is found among us and has the power to turn a good day into a great day.

For further thought

• Pick someone you don't know very well, perhaps even a stranger. Tell him or her something nice that you sincerely mean. What happens?

Faith holds something more

1 Corinthians 1:18–25
Has not God made foolish the wisdom of the world? (verse 20)

Sweden is one of the world's most secularised countries.

You don't often meet people who have an outspoken faith in God. And science and faith tend to be pitted against each other, with science ranked higher.

But I would say I grew up with love for both science and religion, with a medical doctor for a dad and a priest for a mom. And the Swedish Church has a tradition of acknowledging science as important. Our Archbishop Antje Jackelén has a big heart for science. So to me they go together, science and faith, because they are two different things.

I don't read these words from the 1 Corinthians 1 as words opposed to the wisdom of the world. Rather I think they tell us that there is more to the world than we can see, capture and understand. In Sweden today I would say that these words serve to remind us that science isn't everything.

Martin Luther claimed that faith means allowing ourselves to be seized by the things we do not see. The world's wisdom, and science are what we know; faith brings us something else. We can know how we feel today, how the world looks today. We don't know about tomorrow. But we can believe and have faith in how tomorrow will be. In faith there is hope. Faith keeps a little window open when the world's knowledge and facts close doors in front of us. With faith in a loving God we have a little window of love, allowing us to hope and dream.

† God of life, give me faith that carries the hope that will not turn into worrisome awe, no matter what I might know about today or tomorrow.

For further thought
• Read about a scientist you like. Try to picture him or her without hopeful faith in their work. Would they still have come that far?

Here I stand – Krtistina Andréasson

November

321

Wednesday 15 November
Seek God's grace

Galatians 2:15–21

I do not nullify the grace of God; for if justification comes through the law, then Christ died for nothing. (verse 21)

A friend and I often take long walks in London to explore different neighbourhoods, and we try to be open to small details along the way. I love taking these walks.

Not far from the busy station at King's Cross, you can find a beautiful old-fashioned street with old houses and street lanterns. The street is narrow and the ground has wobbly stones. Only horse and carriage missing.

On a walk on a bridge over the Thames, you can discover that discarded pieces of chewing gum on the ground are in fact not only that. Someone has made colourful miniature pieces of art by painting on the gum.

On a windless night, it is amazing what someone busking along the Thames can do to the atmosphere. Music can fill the air when you walk along Southbank, and a song can put lyrics to your walk and touch your heart.

'Do not nullify the grace of God'. Maybe it's about seeking and being open to God's grace.

I love these walks because I have felt how glimpses of God's grace have shone through ordinary places and things. It reminds me to seek God's grace also in my walk through life. Although that grace might seem tiny some days, it must not be nullified. It can lead you down an unexpected path, put colour into a grey day or fill your heart with music. It can turn an ordinary walk, an ordinary day, into something more.

† God of life, thank you for your grace, that it is there to be found, if even in small glimpses, as something to hold on to day by day in my walk through life.

For further thought

- Go for a walk and watch for tiny details. When you find something, let it capture your attention. How does it make you feel?

Thursday 16 November
A loving link between us all

Galatians 3:23–29

As many of you as were baptised into Christ have clothed yourselves with Christ. There is no longer Jew or Greek, there is no longer slave or free, there is no longer male and female; for all of you are one in Christ Jesus. (verses 27–28)

My personal trainer at the gym and I sometimes talk about faith, God, Jesus and the Bible during breaks. He was born in Nigeria and grew up in the UK, and he comes with other perspectives, so it enriches me to talk to him. When I first met him, both London and stepping into a gym were very new to me. But we had church and faith in common. In that we connected.

One time during his boxing class, I took a closer look at the group. We were men and women of different ages from different backgrounds. And many nationalities were to be found in the group that evening: UK, France, Turkey, Sweden, Romania, Italy and Nigeria. Different lives put in a context where we all could connect, have fun and interact.

I don't know about the others' faith or views on life. But perhaps it doesn't matter. God is greater, as my archbishop in Sweden says. The God of baptism became present to me, telling me that we are all connected to each other in some way, despite different lives, ages, backgrounds; yes, all the things that are different and sometimes take the upper hand. There is a loving link between us people! And baptism tells us that God invites us all into that loving context.

My trainer helps me become stronger. But he has also opened up for me moments that have strengthened my faith. My faith is that it is always possible to find a loving way to connect with people. Because every day God welcomes us all, saying we belong together.

† God of life, thank you for the amazing ways you become present and open up for us moments where we can connect with each other.

For further thought

• Where have you recently found astonishing fellowship with others?

Here I stand – Krtistina Andréasson

November

When faith is challenging

> **Philippians 3:7–11**
>
> *I regard everything as a loss because of the surpassing value of knowing Christ Jesus my Lord. For his sake I have suffered the loss of all things, and I regard them as rubbish. (verse 8)*

Sometimes I hear things like: 'Choosing God is choosing to say No to many other things'. I agree to disagree.

Sure, as a younger female priest in a secularised country like Sweden I know what it's like to feel a bit different in ways that aren't always comfortable. And there have been dinner parties where I've wished I didn't have to defend different Bible verses or explain the history of Christianity. So … yes, I get the point. Some things would have maybe been easier in life with another profession, without my lifelong connection to the church.

Yet, I've never felt it as a hard choice, belonging to church or studying to become a priest. It never actually felt like a choice. Martin Luther speaks about faith as a gift put in our hearts. And maybe that's just it. My faith feels more like a gift than a choice, something I cherish. And the things I stand to lose because of my faith! Well, in the Swedish translation of the Letter to the Philippians we read, 'I throw them on the pile of garbage'! For me, those words are quite refreshing.

Priest or not, my faith is a gift that gives me hope, helps me to remember my neighbour, gives me a love to bounce back upon when I fall, and gives me a loving standard to try to follow. What stands in the way of that might as well be thrown on the pile of garbage. The faith you have in your heart is a gift to treasure.

† God of life, I do want to stand up for what I believe. But in times of doubts and loneliness, strengthen me. Remind about the faith in my heart, a gift I treasure.

For further thought

- Many different things are important in life. But in what do you find your peace at night? Perhaps that is what should be treasured.

God is love

Ephesians 2:1–10

But God who is rich in mercy, out of the great love which he loved us even when we were dead through our trespasses, made us alive together with Christ. (verses 4–5)

In the Swedish Church in London you will find a quite simple altarpiece. Big dark letters on a golden background spell out 'GOD IS LOVE'. When I saw it for the first time, it was like a part of me was home, an affirmation of my heart's conviction.

We live in a world with a lot of grey areas. It is often hard to be completely black or white, with clear yes or no answers. Different ethics or morals are adaptable in different situations. Laws and rules are there to make our world work in the best way, but they are black and white, in a world of many grey areas. In those areas, we need love. Because love has different rules.

The altarpiece. I like how the only thing not black or white is to be found in very clear letters: God is love. We come to church for so many reasons: in joyful moments, in sadness, in times of hope, in times of fear, in times of shame or regret. Yet the altarpiece always seems to fit, telling us about a love that exists for every one of us, no matter what. I think that is what faith in God's grace and mercy is about. It's telling me that love is always there to be found, even if just in one little spark. In a world of grey areas, I know that holding on to love will keep me on track. And through God's grace and mercy, love is there for us every day, helping us not just to live but making us fully alive.

† God of life, show me your everlasting love that bears all things, hopes all things and endures all things.

For further thought

• Choose a tricky life question and try to answer it from love's perspective. Will there be a clear answer? Imagine Love judging us all.

Here I stand – Krtistina Andréasson

November

Readings in Matthew (4)
Jesus – challenged and challenging

Notes based on the New Revised Standard Version by **John Holder**

 John Holder is Archbishop of the Anglican Province of the West Indies. John was born in Barbados. He also studied for ministry in Barbados and has taught Old Testament in theological college there. He has contributed to *The Africana Bible* (Fortress, 2010) and to many other publications. He and his wife, Betty, have one son.

Sunday 19 November
Letting go and stepping out is faith

Matthew 22:1–14

Tell those who have been invited: Look, I have prepared my dinner, my oxen and my fat calves have been slaughtered, and everything is ready; come to the wedding banquet. (verse 4)

The parable in Matthew 22:1–14 highlights some of the challenges that Jesus faced in his ministry. It also issues challenges to those who follow him as their Lord and saviour.

The primary challenge faced by Jesus is one of creating a new understanding of God's relationship with his children in a context that was not friendly to this understanding. The new understanding that Jesus is offering is like a wedding celebration, an exciting event for bride and groom, parents and guests.

It offers an experience that merits letting go of all other commitments and joining in the celebrations. That the invitations are rejected and the king is snubbed, only testify to the failure of those invited to grasp the significance of the event to which they are invited.

The parable issues a challenge to Christians and indeed to all persons, to develop the courage to let go and step out in faith when we need to do so. God provides for us new and exciting ways of responding to him: the Holy Spirit is with us at all times as our guide and support when we find the courage to step out in faith. How will you step out this week in the strength of this celebratory understanding of God?

† O God, when faced with the difficulty of letting go and stepping out in faith, grant us your grace to guide and support us.

The power of Caesar versus the power of God

Matthew 22:15–22

Then he said to them, 'Give therefore to the emperor the things that are the emperor's, and to God the things that are God's'. (verse 21)

The challenges to Jesus' ministry continue in this story. He is being asked to make an awkward choice between God and Caesar, captured in the tone of verse 18: 'But Jesus, aware of their malice, said, "Why are you putting me to the test, you hypocrites?"' The assumption behind the requests seems to be the conviction that God and Caesar represent two antagonistic forces that can never be reconciled.

The discussion revolves around ownership and power. Those of Caesar are symbolised by the coin on display: 'And they brought him a denarius. Then he said to them, "Whose head is this, and whose title?"' The coin is also the symbol of limitation as it is of power. It can be lost, become dated and powerless. It can be devalued.

But God as proclaimed by Jesus in St Matthew is neither dated nor powerless. His control is comprehensive, his power limitless; yet he shares this with humanity, even with Caesar.

This profound understanding of power is one that remains ever relevant for the world. Like the 'grass of the field' (Matthew 5:30) it is here today and gone tomorrow. This elusive nature of power should help us to place this human experience in its true context.

† Grant us, O God, to use the power you entrust to us with wisdom and compassion.

For further thought

• How are you using the power entrusted to you? Let us pray for God's guidance to use it to reflect his goodness.

Readings in Matthew (4) – John Holder

The power of death and the power of God

Matthew 22:23–33

The same day some Sadducees came to him, saying there is no resurrection … (verse 23)

This verse sets the tone of the discussion that is to follow. The belief in resurrection pre-dates the time of Jesus, who incorporates the belief into his message. It became the basis upon which his followers constructed Christianity. The story is written from the perspective of the deep-rooted Christian belief in the resurrection. The Sadducees in the story try to demonstrate how ridiculous the belief really is. They cite a test case that seems to contain the potency to destroy the belief once and for all. But it does not. Jesus dismisses their propositions and lifts the discussion to another level by citing the power of God. Jesus answered them, 'You are wrong, because you know neither the scriptures nor the power of God' (verse 30).

As in the case of the invitation to the wedding and paying taxes to Caesar, there is another level missed by those who are locked into the lower level. For in the resurrection they neither marry nor are given in marriage, but are like angels in heaven. Resurrection cannot be reduced to a mathematical construct or formula that can be varied by juggling numbers. It is a matter of faith that affirms the power of God over life and death. Out of this challenge faced by Jesus, there emerges the call to renew our faith in the power of God.

† Strengthen in us, O Lord, the belief in your power over life and death.

For further thought

• The belief in the power of God over all human experiences, including death, offers assurance to us as we encounter the challenges of life.

Wednesday 22 November
Loving God and loving neighbour

Matthew 22:34–46

When the Pharisees heard that he had silenced the Sadducees, they gathered together, and one of them, a lawyer, asked him a question to test him. (verses 34–35)

The themes of the 'challenged and the challenging' are also present in this week's readings. They are captured first of all in the presence of the Sadducees and the Pharisees, two groups that differ in the belief in resurrection.

Having a common enemy can draw two opposing groups together for a common goal! The goal in this case is proving the limitations and indeed the errors of the teachings of Jesus. The challenge placed before Jesus is identifying the greatest commandment. Is it really possible to do so? Surely each commandment identifies a dimension of our relationship with God and neighbour that may not be captured in any other.

Once more Jesus moves the discussion to a new level, saying to the lawyer, 'You shall love the Lord your God with all your heart, and with all your soul, and with all your mind. This is the greatest and first commandment.' The 'greatest' is about love. But there is another connection that anchors love in relationships: '"You shall love your neighbour as yourself." On these two commandments hang all the law and the prophets.'

The answer provided by Jesus identifies a threesome – God, self and neighbour – whose relationships are connected by love. This understanding of love is one that each Christian is called to embrace.

† O Lord, make us instruments of your love.

For further thought
• Which member of the love 'triangle' identified by Jesus – God, self and neighbour – needs strengthening in your life at the moment?

Humility and servanthood:
the way of true greatness

Matthew 23:1–12

The greatest among you will be your servant. All who exalt themselves will be humbled, and all who humble themselves will be exalted. (verses 11–12)

Greatness and servanthood, like humility and exaltation, are not naturally compatible couples. One tends to cast a shadow over the other. Their presence together can generate tension and produce an intense struggle for supremacy. They are cast together in this section of Jesus' teaching, but with the clear statement of what the options are for the Christian. The statement 'The greatest among you will be your servant' identifies the rendering service as a clear option for the follower of Jesus. This is the greatest of Christian qualities. It removes any element of privilege and introduces one of dependence, and it can run counter to what obtains in our modern context where we emphasise independence. The point here, however, is about showing another way that can counter an understanding of greatness that is cemented to power.

This is the challenge we face as Christians. But Jesus is challenging us here to rise to the challenge. We do so fully conscious of the warning and promise attached: 'All who exalt themselves will be humbled, and all who humble themselves will be exalted' (verses 11–12).

† O Lord, increase in us the great virtue of humility.

For further thought

• We should walk the Christian way conscious of this warning and promise, striving daily to great examples of humility as Our Lord requires.

Challenges of the new emerging from the old

Matthew 23:29–39

For I tell you, you will not see me again until you say, 'Blessed is the one who comes in the name of the Lord.' (verse 39)

The tension between the early Jewish-Christian movement and other forms of Judaism surfaces at several places in the New Testament. In Matthew 23, it reaches a high level of intensity. One of the greatest challenges facing the first Christians was that of asserting their faith as a legitimate religion, quashing any idea that it was simply a breakaway radical faction of Judaism. St Matthew like St Paul in the Epistle to the Romans is addressing this challenge. The denunciation of the religion practised by the Pharisees, is however more that the creation of a 'better than you' slogan. It is an attempt to liberate an understanding of God that was dulled by years of ritual and tradition.

The message of Jesus was the new and fresh way of liberation being offered. The message is a call to have the insight to recognise the limitations of the old system and the courage to move on.

The message is a pull to the future, without ignoring the past (Matthew 23:2). The full experience of the new way is somewhere in the future: 'For I tell you, you will not see me again until you say, "Blessed is the one who comes in the name of the Lord."'

In the future is a messianic experience that will sort out all contradictions listed in chapter 23. This is the hope on which the new faith, Christianity, is founded.

† Give us, O Lord, the insight and the courage to live by this hope as we press on to greater experiences of your love.

For further thought

• Where is the newness in your life today?

Readings in Matthew (4) – John Holder

November

The rugged way to a glorious victory

Matthew 24:1–14

And this good news of the kingdom will be proclaimed throughout the world, as a testimony to all the nations; and then the end will come. (verse 14)

This section of St Matthew's Gospel focuses on the end time. It reflects the belief that eventually all the contradictions of life, including those in chapter 23, will be resolved. Verse 14 speaks of this victory, the sharing of the good news throughout the world. The road to victory is, however, not an easy and smooth one. The destruction of the Temple, the deceptions described in verse 5, the military conflicts and natural disasters, persecutions and the lack of commitment in verses 11–12 are some of the frightening, painful and challenging experiences along the way. Faced with these conditions, the Christian is urged to 'hang in there' and endure to the end. Experiences of salvation await those who are able to do so.

The passage sustains a measure of realism. It paints a picture of unease, given the conditions of the world. This is the realism of Christian witness as seen by St Matthew in his time. The tension between the Christian way of life and that of the 'world' has affected Christians in every generation. The great Christian ideals do not easily take root and bear the type of fruit expected. We are, however, assured of God's presence and support as we push on, buttressed by hope and determined to endure to the end.

† O God, grant us your grace to endure to the end.

For further thought

• Do you find this a hopeful passage? Why or why not?

Readings in Matthew (4)
How God judges

Notes based on the New King James Version by **Richard M Benda**

 Dr Richard M Benda is a Rwandan academic and researcher. He was born a Roman Catholic and attended a junior seminary before converting to Pentecostalism when he was 20 years old. Nine years later, he joined the UK-based missionary charity Careforce and worked as a volunteer-missionary in two Anglican churches where he has been worshipping and ministering since 2002. Richard is a research fellow at Luther King House College/University of Manchester. He holds a PhD in religions and political life (University of Manchester) and a master's degree in law (Kigali Independent University). His current research focuses on intergenerational guilt and transmissibility of political responsibility.

Sunday 26 November
You've been summonsed!

Matthew 24:15–28

Then let those who are in Judea flee to the mountains. Let him who is on the housetop not go down to take anything out of his house. (verses 16–17)

The biblical message concerning the ultimate fate of our universe, and humanity in particular, is very clear. We are headed towards a day of cosmic reckoning! On this day, God will judge the universe.

A fair trial in a court of law only happens after parties have been served a summons giving such details as the place, the date and the parties. Today's reading serves as a summons. Jesus is telling us that what is important is not to be obsessed with details that are beyond our control, such as the nature of Daniel's abomination or end times dates. Indeed, if we were to believe the peddlers of dates and signs, the world would have ended many times over; the most recent being 2012!

Rather, there is an invitation to stand vigilant and avoid being found in the wrong places or state of mind. The encouragement is to find a higher spiritual ground where the line of our inner sight is not obscured, in order to distinguish between truth and shadows. In this way, we are in a position to focus on what really matters, namely the momentous encounter with the ultimate judge who holds the key to eternal truth.

† Start by thinking about what might be obscuring your spiritual vision. What would be your higher ground, and how could today's reading guide you there?

Monday 27 November
No worries ... we know the Judge!

> ### Matthew 24:29–31
>
> *... They will see the Son of Man coming on the clouds of heaven with power and great glory. And he will send his angels with a great sound of a trumpet and they will gather together his elect from the four winds, from one end of the heaven to the other. (verses 30–31)*

I have been in a courtroom three times. First, I was wrongly accused of office supplies theft. On the second occasion, I was a witness in a genocide case in a Rwandan *Gacaca* tribunal. The third occasion was an immigration hearing to decide my residence. Each time I found the experience emotionally daunting and rather frightening. Matthew describes a trial the drama of which sounds as majestic as it is frightening. However, for the watchful believer, there is one thing that makes this event quite exciting: we know the Judge who has overall control over these end times. It is Jesus Christ, the Son of God, God himself and most importantly, the Son of Man.

This knowledge is not a one-way phenomenon, either. Jesus, the Judge who is to come, knows us intimately. You see, the amazing thing about this statement is that this future judge is presently our advocate. Paul calls him our Great Priest who has passed through the heavens, one who knows and sympathises with our human condition because he experienced it, and currently, he daily pleads our case before the throne of grace (Hebrews 4:24–16).

If you were a defendant in trial where everything is at risk, would you not want to have a judge like this? One who knows your case inside out, one who knows your character and circumstances intimately and, to top it all, one who acted as your defence advocate before being appointed as judge? Human justice would scream about conflict of interest and say it is impossible to be both judge and party. In his work and person, Jesus has ended this conflict.

† Using Paul's prayer in Ephesians 1:15–23, ask Jesus to give you the wisdom to know him as he knows you.

For further thought
• Imagine Jesus pleading your case. What would he say?

Tuesday 28 November
An unexpected hour

> ### Matthew 24:32–44
> *Therefore you also be ready, for the Son of Man is coming at an hour you do not expect. (verse 44)*

Back in the days when I was studying in a Catholic seminary, teachers had an interesting evaluation device, namely unscheduled tests. Over time, I noticed two things. On one hand, some students were never ruffled by unscheduled tests. On the other hand, knowing the date for an exam was not a guarantee of success or peace of mind. I saw a fair share of classmates falling apart as exam period approached while others tried to cheat their way through exams. The key to success was not the knowledge of when the exam would be but the state of readiness on the day.

Time and again in the final chapters of Matthew's Gospel, Jesus reminds us through his disciples not to waste our spiritual energies on improbable calculations or conspiracies about his return. Some texts suggest that even Jesus does not know the day or the hour. Our time is now and our spiritual task is to be found ready for the many riches of revelation that God has in store for us each day. Elite soldiers hone their readiness through daily drills, going through the same routine even when there is no rumour of war or impeding battle. It is the same with elite athletes who remain in top form through daily training and conditioning.

Our challenge today, and an exciting one at that, is to understand spiritual readiness in our daily living. Are we polishing our daily routines of prayer, worship and reading scripture? Are we busy refining our love, generosity, justice and other Christian virtues? If so, then we will be ready!

† O Lord of times, take my mind away from speculations and train it to find joy in the readiness of your revelation in the here and now of our lives.

For further thought

- Martin Luther is said to have remarked: 'If I knew the world were ending tomorrow, I would plant an apple tree today.' What can you plant today?

Wednesday 29 November
Building a winning case

Matthew 24:45–51

Who then is the faithful and wise servant, whom his master made ruler over his household, to give them food in due season? Blessed is that servant whom his master, when he comes, will find so doing. (verses 45–46)

In the film *The Shawshank Redemption*, the character played by Tim Robbins tells his fellow prison inmate (played by Morgan Freeman) that we all have a choice to get busy living, or dying. Yesterday, we reflected on the virtue of readiness. I am the first to acknowledge how difficult it is to maintain a state of constant alertness for an unknown future event. Sometimes, attempting to do so can lead either to great levels of stress or destructive boredom.

Fortunately, Jesus offers us insight into how to make this seemingly impossible situation achievable. The wisdom of active readiness is one that is turned towards concrete action within the framework of daily and faithful stewardship.

It is a general principle in criminal law that crime and punishment are not determined arbitrarily; they must have legal grounds. So it is with God's judgement. The verdict of guilt or innocence will not be baseless or gratuitous. It will be grounded in our actions and, more concretely, in the many practical ways in which we discharge our duties as stewards of God's creation.

Jesus tells us that in the here and now we make a case for our victory at the end. How? By being channels of God's gift of life to other people as well as to the ecosystem we inhabit; by being busy and ready through holy living and making it possible for life to flourish. If we fail to do so, our carelessness might fail to challenge social and ecological injustices, and even lead to self-destructive behaviours.

† Great Steward of our lives, teach us to do justice, to love mercy, walk humbly with you and be found doing so each day we call today.

For further thought

• Living on high alert, at times of war, for example, can be stressful. Is this the case with the Christian life? Why not?

Thursday 30 November
What has light got to do with it?

Matthew 25:1–13

But while the groom was delayed, they all slumbered and slept ... And the foolish said to the wise, 'Give us some of your oil, for our lamps are going out'. (verses 5 and 8)

Most of us have heard many sermons or read many meditations about this passage! For some reason, the story reminds me of the many prayer vigils I have attended in my young Pentecostal days! I always succumbed to slumber and sleep past 2am! I confided in one of my elders who wisely replied, 'You are still young so you need sleep, and you tend to do too much too early.' Translation: inexperienced and overenthusiastic!

Reading this passage, at first I could imagine something similar happening to these five young women. I struggled with the idea that God would judge us because of our natural limitations. Then, it struck me that the issue was not physical exhaustion and sleep but the running out of oil and the lack of light. Jesus is warning us about the ultimate consequences of not keeping the light in the dark and confusing times before Christ returns.

In Psalm 119, David proclaimed that God's word is a lamp to our feet and a light to our path (verse 105). In fact, in this psalm as a whole and indeed in most of the Old Testament/Hebrew Bible, the word of God and God's law are one and the same thing. Jesus sublimely collapsed the entirety of this law into one commandment: loving God and others. Light is law and the only law is love. It is this light Jesus is encouraging us to keep alight through the tireless work of the Holy Spirit. It is the substance behind our readiness and the empowering strength behind our active stewardship.

† O Holy Spirit! Keep my heart afire with love; undying love for my God, my fellow human beings and my world!

For further thought
• Notice the play of light around you today on leaves, car windows or water. What can light tell you about God's providence and character?

Readings in Matthew (4) – Richard M Benda

November

Punishable ignorance

Matthew 25:14–30

Lord, I knew you to be a hard man, reaping where you have not sown, and gathering where you have not scattered seed. And I was afraid, and went and hid your talent in the ground. (verses 24–25)

This is certainly one of the most tragic passages in the Bible! To have so much and yet do so little or nothing with it. To mistake God's gift for a usury investment and assimilate God to a mere loan shark!

Sometimes ignorance can be disguised as profound knowledge, and this sort of ignorance is truly harmful because it cannot be easily remedied. In most legal systems, ignorance of a legal norm lawfully publicised is culpable and cannot be used as grounds for excuse in a trial. However, genuine ignorance can mitigate a defendant's circumstances. Criminal and sinful ignorance knows what is right and good and chooses to act falsely and wickedly (James 2:7).

'Lord, I knew you …'! Really? I do not think so. Knowing the Lord as the first and second servants knew him is to fully understand the bountiful generosity behind his many gifts. It is knowing his delight when he sees us tap into this abundant provision to bless others and grow spiritually. It is investing these numerous spiritual, moral, intellectual and material capabilities in the business of flourishing lives in the here and now as well as seizing the opportunities to prepare ourselves and others for God's kingdom.

What God has given to us is ours to fully own and enjoy without fear, and to use responsibly. There are aspects in our lives and areas in our world that depend on this active and purposeful reinvestment. Put simply we have the tools to generate rich lives and a vibrant world. Let us not choose the sterile and poor option of lazy ignorance.

† Think of an aspect in your life or a person that you can associate with the phrase 'missed opportunity'. Ask the Holy Spirit to transform this situation into an abundant channel of God's blessings.

For further thought

• What does the parable tell you about God's attitude to human effort? What are you keeping buried that you could be using?

Saturday 2 December
A great day for the carers!

Matthew 25:31–46
Lord, when did we see You hungry and feed You, or thirsty and give You drink? When did we see You a stranger and take You in, or naked and clothe You? Or when did we see You sick, or in prison, and come to You? (verses 37–39)

I was both unfortunate and privileged to live in Rwanda through and after the genocide of 1994. Unfortunate to live through and witness so much evil, suffering and death; privileged to witness the caring heroism of many Christians and non-Christians who took extreme risks to shelter, feed, rescue and take strangers to safety. In those dark days, I was struck by the unlikely and surprising sources of goodness and grace – like JP, a man I did not know before the genocide and yet who sheltered me and my friend despite real threats to his life.

Most people go through their lives without experiencing such dramatic times. However, we are all confronted daily with people in various positions of need and vulnerability. People that mattered to Jesus, will matter in the end and matter to him today. As I write this, I am looking at an arresting image: an old Syrian woman in a wheelchair stuck in the mud at the border between Croatia, Hungary and Serbia. She is crying and the European borders are closed. On the other hand, I have just heard on the radio that three former Manchester United players have given authorisation for homeless people to use their unfinished luxury hotel as a temporary shelter for the homeless until the winter is out.

Judgement day, heaven and hell, sheep and goats ... God's final day is shrouded in mystery and spiritual imagery, but do not be fooled. The day will belong to those who chose to see and care for the needy, most likely without even a second thought about the rewards. Want to be a sheep on that day? Be a carer today! It sounds like a weird advert line but trust me, it makes sense!

† Sing or pray the hymn 'Open our eyes, Lord, we want to see Jesus, to reach out and touch him and say that we love him.' Sit for a moment or two and feel God's invitation in the stillness.

For further thought
• Where will you see Jesus today?

Readings in Matthew (4) – Richard M Benda

December

Covenants and promises
Promises of new life

Notes from the New Revised Standard Version by **Dafne Plou**

Dafne Plou is a journalist and social communicator who works on technology for development in an international organisation. Her work includes travelling to other Latin American countries to lead workshops and seminars, and to speak in conferences. She's a member of the Methodist Church in Argentina. In her local church, in Buenos Aires' suburbs, she works in the area of 'Community building and fellowship in liturgy'. She's also a women's rights activist and participates in the women's movement in her country. She loves baking cookies for her nine grandchildren.

Sunday 3 December (Advent Sunday)
Blessed rain

Genesis 9:8–17

God said, 'This is the sign of the covenant that I make between me and you and every living creature that is with you, for all future generations: I have set my bow in the clouds, and it shall be a sign of the covenant between me and the earth.' (verses 12–13)

Long, rainy weeks were usual at wintertime in my country. But this had been a very dry winter. After weeks and weeks with no rain, the grass in the gardens and parks was drying out and we could feel the dryness in our hair and on our skin. It was awful for plants and crops. In a country where the economy is mostly based on agriculture and cattle breeding, the situation was disastrous. Climate change? Or just too much pollution, exploitation of land and woods, neglect for water resources or careless consumerism?

Everybody longed for rain. But when it came, it was just a soft, gentle drizzle. No umbrella needed when going out. You call this rain? Still, when looking around, the pavements looked shiny and the flowerbeds were well watered. Silently, the parks and fields seemed greener and the birds dared to come out and enjoy the light shower. Rare as it might look, but beautiful as usual, a shy rainbow appeared, brightening the grey old buildings. People didn't want rain to stop this time, but still this rainbow was reminding them that God's promise was there to stay. The rainbow, fading under the refreshing drizzle, announced that life would revive and keep going strong.

† As we get ready to celebrate Christmas, inspire us, Jesus, to announce your promises in a world that looks dry and neglected.

Monday 4 December
Love for the unloved

> **Genesis 16:1–14**
> *The angel of the Lord found her by a spring of water in the wilderness, the spring on the way to Shur. And he said, 'Hagar, slave-girl of Sarai, where have you come from and where are you going?' (verses 7–8)*

It has been announced that a crèche will be inaugurated at the secondary school. A crèche there? Is the secondary school a place suitable for babies? Whether people like it or not, it is. One of the big problems in the area is the high number of boys and girls dropping out of school when they get to 15 or 16 years old. About one million youngsters between 15 and 24 years old in Argentina are under the category of 'ni-ni' – the 'no school, no job' generation.

Statistics are clear and blunt. Seventy per cent of these 'ni-ni' teenagers are girls. And 55 per cent of them declare themselves to be dedicated to unpaid domestic or care work. Why? Because teenage pregnancies have grown dramatically, and these young mothers have no place at school nor in the job market and, what's worse, in many cases no place even at home.

These girls surely suffer the same exclusion, vulnerability and stigma Hagar faced when she decided to run away to the desert. The angel's questions shake us up; we, who would rather look elsewhere.

'Where are these girls and their babies coming from? Where are they going?' the angel asks.

We can't simply say we don't know. We must offer them our love and embrace them as family, as Jesus calls us to do. Let's open their lives, and ours, to trust and hope.

† Challenge us, God, to include in our fellowship those who are easily discriminated against. Help us to share your infinite love and acceptance.

For further thought

- Have you ever shown interest in the needs of students and teachers at your local secondary school? Talk about it in your church group and think of the best way to approach their concerns.

Covenants and promises – Dafne Plou

December

341

Tuesday 5 December
Sarah and Mary

Genesis 18:1–15

The Lord said to Abraham, 'Why did Sarah laugh, and say, "Shall I indeed bear a child, now that I am old?" Is anything too wonderful for the Lord?' (verses 13–14)

Why should we think of Sarah at this time of the year? Sceptical woman. She was not at peace; she laughed not with happiness but with irony, perhaps in a hurtful way. And the Lord got the stinging message, her hidden doubt and disdain. Sarah showed anything but goodwill, and she even lied trying to conceal her real feelings. So, should the Lord have kept his promise or should he have just left her alone?

'There is nothing too difficult for me', said God, assuring Sarah of his transforming power. It was not only a pregnancy that God was planning. It was a deep change in attitude and spiritual willingness in this unconvinced woman who asked herself if she 'would really know such happiness' – the happiness of having her own child and recovering the respect of her husband, her family and even herself.

Sarah had done her best. She had kept the traditions, offering her servant to her husband. She had shown goodwill. But submission was not for her and she wouldn't stand being despised. Once pregnant, would she be able to sing what Mary sang many centuries afterwards: 'God All-Powerful has done great things for me, and his name is holy'?

Advent is a time to prepare the way and to get ready spiritually to celebrate Jesus' birth once more. We are surrounded by sceptical people, who perhaps consider our beliefs to be nonsense. But let us remember that nothing is too difficult for the Lord and that he can transform our lives and the world, doing great things for his children and his creation.

† Jesus, help us to announce this Advent your peace for all people of good will.

For further thought

• How can you share God's promises and his call for spiritual renewal in your community during this Advent season?

Covenants and promises – Dafne Plou

December

342

Wednesday 6 December
Deliverance from bondage

Exodus 6:2–9

I have also heard the groaning of the Israelites whom the Egyptians are holding as slaves, and I have remembered my covenant. (verse 5)

Will war ever end? Will peace in the world have a chance some day? During 2015, TV news showed us the darkest side of world events: thousands of refugees and forced migrants trying to get to new lands where they and their families could have a chance for a better life; a life with no bloody battles, bombing, hunger or death. The photos of people sailing in unfit boats facing perils and death, the scenes showing the long marches of those deprived by war trying to overcome all sorts of barriers, even human barriers, and the interviews with a people who spoke with sorrow, but also with great dignity helped to open new possibilities for many.

Can Christians speak meaningfully about peace when these dramatic reports shake our world daily? In today's reading, God reminds us that he is the God Almighty and that he sees the suffering of this people and is ready for action to keep his promise real. When God sent his son Jesus to share our life in this world, he wanted to transform power relations and open heads and hearts to justice, peace and reconciliation.

How can God's promises come true if he cannot count on our commitment and solidarity with our fellow humanity? TV news shows us suffering and discrimination but also engagement, openness and community involvement in accepting others in need and preparing for them a decent place where to stay in a new land.

In Advent we announce that our Saviour is coming soon. Let us reinforce our commitment to build one world and one humanity in peace, with all people of goodwill!

† Keep us firm in our faith to face turbulent times, dear God, and let us be ready to open doors for those in need.

For further thought

• What opportunities are there where you live for help and engagement with refugees?

Thursday 7 December
Hannah's prayer

1 Samuel 2:1–10

Talk no more so very proudly, let not arrogance come from your mouth; for the Lord is a God of knowledge, and by him actions are weighed. (verse 3)

Every week a national newspaper in Argentina publishes a section on how to make the most of leisure time. Journalists have even invented a name for those who are introduced like a kind of new urban tribe, the 'experts' in leisure time. These characters are not considered mere idlers, but specialists in making the best of their free time, leaving worries and sorrows aside. They all look alike, young, handsome and beautiful, well-dressed and with a full wallet or purse, including generous credit cards. Ready to make us believe that happiness and consumerism go hand-in-hand!

But what about those who cannot get to this golden realm because they cannot afford it? Are they expected to put their effort into entering the circle, perhaps at least in appearance, expending more than their budget allows? Our enemies are not only those who use weapons and deadly means to kill and destroy, but also those who have an attractive, easy-going message to make us believe that happiness lies in what we can buy. Are we clear that we need to be rescued to avoid falling into this trap?

When Hannah prays, she refers to the 'proud people' as those who should stop being selfish, thinking high of themselves, and start putting their lives and hopes in the God who can rescue them and make them strong and happy. Are we ready to laugh at today's 'enemies' who proclaim selfishness and consumerism as a 'new expertise' to take pride in? To announce a new life in Jesus challenges us to do so.

† Guide us, God, to make this Advent a time to look at ourselves and consider where our trust truly is. Help us to put our hopes and confidence in your hands.

For further thought
- Is it possible to get ready for a simple Christmas celebration? What things would you leave aside? What practices would you keep?

Covenants and promises – Dafne Plou

December

344

Friday 8 December
Steadfast love

Psalm 89:1–18

Righteousness and justice are the foundation of your throne; steadfast love and faithfulness go before you. (verse 14)

It is time for general elections in my country and candidates, their speeches and their promises are present in all the media. But this time, the Internet and social networks are playing a big role. A group of independent journalists have started a project called chequeado.com ('CheckedOver.com'), a very active website where the candidates' discourses are thoroughly inspected. The tags 'false', 'half-true' and 'true' are the sites' big stars and many days the results of these examinations make the headlines in mainstream media, especially when data and facts are distorted by a candidate to accommodate results in his/her favour.

People want strong leaders in their countries – men and women who can assure them that their interests will be looked after and that justice and fairness will increase everybody's well-being. But is this enough? This psalm adds two more attributes to good governance: love and faithfulness. It's difficult to attribute these to a ruler, but someone who is neither committed to the people nor trustworthy will surely get into trouble soon.

Our leader, God, has proved again and again that he wants to lead us with justice, fairness, love and faithfulness. We don't need to check his promises over. As we get ready for the celebration of Christmas and join this festival of grace, we are assured that God's steadfast love protects us like a shield and his saving power will always sustain us in faith.

† Guide us, dear God, to share with others your promises and your faithfulness, letting them know that your love and protection embrace all peoples and the whole of creation.

For further thought

• Like www.chequeado.com, why don't you try to hold God to his promises to his people? Find out how his steadfast love is always at work!

Covenants and promises – Dafne Plou

Saturday 9 December
Finding your voice

Luke 1:13–23

He will turn many of the people of Israel to the Lord their God. With the spirit and power of Elijah he will go before him, to turn the hearts of parents to their children, and the disobedient to the wisdom of the righteous, to make ready a people prepared for the Lord. (verses 16–17)

If you are like me, we often feel our generation is the one going astray – the rebellious one, made up of people who only trample on the values and principles that used to be their society's pillars. But as we read the scriptures, we find these characters now and again. Disobedience, double-standards, cheating and disloyalty have always been there and God has proved his patience and mighty love again and again.

Zechariah was struck dumb not only because he got confused and was afraid of the angel's presence, but because the challenges put in front of his future son were hazardous. He knew very well what Elijah had to face when confronting Baal's priests, and in his persecutions. Calling Israel to turn back to God would be a risky task and his child, not yet born, would have to be brave.

But the promise kept Zechariah going, for he had a role to play if he wanted his son to become a true and faithful prophet. John was to have such an influence that he would even make parents more thoughtful of their children, and of the world's future.

When we get ready to celebrate Christmas, we think of children a lot, but mainly because of the presents they ask for and we are expected to buy. Do we think of their spirituality, of their need of God, of their wishes for a peaceful life at home, at school, in the world? Advent is the time to talk to them about our faith and belief in Jesus, our Saviour. Let's not stay dumb!

† Dear God, make our words simple and loving, so that we might share with our children the centrality of Jesus' birth and mission in our Christmas celebration.

For further thought

- As we get ready to decorate our Christmas trees at home, at church, in community spaces, think of ornaments that meaningfully reflect the Christmas message and invite participants of all ages to contribute with their creativity.

Covenants and promises
Warnings of consequences

Notes based on the New Revised Standard Version by **Sham P Thomas**

Revd Dr Sham P Thomas is an ordained priest serving The Mar Thoma Syrian Church Bangalore, India. He was the James S Stewart scholar at the University of Edinburgh and professor of communication at the United Theological College, Bangalore. He continues to lead conferences and retreats.

Sunday 10 December
Your choices

Deuteronomy 28:1–6, 15–19

If you will only obey the Lord your God, by diligently observing all his commandments that I am commanding you today, the Lord your God will set you high above all the nations of the earth. (verse 1)

The Bible portrays the magnanimity of God in not programming creation to function together with the will of the creator alone. God, distinctly different from us, gave freedom to creation either to walk with or against God. This choice, however, has specific implications. Those who obey the will and fulfil the plan of God will be blessed and those who deviate will be cursed.

Warnings of disastrous consequences have been conscience keepers of our life from early childhood. Some of the commonest alerts like 'Beware of fire', 'Follow traffic rules', 'Cigarette smoking is harmful' crowd our city roads and streets. These warnings are preventive rather than punitive actions. Warnings are pieces of information to help us making judicious choices in life and engage in responsible actions. Warnings, thus, become gestures of caring and love!

God's warnings also reveal the agony and kindness of God who waits anxiously to see whether we will, in our free will, choose to gladden God and consequently become fruitful. God, ultimately, does not want us to be punished or to perish.

† Lord God, help us to be a channel of your blessing and bring joy unto you through our conscientious behaviour as your children.

Barking dogs!

Ezekiel 33:1–16

But if the sentinel sees the sword coming and does not blow the trumpet, so that the people are not warned, and the sword comes and takes any of them, they are taken away in their iniquity, but their blood I will require at the sentinel's hand. (verse 6)

One of my childhood curiosities was to watch how the household hen would signal a warning on sensing an eagle or an owl in the vicinity, and how the chicks would instinctively seek shelter under their mother's wings.

Warnings are essential because most are not aware of dangers on their own. It may be beyond their prudence or even their imagination. One of the reasons the prophets were known as barking dogs in the history of Israel was because of their warnings to the people in their journey of faith. Prophets were the built-in warning system in Israel as a guard against the kings and the people in their personal and public life. This is made explicit in the command to prophet Ezekiel to be a watchman. Importantly, his destiny was linked with his duty as a watchman.

The purpose of watchmen, barking dogs or a clucking hen is to avert a disaster. In the present world, such warning mechanisms have come into place in all walks of life. They may range from the appointment of security guards or the setting of burglar alarms to sophisticated weather satellites. We also have various forums like citizen watches, media watches and human rights watches that perform the function of monitoring and warning for the health and safety of the world. If they do their duty, others can live with a sense of peace, as they don't have to keep watch over their shoulder all the time. What is not expected of them is silence or dereliction of duty.

† Lord, in the face of injustice may we not be mute spectators. Give us the voice to bark when necessary!

For further thought

• What watch group do you rely on every day? Give thanks to God for meteorologists and anyone else who comes to mind.

Covenants and promises – Sham P Thomas

December

Tuesday 12 December
Watch out

Ezekiel 34:1–16

Thus says the Lord God, I am against the shepherds; and I will demand my sheep at their hand, and put a stop to their feeding the sheep; ... I will rescue my sheep from their mouths, so that they may not be food for them. (verse 10)

A news item like, an 'anti-graft ombudsman was taken into police custody for being part of an extortion racket' would have made banner headlines a few decades ago. This may not be the case anymore! When corruption becomes rampant, and institutions and systems appointed to safeguard us from such happenings become complacent, it becomes ironical and comical. What is more surprising is that when barking dogs become lap dogs many of us are not even surprised!

The prophet Ezekiel draws our attention to the abuse of power and positions of a least expected group – religious leaders. Shepherds earned their name because of their life and leadership in protecting and nurturing the sheep, strengthening the weak and the vulnerable. Some of them sacrificed their lives in ensuring the well-being of their flock. It is no wonder that God was called a shepherd. But how would we understand and explain when such a moral and spiritual office crumbles under the weight of their own misdeeds? If the shepherds start devouring the sheep what is their distinction from thieves and wild animals? What would we call the shepherds who use their privileged access and proximity to the sheep to misuse them for protecting and promoting their own vested interests?

This may be a recipe for frustration and loss of hope, but God will not allow this to continue even though God can be doubted or even blamed at times. God's intervention is the only ray of hope!

† Lord, forgive us for not using our authority and leadership in a pastoral way. May we not be self-obsessed leaders.

For further thought

• How can we explain God's presence when the church and her leaders are involved in corruption and power abuse, or when they become insensitive and arrogant?

Covenants and promises – Sham P Thomas

Wednesday 13 December
Watch yourself

Luke 3:1–14

'... Even now the ax is lying at the root of the trees; every tree therefore that does not bear good fruit is cut down and thrown into the fire'. And the crowds asked him, 'What then should we do?' (verses 9–10)

John the Baptist here directs warnings to the self-righteous people who absolve themselves of the need for repentance. It is noteworthy that Jesus also never discounted such acts and never withheld harsh words against such people. Both John and Jesus declared that none can claim immunity from divine judgement by dint of their racial supremacy or spiritual pedigree. Everyone has to stand scrutiny before God and be accountable for their actions.

John called for repentance and reformation as the route to avoid the axe of judgement. Repentance is not just an emotional expression of feeling sorry for certain wrongdoings. It is a conscientious recognition of our fallibility and the folly of romanticising either the past or the present as if they were absolutes. Repentance thus becomes a self-critical and crucial introspection into the past and the present in conjunction with God's demands on us.

Repentance is only partial if not complemented with a change in our habits. It involves changing everyday life and practices, modes and values impacting our personal, social and financial world. Accordingly, John called for prudent sharing of resources in the midst of poverty, strengthening the values of transparency and a freedom from the lust for money. As was the case for John himself, our homes, clothes and even the food we eat will need to bear trademarks of the repentance and renewal that we internalise and proclaim.

† Lord, may we be prudent torchbearers for you. May our life be a patent of repentance and renewal.

For further thought

- The season of Advent is a time of repentance and renewal in some of the church traditions. How would you understand repentance in your context?

Thursday 14 December
False alarms

Mark 13:3–13

Many will come in my name and say, 'I am he!' and they will lead many astray. When you hear of wars and rumours of wars, do not be alarmed; this must take place, but the end is still to come. (verses 6–7)

False warnings may have dangerous consequences. One of the folk stories I heard in my early childhood is about a lad who was rearing sheep in the outskirts of the village. One night he cried out, 'Tiger, Tiger.' The villagers rushed out to defend him but to their dismay there was no tiger, only peals of laughter from the naughty lad. He played this prank more than once. One fine day to the utter surprise of the lad an actual tiger was on the prowl and his genuine cry for help fell on deaf ears. Through this narrative my grandmother emphasised that one should never raise a false alarm, as it will discredit the caller. While mock alarms may validate the security system, false alarm can do great harm.

One of the false alarms that misled believers many times in history was about the end times and the second coming of Christ. It is a pity that, in spite of Jesus' warning, many had fallen victims of self-styled prophets and their false predictions. Of course, there will be an end time, but God alone knows and decides the time, mode and location. No one else is given this knowledge and we are to accept this limitation, as Jesus himself had done. While prayerfully and expectantly waiting for his coming, our call is to live in this world as his witnesses even when we are persecuted for our faith.

† Lord, help us to be discerning the signs of the times without prejudging your knowledge and plan.

For further thought

• How do we debate with those who graphically portray the second coming of Christ with absolute certainty?

Unity is the watchword

One of the crises in our world is increasing fundamentalism and terrorism. These are nurtured by intolerance for diversity and a penchant for uniformity and homogeneity. The fundamentalists and terrorists have rigid views on the rights of the other who is different from them in terms of race, region, religion, creed and cultures. For them, the other should mirror them or at least be pliable. If the world has to exist and grow in harmony such traits need to be identified, isolated and changed in all walks of life. So also, we need to champion a guiding principle like 'unity in diversity'. Unity does not mean an uncritical acceptance or passive tolerance of the other, but a conscious affirmation of the other. It is a commitment to respectful relation with each other even while being distinct. It is also an affirmation that people of different colours, creed and customs are inevitable for the growth of a vibrant and dynamic world.

This affirmation is important for the church as well. Even within a particular church denomination a certain doctrine, office, pattern or ritual can become dominant and consequently a threat to others. We must take seriously Paul's assertion that the gift of different gifts, vocations and offices is not a recipe for competition or fragmentation. Rather it cements the compatibility and sustainability of the church. It is in affirming the oneness in the midst of diversity that threads are woven into making God's signature fabric: 'The Blessed World'.

† Lord of Unity, help us to find ways of respecting the others even while being sensitive of the differences and even divergence.

For further thought

• What examples can you think of in which different parts work together for the sake of greater unity?

Saturday 16 December
Virtues on foot

Ephesians 5:1–14

Try to find out what is pleasing to the Lord. Take no part in the unfruitful works of darkness, but instead expose them. (verses 10–11)

Being naive is not a virtue. The Bible does not envisage the world as an ideal one and ask that we live in it. The Bible warns us to be alert, vigilant and wise in recognising those forces that work overtime in their determination to derail God's purposes and kingdom. Hence Jesus' request that his disciples pray that they may not be led into temptation and be delivered from the evil one. The evil one has the possibility of leading people away from God.

Paul suggests three things in order to move with God. First, we have to consciously move away from the un-gods. These may be anything that claim supreme allegiance in our lives and thereby compromise or even replace God. Second, we have to courageously expose the forces of darkness by sensitising ourselves and others to how certain conversations, practices and passion are subtly and covertly subverting God's interests and leading God's people away. Third, while defending ourselves from the evil one, we need to make a consistent decision to stay on course with God. This is the minimum gesture required of us for the gracious forgiveness and freedom given by Christ. Life is distinct only if it is lived as a love story with the Lord. Only then will we take part in the evolution of the world into a splendid haven through our presence.

† Gracious Lord, who has given us a new window of life as a gift through your Son Jesus Christ: enable us to lead a worthy life.

For further thought
• Which are the forces of darkness in your life that you can identify? How can you oppose them?

Covenants and promises – Sham P Thomas

Covenants and promises
Deals negotiated

Notes based on the New International Version (UK) and the New King James Version by **Michiko Ete-Lima**

Michiko Ete-Lima currently works as a legal officer for the Congregational Christian Church of Samoa. She also lectures part time at Malua Theological College, Samoa, in the area of theology and academic skills. She is married to Peletisala Lima who lectures full time at MTC, and she is the mother of two daughters. She is also an accredited mediator and is a member of the Accredited Mediators of Samoa. She enjoys playing tennis and zumba. She loves her quiet times, reading and meditating on God's word.

Sunday 17 December
Abraham argues with God

Genesis 18:16–33

Then Abraham approached him and said: 'Will you sweep away the righteous with the wicked? What if there are fifty righteous people in the city?' (verses 23–24a, NIV)

This week's theme of bargaining with God reminds me of my work as mediator. In this role, I am required to allow the parties to reach their own solution that is beneficial and equitable for both parties.

I see myself as a mediator listening to the discussion that is taking place between God and Abraham. Abraham starts off with the number 50 and ends with the number 10. Evidently, God is willing to save the sinful city even if there were a few good people. But I cannot help but feel that there is an imbalance in the outcome of this negotiation! A whole city is about to be saved, and yet there are only a few good people.

I wonder what God's response would have been had there only been one righteous person? The answer is not explored in this dialogue, but I am confident that God would have saved the city even if there was only one person. My quiet confidence is because God gave his one and only son, Jesus Christ for the world. In the death and resurrection of his one and only Son, the whole world was saved.

May this quiet confidence grow as we explore God's dealings with others this week.

† Dear God, thank you for your one and only Son Jesus Christ who died so that we may be saved from our sins and have eternal life.

Monday 18 December
A grave for Sarah

Genesis 23:1–20

Ephron answered Abraham, saying to him, 'My lord, listen to me; the land is worth four hundred shekels of silver. What is that between you and me? So bury your dead.' (verses 14–15, NKJV)

On the hills of Mount Vaea in Samoa lies the grave of the famous author Robert Louis Stevenson. Stevenson, despite being a foreigner, had earned the Samoan people's loyalty and respect in his last years living in Samoa; he even took the Samoan name Tusitala. After his death, he was granted the choicest piece of land in which to be buried.

This is not unlike the story we have of Abraham, when he was given the choicest field to bury his beloved wife. When Abraham requested the land, it was easily accepted by the people for he was a man of integrity.

In any agreement made, a person's reputation is critical. It serves as a key factor in the willingness of others to enter into an agreement with you. In this case, Abraham's reputation preceded him. This was evident also in the life of Robert Louis Stevenson. The request that he be buried on the hills was easily accepted by the Samoan people, because of his character.

We need to ask ourselves if we have a reputation that is one of integrity. Are we people with whom people will willingly enter into agreements, or is our reputation riddled with disrepute? Abraham shows us how our character is crucial in all our dealings with God, and with others.

† Lord, help us to live a life of good repute that others may see you in our lives and that they can easily work alongside and with us. Blessed be your name, Jesus Christ.

For further thought
• What person in your life today or in the past is a person of integrity? What traits do they have?

Covenants and promises – Michiko Ete-Lima

Tuesday 19 December
Covenant to prosper

Deuteronomy 29:1–15
Therefore keep the words of this covenant, and do them, that you may prosper in all that you do. (verse 9, NKJV)

As a legal officer, I am expected to draft and review various contracts and agreements for the Congregational Christian Church of Samoa. In many of these contracts, 'scope of duties' will feature the outlines of the duties that parties must abide by in order to fulfil the contract. The non-performance of these duties would eventually be considered a breach of contract. There is always an underlying understanding that if there is no breach, both parties will duly benefit.

God's covenant given to the Israelites assures their prosperity when they adhere to the terms given. Accordingly, if the people perform the 'scope of duties' that have been outlined in the covenant, they will duly prosper. It's a promise that is easy to believe, because Moses reminds them of God's goodness while they were on their journey from Egypt. The Israelites would have easily trusted this promise as they have already encountered the goodness of God throughout their lives.

The covenant is amazingly inclusive. Even strangers will be blessed if they are obedient to the terms of the covenant. This is indicative of God and his love that knows no boundaries. God is not exclusive, but rather his grace reaches and envelops all! God's purpose for this covenant is so that all may be blessed when they live in true obedience.

† Dear Lord, help us to be obedient to your word so that we may see your blessings and prosperity in our lives.

For further thought
• The blessing the Israelites received was very practical – a promise of land, rain and a healthy harvest. Count your blessings today, and give thanks.

Wednesday 20 December
Boaz redeems Ruth

Ruth 4:1–12

And the close relative said, 'I cannot redeem it for myself, lest I ruin my own inheritance. You redeem my right of redemption for yourself, for I cannot redeem it.' (verse 6, NKJV)

There is a real sense of transparency and urgency in the process that Boaz has taken in order to redeem Ruth. He insists on witnesses so as to ensure authenticity. Boaz leaves no room for error. It's indicative of his genuine love for Ruth.

In Boaz's actions, he is tactful in outlining the total situation to the next of kin. The next of kin rejects the offer – but I can almost hear Boaz's heart skip a beat lest the relative insist on redeeming the land. The confidence and the relief that Boaz must have felt would have been immense.

The final part of the reading is of some interest whereby the community have given Boaz a blessing for what has taken place. This is a common custom in Samoa and I am sure in many other cultures; the community will gather and give their blessings. This may be for the person who is getting married, or about to travel or about to enter a new position. It is these blessings that the person will take and hold dear. For them, it is these blessings that will help them throughout their new endeavour.

This, then, is not unlike the blessing for Boaz by the community, which, in the turn of events, became a prophecy. In the end, it was through the lineage of Boaz and Ruth that Jesus descends from – Jesus Christ who, like Boaz, is a redeemer.

† Lord Jesus Christ, we are truly thankful, for you have redeemed us.

For further thought

• How does this very practical and cultural context for the word 'redeemer' help you see Jesus as redeemer?

Covenants and promises – Michiko Ete-Lima

David's throne established

> **2 Samuel 7:4–17**
>
> *He shall build a house for My name, and I will establish the throne of his kingdom forever. I will be his Father, and he shall be My son. (verses 13–14, NKJV)*

For members of the Congregational Christian Church of Samoa, the existence of a church building is vital. In many of the local parishes, the initiative for the construction of a church building is usually from the local pastor. This is easily supported by church members in their desire to build a house for God. Their mindset and their desire is not unlike that of David.

However, unlike David, no such specific instructions were given to them to not construct a church building. I am convinced, however, that if such specific instructions were given, many would have heeded the word of God and obeyed. The instructions would be well received, for they would have included a prophetic assurance that an heir would build the church.

The realisation that one day your own desires and yearnings would one day be fulfilled by your own children is truly overwhelming. It speaks of God's perfect timing and perfect will in our lives. At times when we feel that our desires and our dreams are not being realised, we need to give it to God and allow God to do his perfect will with them.

As a parent, we all would like for our children to carry on our legacy. And when this legacy is carried on in God's will, there is nothing more satisfying!

† Lord, help us to be patient and understand that only in giving you the desires of our hearts will your perfect will be done.

For further thought

• What deep desire might you need to listen to today? What might you need to let go of?

Friday 22 December
Richly blessed

Isaiah 55:1–5

Incline your ear, and come to Me. Hear, and your soul shall live; And I will make an everlasting covenant with you – the sure mercies of David. (verse 3, NKJV)

The Congregational Christian Church of Samoa refer to their pastors as *fa'afeagaiga*. The term is made up of two words, *fa'a* and *feagaiga*. The word *fa'a* means 'to do' or 'to be' and the word *feagaiga* means 'covenant'. In effect, the term can be translated as 'to be the covenant'. It connotes a sense of importance and high regard for the pastor when they take on their calling in their parish.

When the pastor is called to their parish, there is a *osiga feagaiga*, which literally translates to mean 'the establishment of the covenant'. As with any covenant, the parties will abide by the terms accordingly, and if any of the terms are not adhered to, the covenant is broken. If this covenant is ever broken by the pastor or his family, they must leave the parish and this is known as the *tatalaga feagaiga,* or the breaking of the covenant.

In today's passage, however, we read about a covenant that cannot be broken. It is an everlasting covenant that is offered to all. It suggests those who enter into this covenant will be truly blessed, and blessed abundantly. It is a covenant that is unlike a human covenant that will have certain rules that one must abide by in order to gain the maximum benefits from it. This is an everlasting covenant that, in the end, glorifies those who enter into it.

† Lord, we are thankful that you are the author of the everlasting covenant that you called us into. We are richly and fully blessed.

For further thought

• What covenants, legal or otherwise, underlie your community and make it safe?

Covenants and promises – Michiko Ete-Lima

Saturday 23 December
Jeremiah's deal

Jeremiah 32:6–25

And though the city will be given into the hands of the Babylonians, you, Sovereign Lord, say to me, 'Buy the field with silver and have the transaction witnessed.' (verse 25, NIV)

In my capacity as a lawyer, I am often asked to sign and witness deeds or agreements. I would duly sign as a witness with true confidence that both parties agree to the terms and conditions of the agreement. The parties have entered into the agreement with the knowledge that they will both be receiving something that is equitable. For instance, the buyer of the land happily agrees to give over money for the land that they know is worth what they are paying for it.

However, one cannot help but feel that in the case of Jeremiah, he is entering into an agreement that is inequitable and unfair. Jeremiah, however, does not hesitate to do the will of God. No matter how ridiculous and preposterous the situation may seem, he enters into this agreement willingly as a satisfied customer.

It indicates the strength and the depth of Jeremiah's faith and obedience that, despite what is seemingly a ridiculous situation, he does not hesitate. He carries out the will of God and knows that in his obedience, all is well.

At times, we may encounter situations that may appear to be ludicrous and nonsensical. Others will second-guess the reasoning behind our seemingly ridiculous actions, but when we do it in the quiet confidence that we are doing God's will, then we are blessed with the peaceful assurance that God's will is the only will!

† Lord, let our faith and our trust be built upon your wisdom and knowledge, for you alone know what is best in our lives.

For further thought

• Take time out today to consider and reflect on what God's will is for you in a particularly difficult situation.

Covenants and promises – Michiko Ete-Lima

December

360

Covenants and promises
Visions of a better future

Notes based on the New Revised Standard Version by **Andy Nagy-Benson**

 Revd Andy Nagy-Benson is the pastor of The Congregational Church, United Church of Christ, in Middlebury, Vermont (USA). Prior to his studies at Yale Divinity School (M.Div.), Andy worked on the salmon docks of Alaska, taught English and environmental education in Costa Rica, and taught English at an independent secondary school in New York. Since his ordination in 1998, Andy has served as pastor of three churches in New England. Andy and his wife, Gwendolyn, have three daughters.

Sunday 24 December
A Second Chance

Jeremiah 31:31–34

This is the covenant I will make with the house of Israel after those days, says the Lord: I will put my law in their minds and write it on their hearts. I will be their God, and they shall be my people. (verse 33)

When I was in Los Angeles in the early 1990s, the city had the highest concentration of gang activity in the United States. In the fray of that urban violence, Father Greg Boyle SJ and his parish sought to improve the health and safety of their community. They started by finding local business owners who were willing to hire former gang members. The roots of that initiative, 'Jobs for a Future', have grown deep and wide for nearly 30 years. Today, Homeboy Industries is a lauded organisation that supports thousands of high-risk youth and gang members who are eager for a fresh start.

Life on the streets of Los Angeles is as familiar to some as it is foreign to others, but we all know the power of new beginnings. Perhaps that is why Jeremiah's words still shimmer. God's promise of a renewed and lasting connection with Israel gives hope to those who have forgotten who and whose they are.

A better day is coming, says the prophet. Still, there is a choice to make today. Will God's forward-looking promise animate us here and now? Will we choose to hope? Will we encourage hope in others?

† Gracious God, when hope recoils, when all that is broken is all I can see, call me back to the path of your faithfulness.

Monday 25 December (Christmas Day)
Consider the little ones

Micah 5:1–4

But you, O Bethlehem of Ephrathah, who are one of the little clans of Judah, from you shall come forth for me one who is to rule in Israel, whose origin is from of old, from ancient days. (verse 2)

Christmas socks. For the past 20 years, my wife and I have given each other a pair of wool socks for Christmas. Not very romantic? Okay. A rejection of the consumerism that runs amok this time of year? Maybe. But, more than anything, the 'sock swap' is a celebration of little things that matter. These are not anti-gifts. New wool socks help us endure the long, frozen months of New England winters. The socks are carefully selected (inventories have grown over the years) and are received with laughter and a seasoned refrain: 'Socks!'

Two thousand seven hundred years separate us from Micah. In many ways, the prophet's world and ours are very different. Still, I have a sense that Micah might agree that an affinity for little things is one way to approach Bethlehem and to glimpse something important about God.

At a time when a divided nation was mired in disappointing leadership, anaemic religious observance and rampant violence, Micah foretold a new kind of ruler. That ruler will come from Bethlehem, the small town where a young shepherd was once anointed king. In David's day, as in Micah's, Bethlehem was a modest address far from the seat of power, 'one of the little clans'.

The prophet stands in a long line of Israel's faithful who have learned to look for God-in-action in unassuming people in out-of-the-way places. In the youngest son who watches his flock in the middle of nowhere. In a baby born in a barn to an unmarried couple. In little gifts, even socks, given with love.

† God, on this holy day, in this quiet moment, hear my thanks for the almost unnoticeable ways your grace touches down in my life.

For further thought

- Where in your community would you least expect to find evidence of incarnate love? Would you be willing to go there and look more closely?

Tuesday 26 December
As good as done

Luke 1:46–55

God has brought down the powerful from their thrones, and lifted up the lowly. (verse 52)

One of my oldest friends is a professional photographer. He recently gave me one of his photographs: a snowy mountaintop at play with morning mist and pink light. I took the enlarged print to a local frame store, and the shopkeeper guided me through the selection process with patience and skill. When the decision was made – this glass, that frame – he extended his tattooed arm and shook my hand. He looked at me and said, 'Done.' Of course, the framing project was not done; it had just begun. But, his final word was reassuring. It gave me confidence that the job was well within his grasp.

I think that shopkeeper has something in common with Mary. When I try to shake loose from the familiarity of Mary's Magnificat, I rediscover what I too often forget. For the most part, her song is framed in the past tense. She sings of God who 'has done great things' and 'has brought down the powerful from their thrones, and lifted up the lowly'. Mary surely knows that this has not yet been accomplished. But she conveys confidence that God's mercy and justice are as good as done. She trusts that her child will do what God has always done: lift up the lowly, free the enslaved, feed the hungry, give justice to the widow, the orphan and the sojourner.

Isn't that an expression of profound faith? Despite the uncertainties of today, we trust not only that all shall be well but that the victory's won. It's done.

† God, your past provision feeds my confidence. Your faithfulness animates my hope. Hear my song of thanks in my living of this day.

For further thought

• Is there a song in your music library that conveys the faith that Mary sings? That echoes her confidence?

Covenants and promises – Andy Nagy-Benson

December

363

The unbroken circle of God's concern

Luke 1:67–79

Thus he has shown the mercy promised to our ancestors, and has remembered his holy covenant ... (verse 72)

I was born on Mother's Day in the United States, 10 May, which would have had a certain charm if I had been due to arrive in early May. My parents expected me a month later. Of course, my premature birth would hardly register on today's scale of precarious deliveries, but in 1970 a baby born four weeks early was a concern. Over the years, my parents have shared little with me about those weeks in the hospital, but my uncles and aunts have been more forthcoming. My late Uncle Bob once told me that my father did not leave the hospital during my four-week stay. That piece of my story returned to me with force when my oldest daughter was born a month early. Her hospital stay was shorter than mine, but during that unsettling, first week of parenthood I began to see how my care for Ella belonged to an older story, the story of my parents' care for me.

In a similar light, Zechariah and Elizabeth see the birth of their son, John, as part of a much longer story. Like Sarah, Elizabeth carries and delivers a child in her old age. Like Abraham, Zechariah marvels at the arrival of his long hoped for son. The covenant that God made with Abraham and Sarah is an ever-flowing stream that brings new life to Elizabeth and Zechariah's lives.

When we find ourselves carried by the ancient current of God's faithfulness, perhaps we, like Zechariah, feel words of praise welling up in us.

† God of ancient days and of this day, I give thanks for the sacred story of grace that began long before I arrived and will continue long after I'm gone.

For further thought

- Is there a family tradition that gives you a sense of living as part of a much larger whole? If so, what is the tradition? Why is it important to you?

Thursday 28 December
First impressions

Luke 2:25–38

Guided by the Spirit, Simeon came into the temple; and when the parents brought in the child Jesus, to do for him what was customary under the law, Simeon took him in his arms and praised God. (verse 27)

Simeon and Anna take one look at two-month-old Jesus and see something. In an instant, they know more about Jesus than they could reasonably explain. It is difficult to say how that happened, but we know it can happen. Many years ago a friend saw a photograph of a young woman on a colleague's bulletin board and blurted out, 'I'm going to marry her.' What an odd thing to say! But, in time, those two would meet, become friends and exchange vows. Malcolm Gladwell would like that. In his best-selling 2005 book, *Blink*, he tells of an ornithologist who once spotted a bird in flight more than 100 metres away and he knew, instantly, that it was a ruff (a rare sandpiper). The birder had not seen one in flight before, and yet he was able to capture what birdwatchers call the bird's 'giss' – its essence.

So, what is the giss Simeon and Anna see? Based on what Simeon says (or sings), when he sees Jesus he glimpses the assurance that God has kept the promises made to the Israelites. In a blink, he and Anna sense God is with them in this child. The moment they waited for has arrived. The Messiah is looking back at them.

In some Christian traditions, Simeon's song is sung after Holy Communion. Like Simeon, we sense (see, touch, smell, taste) the promised presence of Christ in the bread and wine. And, like Simeon, we find new confidence and courage to live as people who belong to God in life and in death.

† Gracious God, look upon all people with kindness and grant us peace.

For further thought

• I invite you to read George Herbert's poem 'Love (III)' and to contemplate the poet's phrase 'quick-eyed Love'. What does it say about Jesus? What does it suggest about living a Christian life?

Covenants and promises – Andy Nagy-Benson

A season for big ideas

Isaiah 65:17–25

For I am about to create new heavens and a new earth. … (verse 17)

A beloved member of the church I serve slipped me a note after worship last fall. I consider her one of the living saints, someone who models for me and many others the walk of faithfulness. When I returned to my study, I opened the folded paper with anticipation. There, in my friend's shaky handwriting, I read words of the famous sculptor Henri Moore. It had to do with the 'secret of life', with devoting yourself entirely to a task that you cannot possibly do.

I laughed with recognition. It was no coincidence that she passed along those words after a sermon on Isaiah 65. We had just heard the promises of God in the mouth of the prophet. 'I am about to create new heavens and a new earth,' says the Lord. 'The wolf and the lamb shall feed together,' says the Lord. I had just spoken about aspiring to God-sized ideals, to possibilities that seem impossible.

Some may say that the world the prophet forecasts does not closely resemble the world in which we live. Others might think that such harmony and fullness of life are not possible. And yet, from generation to generation, too-good-to-be-true is the soil in which faith has taken root. If God's word is as good as Isaiah's prophetic vision sounds, then here's an invitation to dream bigger than we've dreamed before, to give ourselves completely to whatever seems impossibly out of reach, and to trust that God will, again, lead us to a better tomorrow.

† God, where I see that which is broken, help me see what is healed. Where I see want, help me dream of dreams fulfilled.

For further thought

• What is the biggest dream you dream for your life? Mary Oliver's poem, 'Evidence', may be a good companion as you sit with that question.

Saturday 30 December
How far away is heaven?

Revelation 21:1–7

See, the home of God is among mortals. He will dwell with them as their God; they will be his peoples, and God himself will be with them. (verse 3)

Humans have dreamed of heaven for thousands of years. The 'history of heaven' is long and textured. Visions of our eternal union with God are as varied as we are. Our ideas of heaven span broadly, but from Jewish and Christian scripture to the poetic visions of Dante to our own attempts to explain where loved ones go after they die, the direction of heaven is 'up'. Perhaps that is why John's vision of heaven stops us and draws us in. He invites us to see something more. For John, the day is coming when heaven will come down to earth in the form a holy city, a New Jerusalem.

Despite all that reminds us that heaven has not yet fully arrived, John invites us to trust that a new and better day is possible. And, in the meantime, we may wonder: Is there anything I can do to move things along? What can I do to help?

I am not sure God needs our help, but I believe God welcomes it. Yesterday, I watched a homeless man (who I've come to know and admire) pull up the grass from the cracks in the pavement on Main Street. He was in the neighbourhood to have a warm meal at our church, and for the 15 minutes before the doors opened, he thought to beautify a stretch of pavement. His story and present struggles are far from a celestial paradise, but seeing him across the road made me wonder if heaven was a little closer than I realised.

† Loving God, let the promise of heaven on earth find a home in me, that I may have eyes to see 'thy kingdom come'.

For further thought

- Recalling the journey of the past year, would you say 'heaven' touched down in your life, if briefly?

Sunday 31 December
On the shoulders of the saints

Revelation 21:9–26

And the wall of the city has twelve foundations, and on them are the twelve names of the twelve apostles of the Lamb. (verse 14)

Recently, I participated in an examination of an ordination candidate. She summarised her excellent ordination paper and responded to questions. When asked to elaborate on how she got to this point on her journey, she said, 'I stand on the shoulders of many,' and she proceeded to celebrate the people in her life who planted and nurtured her growth as a follower of Christ. One by one, she named people in her life who lifted her up and encouraged her to see her gifts and graces for ordained ministry. It was beautiful.

That conversation reinforced what I have witnessed in my own life and the lives of many I have served. On this journey of faith, we walk with companions who encourage us, and we follow the footsteps of faithful people who have gone before us. Their faces and names come readily to mind.

In this spirit, as I spy the names of the apostles carved into the foundation stones of New Jerusalem, I wonder whether they might bear more names by the time the city arrives. The names of people who have shown us what it means to love others as Christ loves us.

† God, thank you for the faithful of every generation. May I, too, have the grace to carry love's light within me and to let it shine.

IBRA International Fund: would you help us?

Will you work with us and help us to enable Christians from different parts of the world to grow in knowledge and appreciation of the word of God by making a donation of £5, £10 or even £50? 100 per cent of your donation will be used to support people overseas.

How your donations make a difference:

- **£5.00** buys 3 copies of *Fresh From the Word* in Fiji
- **£10.00** prints 12 copies in India
- **£25.00** prints 30 translated copies of IBRA notes in Ghana
- **£50.00** buys 70 copies of *Fresh From the Word* in India

If you would like to make a donation, please use the envelope inserted in this book, send a cheque to International Bible Reading Association, 5–6 Imperial Court, 12 Sovereign Road, Birmingham, B30 3FH or go online to shop.christianeducation.org.uk and click the 'Donate' button at the top of the page.

Since the International Bible Reading Association was founded in 1882, our UK readers have been making donations to the IBRA International Fund with the aim of supporting our overseas readers through the network of IBRA partners.

Our partners are based in 16 countries but the benefit flows over borders to at least 32 countries all over the world. Partners work tirelessly and often without pay to organise the translation, printing and distribution of IBRA Bible study notes and lists into many different languages from Ewe, Yoruba and Twi to Portuguese, Samoan and Telugu!

For over 130 years, IBRA readers' donations have helped to support them, and we guarantee that 100 per cent of your donations to the international fund go to support our international brothers and sisters in Christ.

Making a difference

Donations to the IBRA International Fund have supported Asempa publishers, our partner in Ghana, for nearly 30 years. Throughout the early 1990s and 2000s IBRA supplied large consignments of many publications and songbooks for local distribution. Since the mid-2000s, Asempa have focused on the translations and production of IBRA daily reading notes.

Asempa currently translate *Fresh From the Word* in to 4 local languages; Twi, Ewe, Fante and Ga, as well as printing copies in English. Each year they distribute over 20,000 copies; many of these to extremely rural areas of Ghana. In 2016, Asempa told us that direct sales to church groups enabled them to reach some more first-time users of IBRA daily reading notes.

Your donation can help Asempa translate into more languages, and to reach even more people in remote areas. Just £10.00 can fund the printing of 12 copies of *Fresh From the Word* in a local language.

Where people are following IBRA daily readings:

Global community

Our partners enable IBRA readings to be enjoyed all over the world; from Spain to Samoa, New Zealand to Cameroon. Each day when you read your copy of *Fresh From the Word* you are joining a global community of nearly 1 million people who are also reading the same passages. Here is how our readings impact people across the globe:

American Samoa

The Congregational Christian Church in American Samoa say the following about IBRA daily readings:

66 The IBRA materials encourage you to read the Bible every day and meditate on the Word. It empowers people to know God in their own terms. It strengthens and bonds families together in Christ Jesus. It waters the thirst of our souls with spiritual food. 99

Revd Reupena Alo feels that the IBRA notes help transform people from their self-centred thinking into being mission-oriented, and has seen people going out to help others in need.

India

The Fellowship of Professional Workers in India value the global community of IBRA readers:

66 The uniqueness of the Bible Reading is that the entire readership is focussing on a common theme for each day which is an expression of oneness of the faithful, irrespective of countries and cultures. 99

Cameroon

Revd Dr Peter Evande of the Redemptive Baptist Church in Cameroon has distributed IBRA daily readings for 10 years, and says:

66 The use of writers from different cultural backgrounds makes IBRA notes richer than others. That aspect also attracts people from different backgrounds to love them. The structure and seasons of the Christian year help many people. 99

UK

Sue, from the UK, has read IBRA notes for 22 years:

66 I have had many days where it feels as though the notes have been written just for me. I like the short reading for each day as this can easily be fit into a daily routine and be kept up with. I also really like reading the views of the writers from overseas for an international view. 99

Thank you!

IBRA partners and distributors

A worldwide service of Christian Education at work in five continents

HEADQUARTERS
IBRA
5–6 Imperial Court
12 Sovereign Road
Birmingham
B30 3FH
United Kingdom

www.ibraglobal.org
ibra@christianeducation.org.uk

SAMOA – TOKELAU
Congregational Christian Church in Tokelau
c/o EFKT
Atafu
Tokelau Island

hepuutu@gmail.com

AMERICAN SAMOA
Congregational Christian Church in American Samoa
PO Box 1537
Pago Pago
AS96799

cccasgs@efkas.org / reupenalo@yahoo.com

WESTERN SAMOA
Congregational Christian Church in Western Samoa
CCCS
PO Box 468
Tamaligi
Apia

isalevao@cccs.org.ws / lina@cccs.org.ws

FIJI
Methodist Bookstore
11 Stewart Street
PO Box 354
Suva

mbookstorefiji@yahoo.com

GHANA
Asempa Publishers
Christian Council of Ghana
PO Box GP 919
Accra

gm@asempapublishers.com

NIGERIA
IBRA Nigeria
David Hinderer House
Cathedral Church of St David
Kudeti
PMB 5298 Dugbe
Ibadan
Oyo State

SOUTH AFRICA
Faith For Daily Living Foundation
PO Box 3737
Durban 4000

ffdl@saol.com

IBRA South Africa
The Rectory
Christchurch
c/o Constantia Main and Parish Roads
Constantia 7806
Western Cape
South Africa

Terry@cchconst.org.za

DEMOCRATIC REPUBLIC OF THE CONGO
Baptist Community of the Congo River
8 Avenue Kalemie
Kinshasa Gombe
B.P. 205 & 397
Kinshasa 1

ecc_cbfc@yahoo.fr

CAMEROON
Redemptive Baptist Church
PO Box 65
Limbe
Fako Division
South West Region

evande777@yahoo.com

INDIA
All India Sunday School Association
Plot No. 8, Road 6
Threemurthy Colony
Mahendra Hills
Secunderabad 500 026
Andhra Pradesh

sundayschoolindia@yahoo.co.in

Fellowship of Professional Workers
Samanvay
Deepthi Chambers, Opp. Nin.
Tarnaka
Vijayapuri
Hyderabad 500 017
Andhra Pradesh

fellowship2w@gmail.com

The Christian Literature Society
No. 68, Evening Bazaar Road
Park Town
Chennai 600 003
Post Box No. 501

clschennai@hotmail.com

REPUBLIC OF KIRIBATI
KPC Bookstore
PO Box 80
Bairiki, Antebuka
Tarawa
Republic of Kiribati

Fresh From the Word 2018
Order and donation form

International Bible Reading Association

ISBN 978-0-85721-798-1	Quantity	Price	Total
AA170101 Fresh From the Word 2018		£9.99	
10% discount if ordering 3 or more copies			
UK P&P			
Up to 2 copies		£2.50	
3–8 copies		£5.00	
9–11 copies		£7.50	
12 or more copies		Free	
Western Europe P&P			
1–3 copies		£5.00 per copy	
If ordering 3 or more copies please contact us for revised postage			
Rest of the world P&P			
1–3 copies		£6.00 per copy	
If ordering 3 or more copies please contact us for revised postage			
Donation Yes, I would like to make a donation to IBRA's International Fund to help support our global community of readers.			
		£5.00	
		£10.00	
		£25.00	
		£50.00	
		Other	
TOTAL FOR BOOKS, P&P AND DONATION			

Ebook versions are available. Please see our website: shop.christianeducation.org.uk. A Kindle version can be purchased via Amazon.

Gift Aid declaration *giftaid it*

If you wish to Gift Aid your donation please tick the box below.

I am a UK tax payer and would like IBRA to reclaim the Gift Aid on my donation, increasing my donation by 25p for every £1 I give.

☐ I want IBRA to claim tax back on this gift and any future gifts until I notify you otherwise. I am a UK taxpayer and understand that if I pay less Income Tax and/or Capital Gains Tax than the amount of Gift Aid claimed on all my donations in that tax year it is my responsibility to pay any difference.

Signature: _____   Date: _____

Thank you so much for your generous donation; it will make a real difference and change lives around the world.

Please fill in your address and payment details on the reverse of this page and send back to IBRA.

Please fill in your order on the reverse

Title: _____ First name: _____ Last name: _____

Address: _____

_____

_____

Postcode: _____ Tel: _____

Email: _____

Your order will be dispatched when all books are available. Payments in pounds sterling, please. We do not accept American Express or Maestro International.

☐ I have made a donation

☐ I have Gift Aided my donation

☐ I would like to know more about leaving a legacy to IBRA

☐ I would like to become an IBRA rep

☐ I enclose a cheque (made payable to IBRA)

☐ Please charge my MASTERCARD/VISA

Cardholder Name: _____

Card Number: ☐☐☐☐ ☐☐☐☐ ☐☐☐☐ ☐☐☐☐

Start Date: ☐☐ ☐☐   Expiry Date: ☐☐ ☐☐

Security number (last three digits on back): ☐☐☐

Signature: _____

Please return this form to:

**IBRA
5–6 Imperial Court
12 Sovereign Road
Birmingham
B30 3FH**

You can also order through your local IBRA rep or from:

• website: shop.christianeducation.org.uk
• email: ibra.sales@christianeducation.org.uk
• call: 0121 458 3313

◆IBRA
International Bible Reading Association

Registered Charity number: 1086990